WAS IT ALL JUST A CON?

The Covid Con

How Deception, Lies, and Greed Gave Rise to the Pandemic Dictators

By Brady Willett

The Covid Con. Copyright © 2022 Brady Willett

www.thecovidcon.com

ISBN: 978-0-9687501-1-7

Contents

Introduction

Before SARS-CoV2 (COVID-19) I had never given much thought to vaccinations. As a young boy growing up, I received whatever vaccines the school, my parents, or doctor said I needed and then went about my merry way. There was no group of people - at least from what my wide eyes could see - against the idea that kids need to get injected with certain things not to get sick. You could say my childhood naivety was bliss.

This relative period of calm lasted most of my adult life as well. As I aged, I noticed that vaccines were something adults took in the military before travelling to foreign countries and that many elderly or sick took annual influenza (flu) shots to avoid catching the flu. The very idea that vaccines could be a source of social strife, personal stress, or political gamesmanship was foreign to me. My thought process was quarantined to the fundamental idea/belief that if someone didn't want to take a vaccine, they simply didn't take it.

Before making the jump to my thought process today, it is important first to point out that my outlook on life is typically rooted in the arena of contrarianism. This is to say that if given an idea or statement, my active mind isn't easily agreeable as it analyzes and rummages for contrary thoughts. To use a quick and slightly embellished example, if someone says 'it is cold outside,' my brain's first impulse is to never respond with 'yes, it is' - even if it is, in fact, cold outside. Rather, I respond with something like, 'yes, although last year at this point it was even colder, and the coldest day of the year on average arrives next week.' In my unique way - which most people seem to like and respond to positively - I can disagree with a statement and provide added colour, all while nimbly agreeing to the overriding theme.

As for what happens when I do not have new or contrarian information to add to the conversation, I usually give a juvenile Seinfeld-like reflexive razzing - 'What - Cold outside? No shit Sherlock.' I imagine this reflex or defence mechanism is uncoiled, in part, to convey my sense of humour as well as to help obscure my lack of knowledge on the subject matter. However, I confess there may also be some underlying psychological forces at play. Deploying U.S. Vice President Kamala Harris' suggestion to 'do Google,' some of the reasons why I may be quick to put others down may include:

"The need to feel superior to others, Childhood trauma, Low Self-Esteem, A poor home life, They have been bullied themselves, Insecurity, Poor Education, Lack of Empathy, and Underlying mental health issues." ~ Google Search

Lack of empathy seems to fit (who really cares about the weather anyways?), although some underlying yet-to-be-determined neurosis or mental health issues can certainly not be ruled out. More on this later.

This contrarian spirit has, at times, served me exceptionally well. For example, in the financial markets, those who do not follow the herd, or 'contrarians,' tend to make timely decisions that are beneficial to long-term profits. While being contrarian means you miss out on that which is most popular (i.e., 1990s dot com stocks and Bitcoin/crypto more recently), it also ensures you will be more prepared for when market manias end and the inevitable mad rush to the exit happens.

This contrarian attitude has also been beneficial when trying to learn new things or understand how brilliant people see the world. Some of the most memorable conversations I have had have been with people much smarter than me, some of whom were even *delicate geniuses*[1] (hat tip to George Costanza). Even as I lost most of these debates or arguments, I expanded my mind in ways accomplished only by repetitious intellectual failure. The applicable adage here is that of a bodybuilder, given that the mind, much like the body's muscle tissue, builds itself back stronger after periods of stress or shock. Losing or getting lost in debates, like ripping muscle tissue, can be the point.

---

[1] Through an introduction to Foucault's genealogical methods, Dr. Todd Alway helped me see the world differently.

And, it goes without saying, the contrarian monkey in my cerebral wheelhouse has also got me into troubles that, in retrospect, would not have been so severe if I had been better at reading the situation and less concerned with heated, endless debate. As a quick example, my wife and I made a bet once about whether Pinewood was a soft or hardwood (I dumbly thought the latter). Even though I admitted I was wrong, I found some obscure pine species in South America that was considered a hardwood to forever muddy the waters of the wager (and, in my mind, keep the conversation going). This tact was not amusing to my wife. Suffice to say, contrarianism can sometimes quickly escalate to jackassism.

So, my opinion on vaccination leading up to COVID-19 was that, beyond my limited experiences with vaccines, I really had no opinion at all. If someone told me vaccines were tremendous and they wished there were more of them, I would unintelligently counter that vaccines were crap and we should not have any. Likewise, if someone said vaccines were dangerous because of, say, high mercury levels, I would challenge that vaccines had a long history of helping people and if you don't want mercury in your body, take spirulina or selenium to help detoxify. In my mind debating on either side of the vaccine coin was how I could instigate a knowledge-sharing session. If someone was passionate, informed, and eloquent on the subject of vaccines, I didn't care if they were pro or anti-vaccine (anti-vaxx); I just wanted to argue and learn more from them. The mind needs to rip before it can be built back stronger.

I liken this period, from, say, five years old to 47 years old, to me subconsciously sending out drones in search of answers to the 'vaccine' subject but never having any of the drones reporting back a direct strike. I didn't see mercury in the vaccines as much of a problem, and I didn't think the 'hippy' parents homeschooling unvaccinated kids were good or bad or right or wrong per se. Again, this was because my original and only real semblance of a conclusion was very clear: if you don't want a vaccine, don't take a vaccine. The topic of vaccines wasn't something that occupied my curiosity.

When COVID-19 made the jump from China to the rest of the world, the drones started to send me back information on 'vaccines' with the force and destruction of a tsunami hitting land. My brain, through no fault of my own, absorbed and argued and debated every tidbit of vaccine-related information I could find (which became immensely easier from a time perspective when I lost my job for not disclosing my medical status). I watched and read information about COVID-19 and vaccines until my eyes literally were so dry they could no longer stay open. I read studies and clinical literature until I had devised a system by which to sort through the rubbish and bookmark the potential for later consumption. Finally, I learned that the internet and library were so densely packed with vaccination knowledge that you need to stop and sometimes refresh to avoid entering crazy town. I realized I was never going to dedicate my life toward becoming an epidemiologist or infectious disease specialist, and I knew I would not be taking over for Dr. Fauci when he retires, or he goes to jail, depending upon what source material you fancy reading.

Ultimately what I learned is that I am still learning. I went from being in a state of naive bliss to acquiring knowledge to form opinions. I now believe that the subject matter of vaccines is both malleable and evolving. I do not think, at least at the moment, that the COVID-19 vaccines are a bioweapon intended to thin the human population, but I also don't think mRNA technology is really all that spectacular. What I do think is think. Sometimes too much.

My personal experiences are unique in some respects but hardly uncommon. I arrive at today after great emotional and mental stress, at the expense of family and friends, and after some formidable monetary uncertainties. I don't consider myself a victim, although I will display and openly discuss experiences of being victimized. Quite frankly, I used to be the cheery contrarian bent on adding spice to others' lives through debate and comedy, while today, I am starting to resemble Archie Bunker (archetypal old cranky guy) permanently bent against this COVID-19 nightmare. Again, this isn't precisely victimhood, as my self-help spirit guide tells me the recipe for changing life is baked within me, but it is the unfortunate hole I find myself completely immersed in.

The solar-powered contrarian drones I sent out are still circling, looking for more vaccine targets, although one firm opinion has evolved from a boyhood observation to a fully informed adult conviction: I don't want any of the current COVID-19 vaccines, and I am not taking them! Some would say this posture is akin to a 'hill to die on,' but the newishly cranky man in me instead counters that this is my hill to take a lot of others with me. If this sounds overly aggressive or seems to carelessly splish-splash an aura of suicidal or homicidal thoughts, that is because a small part of me is still irate at the COVID-19 deceptions and lies. I am not proud of some of the thoughts I have had over the last year or so, but they happened nonetheless.

One of the goals of this book is to convey how I and others in Canada have been under attack, both with words and actions, and how the breaking points have become too plentiful to catalogue. And while each person's experience on this matter has been unique, for me, these attacks first arrived in August 2021 - or when the Trudeau government first announced their 'vaccine policy.' Shortly after this ill-warranted policy was announced, The Toronto Star reported the following:

"I have no empathy left for the willfully unvaccinated. Let them die. I honestly don't care if they die from COVID. Not even a little bit. Unvaccinated patients do not deserve ICU beds..."[1]

You would think such vile words would be relegated to the back pages to hide what seems tantamount to hate speech. On the contrary, the above words - which, to be clear, said let unvaccinated people die and do not give them an ICU bed - were stamped in big, bold letters on the front page. That the partly government-funded Toronto Star, Canada's largest daily print newspaper, sanctioned such fiery rhetoric was astonishing and a symptom of an oddly aggressive, coordinated, and sustained attack on medical choice in Canada. This campaign to compel ALL Canadians to receive vaccines simply because the government deemed them necessary continues churning to this day. It is likely it will never completely go away.

What follows isn't meant to be a sermon to indoctrinate you into my way of thinking or to agree with my thoughts. The capacity for change, good or bad, at root, is within you and you alone. This is simply my story, the path I have knitted toward a hardened anti-mandate and pro-medical-choice dogma that is reinforced by facts and, in some instances, logic.

Whether you are unvaccinated or cherish your medical privacy, there is the hope some material found within will be informative and fresh. As for those fully vaccinated and/or boosted (not that there is anything wrong with that), I believe you should always be permitted to make medical choices that are best for you and that are free from any harassment or judgement from politicians or fellow citizens. We are all good enough just as we are, jabbed or not jabbed.

Chapter 1 - August 13, 2021

On March 23, 2022, German MP Christine Anderson stood in front of the European Parliament and stated that Canadian Prime Minister, Justin Trudeau, had violated *'human rights, and the rule of law.'* Ms. Anderson's words - which were spoken within earshot of a despondent (and likely seething) Trudeau - continued to ratchet ever tighter, culminating in a vitriolic-volcanic crescendo:

"Mr. Trudeau, you are a disgrace for any democracy; please spare us your presence."[2]

To those in Canada and around the world that had grown to loathe the Canadian leader since August 13, 2021, Ms. Anderson's words rang out with a magnificent and righteous tone. There was even a brief but exuberant round of applause from many, usually reserved, European Parliament members. The celebratory tweets and posts across various social platforms virally infected the internet. Ms. Anderson was a hero, at least for one day.

Perhaps the most remarkable thing about Ms. Anderson's piercing words wasn't the shock and awe but that they were echoed by others, including Croatia's Mislav Kolakusic. Speaking minutes after Trudeau's speech, Mr. Kolakusic was equally as brusque as Ms. Anderson:

"Canada, once the symbol of the world, has become a symbol for civil rights violations under your quasi-liberal boot in recent months. We watched how you trample women with horses, how you block bank accounts of single parents so they can't even pay their children's education and medicine, that they can't pay utilities and mortgages for their homes. To you, these may be liberal methods; for many citizens of the world, it is a dictatorship of the worst kind...Rest assured that the citizens of the world united can stop any regime that wants to destroy the freedom of citizens, either by bombs or harmful pharmaceutical products."[3]

As Mr. Kolakusic levelled this verbal assault, he even made a point of pausing during his speech and turning to look Trudeau straight in his eyes. This head-turn-pause by Mr. Kolakusic was

quite effective at highlighting the seriousness of his tone. For
Trudeau, a onetime boxer with dubious skill, it must have been
chilling. After all, there isn't exactly a rope-a-dope option
available as world leaders throw 'you are a dictator!' haymakers in
your direction.

Along with speeches from Ms. Anderson and Mr.
Kolakusic, still others, including Romania's Cristian Terheş,
protested Trudeau's speech entirely by refusing to be in
attendance. On his Facebook page, Mr. Terheş noted that Trudeau
*can't come to teach Putin's democracy lessons from the European
Parliament when you pass with horse hoofs over your own citizens
who demand that their fundamental rights be respected.'* As with
Ms. Anderson and Mr. Kolakusic, the horses-trampling-people
theme was, not surprising, prominently referenced (by way of
context, horses did trample two people while trying to wall off
Canadian protesters a few weeks before the EU meeting, and this
was a horrific and terrifying incident to watch. There is no
evidence Trudeau directly sanctioned these actions or that
trampling people was the intent of the horse manoeuvres. There
were, however, blatant lies spread by the police about *the horses*
being attacked by flying bicycles).

Not to be outdone, German MEP member, Bernhard
Zimniok, gave a brief speech pointing out that Trudeau lashed out
against those protesting disproportional COVID-19 measures,
stating, *'Let us not give someone like this any speaking time in this
house of democracy.'* Then there was French politician Virginie
Joron, who didn't lob any verbal hand grenades at Trudeau but did
show up wearing a 'Truckers Freedom Convoy' sweater. The
Twitter response to France's Ms. Joron was Merci du Canada.

Around the same time Trudeau was building unwelcomed
memories in Europe, he was suffering a merciless onslaught of
negative news coverage in North America. On Fox News's Tucker
Carlson Tonight - the number one rated news show in America -
Tucker Carlson correlated the invoking of the Emergency Act with
'Canada cancelled democracy' and *'Justin Trudeau is the dictator
of Canada.'* Similarly, the number one podcaster in America, Joe

Rogan, lashed out at Trudeau, saying he was *'demonizing'* Canadians that choose not to have a medical intervention *'in the worst possible ways, with no evidence.'* Then there was the world's richest man, Elon Musk, who posted a meme of an image of Hitler saying 'Stop Comparing Me to Justin Trudeau' on top and 'I had a budget' below. As far as memedom goes, Musk pulled the right levers to cause a ruckus. Musk later deleted the Tweet.[4]

Eerily quiet during this timeframe was much of the mainstream media (MSM) in Canada. Amazingly, the MSM was still treating Trudeau with what can most politely be described as peculiar professional respect. That multiple EU leaders had openly called Trudeau a dictator to his face wasn't worthy of much of a spotlight, if any. Instead, according to the CBC, the unmemorable speech that Trudeau gave was the real story worth covering:

"Most of the European Parliament members in attendance for Trudeau's speech in Brussels, the Belgian capital, were seen giving the prime minister a standing ovation. The assembly's public galleries were full for the speech."[5]

The CBC conveniently failed to mention that many European Parliament members were not in attendance for Trudeau's speech and that some had not attended in protest. As for the 'public galleries were full' observation, this was akin to saying the naked man ran across the tennis court and the stands were packed, all the while knowing the stands were full to watch the tennis match and not the naked man. European Parliament's webpage notes that approximately a half million people visit the Plenary chamber, where Trudeau spoke, each year and that groups should book at least two months in advance. It is highly improbable that the public galleries were full specifically to see a speech from Trudeau.

As the CBC - regarded as the most biased pro-liberal government mouthpiece in Canada - happily covered Trudeau's lovely pro-democracy speech, other 'news' organizations, including CTV, were in the trenches doing the requisite dirty work:

"Anderson is a member of the right-wing Alternative for Germany party and has falsely claimed that COVID-19 vaccines are "experimental" and "not been properly vetted and tested." She has also refused to be tested for COVID-19."[6]

Apparently, in the mind of the CTV's Sarah Turnbull, before dubbing someone a dictator, you must first accept a COVID-19 vaccination and applaud the COVID-19 vaccine. As for the assertion that Ms. Anderson 'falsely claimed' that the vaccines were 'experimental,' Ms. Turnbull neglected to mention that the Phase 3 clinical trials of Moderna's and Pfizer's mRNA vaccines for COVID-19 are not expected to end until December 29, 2022,[7] and February 8, 2024,[8] respectively.[2] Some could say, and everyone used to say, that vaccines still in Phase 3 long-term trials were indeed 'experimental' given that many vaccines have failed in Phase 3 trials before.[3] Next, the character assassination effort set its gaze on Kolakusic:

"Kolakusic previously compared vaccine mandates to the death penalty and claimed "tens of thousands of citizens" have died due to vaccine side effects. A Reuters Fact Check found that Kolakusic's claim is "mostly triggered by a misunderstanding of information."

A Reuters fact check concluded Kolakusic doesn't understand stuff. OK, but how is Kolakusic's understanding of Trudeau, whom he calls a dictator? As for Kolakusic's math on vaccine-induced deaths, we know people are dying from the vaccines, and the case could certainly be made that if you are forcing something on people that can kill them, and they subsequently die, this could be viewed as 'murder.' This said, the number of deaths from the COVID-19 vaccines is heavily disputed, and Kolakusic could be way off the mark. The curious question here is if the MSM was so confident Kolakusic's numbers are inaccurate, why don't they provide their best estimate of

---

[2] The estimated completion dates of the mRNA COVID-19 vaccine trials have changed since 2020. To see all changes to these studies, click 'History of Changes' when viewing the clinical trials at www.clinicaltrials.gov

[3] Ms. Turnbull did not respond to multiple requests for comment.

vaccine deaths? Is it somehow wrong to ask that if *tens of thousands of citizens* dying from the vaccines is the wrong number, what is the right number?

The ad hominem attacks by Canadian media against anyone speaking badly of Trudeau were well beyond that of slightly slanted nationalistic pride. By way of contrast, world leaders were not attacking Trudeau's character per se; they were merely highlighting an evidentiary-based case and arriving at the deduction that Trudeau was a dictator. If the Canadian press had disagreed with this conclusion, perhaps they should have contended that the evidence lacked full context or was erroneous, or was possibly presented in an overly perfunctory manner. They did not.

Some analysts contended the purpose of Trudeau's oddly timed trips to Europe was to escape the whirlwind of criticism being hurled at him in North America. Ironically, the downpour of disdain actually intensified as Trudeau jetted off to another continent. Even when visiting the UK's Boris Johnson a couple of weeks earlier, Trudeau was forced to enter 10 Downing Street through an 'alternative entrance' to avoid the protests.[9] With so many dubbing him a tyrant or a dictator, it was unfeasible that even Trudeau didn't see a deep irony as he read his pro-democracy scripts.

Incidentally, in Canada, with the notable exception of People's Party of Canada's Maxime Bernier, politicians generally do not call Trudeau a dictator. This is due primarily to the fact that most politicians are duplicitous, spineless, and quisling piles of broken promises, of course, but it is also the result of a heavily indoctrinated Canadian citizenship that often exhibits Stockholm syndrome characteristics. Many Canadian politicians were indeed aghast at Trudeau's antics regarding the unvaccinated and protesters. However, they tended to clam up when it came time to talk about it so as to not upset potential voters.

As the March 23, 2022, speeches against Trudeau aptly demonstrated, the worldwide rage against vaccines, mandates, and authoritarianism that had been building during the pandemic had found a conduit by which to be released - Trudeau! Other world leaders, including the Netherlands' Mark Rutten and Australia's Scott Morrison, to name two, had also adopted aggressive stands against unvaccinated citizens, but only Trudeau declared a state of emergency and rounded up peaceful protesters with brutality. More importantly, none of the leaders intentionally trying to irritate the unvaccinated had the audacity, the unmitigated gall, to attend EU Parliament and deliver a speech on democracy. Trudeau did.

While there are many scandals and potentially criminal activities that could be explored to highlight how Trudeau went from a well-liked and handsome schoolteacher to a well-hated Prime Minister with dictatorial aspirations, the pertinent Trudeau event for today's purposes started on August 13, 2021. On this day, everything in Canada changed, possibly forever, because of an ill-advised decision and the shocking change in the leadership approach of Trudeau. So, after considerable adieu, the reader may justifiably ask - what the heck happened on August 13, 2021, anyways? This:

"Government of Canada to require vaccination of federal workforce and federally regulated transportation sector."[10]

Two days after officially confirming a vaccine mandate would be coming to Canada, a country that has never had such stringent vaccine mandates before, Trudeau shocked the nation again:

"Canadian Prime Minister Justin Trudeau announced snap elections for September 20, two years ahead of schedule, in a bid to capitalize on the country's pandemic response which has received cross-party support."[11]

We were told the pandemic was so horrendous that the rights of Canadians had to be temporarily placed aside for the greater good, and moments later, for some mysterious and not yet fully illuminated reason, we were told it was the opportune time to get out and vote. Many called Trudeau's surprising pandemic election declaration a wedge issue, which it clearly was, and correlated the timing to little more than a power grab. It seemed Trudeau wanted to rise from weak minority leader to King, and he was declaring war on the unvaccinated in an attempt to seal the crown. August 13, 2021, is when this declaration of war was made, and it didn't take Trudeau long to leverage his brand of hate with kamikaze-like glee.

Chapter 2 - My Dream Job

I started doing moving jobs for my dad's company and working in warehouses when I was 13. My first gig outside of moving furniture, Rubbermaid, was an excessively boring and tedious position as I was charged with putting stickers on Rubbermaid containers. Anyone with toddler-level dexterity and walk-down-the-street vision could master this job within 20 minutes. What I learned early on with this first summer job was that getting along with others is the most critical aspect of helping create a thriving work environment. Had I not been an agreeable and hardworking kid, there is no way I would be able to stand listening to primarily old cranky women venting about things like their bingo losses for eight hours a day.

One day at Rubbermaid, a forklift driver went home sick, and the boss asked our section (or the placing stickers on products section) if anyone had any forklift experience. Despite never having driven anything, ever, I immediately threw my hand in the air. The boss smiled and said after lunch, I would be driving a forklift. As he walked away, I began stealthily asking coworkers if anyone knew how to operate a forklift. No one I asked had any experience, which is probably why they didn't raise their hands.

While warehouse goings-on are not often key moments in someone's life, this moment resonated with me on some deeper level. Perhaps it was a lark or the desire to try something new, but I wasn't entirely sure why I raised my hand, and now, as a 13-year-old kid, I was faced with an adult-sized dilemma. Should I come clean and tell the supervisor I was unable to drive these forklifts or just go for it? Remembering I was a kid ensconced in an ultra-boring job and surrounded by primarily chain-smoking older women that liked vodka more than food at lunch, the latter option seemed preferable.

During the lunch shift, I hopped on the massive Toyota forklift and started experimenting with the levers. Once I had up and down mastered, I attempted to drive forward and backward. Thankfully, our lunchroom was a good distance from the warehouse area because my first not-so-gentle clash with one of the poles was much louder than anticipated. Likewise, the slamming of the forks to the ground repeatedly was not something an experienced driver would do. Within 20 minutes of slow-go tinkering, I could drive in a circle, and I quickly learned not to touch the gas while turning and reversing. As a kid, I surmised that accelerating during turns created G-force grade pressures.

The goal after my fellow workers returned from lunch was to pick up a pallet after it was wrapped and take it to one of the many rows deeper in the back of the warehouse. I had watched the other drivers do this for eight hours/day for a few weeks, so the actual job wasn't foreign to me, even if the execution of this task by driving a 3,000 lbs forklift was.

As I started with the first fully-wrapped skid, which I subsequently picked up too high, slammed to the ground, and then picked up too high again, it quickly became evident to anyone that I may have exaggerated having experience. To my surprise, I wasn't reprimanded or told to get off the machine I clearly should not have been driving, which was odd, I thought. Instead, the supervisor kind of looked the other way, and the other forklift drivers gave me a couple of tips. I like to think they took a shine to me because they thought I had potential. The reality may have been that during the tight labour market conditions in Ontario, anyone with a pulse that wanted to drive would suffice. Barely able to move one skid to every five of the other drivers, I was the best available option.

The lesson I learned was that taking the initiative, even when deploying asinine confidence, can unfurl unexpected benefits. Managers sometimes call a variant of this a 'can do' attitude, and it seems, upon reflection, that young people probably have too much of this posture while older people have too little. Regardless, by the end of summer I was one of the best forklift drivers at Rubbermaid. And while I did end up going to bingo a few times with my new lady friends (they were in their 70s, and I was 13), I never did go back to placing stickers on packages. I was shown how to drive the clamp-forklift truck, asked to return the following summer, and promised if I ever wanted a referral, not to hesitate to ask.

After Rubbermaid, I worked for Dominion Citrus at the Ontario Food Terminal driving motorized hand-jacks and picking/hand-bombing fruit. My dad drove a truck for Dominion Citrus while also working at Good-Year tire and doing moving jobs on the side. Even as a 14-year-old kid, I started to see the hierarchical nature of businesses and warehouses. Manually picking products and placing them on the skid was the lowest of the low, while forklift drivers, truck drivers, supervisors, managers, etc., represented the more highly sought after and better-compensated positions. There were even 'cash' jobs at the Ontario Food Terminal, a segment all their own, where you would show up to work, hand-bomb a tractor-trailer full of, say, watermelons, and be handed cash for your effort. Even at my young age, I was entranced by cash jobs.

While working at Dominion Citrus, with mostly older men this go round, I had some real-life experiences. One of the more memorable was when a scruffy-looking man complimented me on my veins. He said my veins were nice, and it was too bad I wasn't a heroin addict. Not really understanding what heroin was or why large veins were important, I nodded acceptingly. As I grew a little older, I realized that this work environment - the pit as it was called - was apparently quite the rough spot.

After Dominion Citrus, I worked at Beckers as a cashier, No Frills as a grocery clerk, Suncrest Groceries in the deli, Flings Fried Chicken frying chicken, and then, when I went to university, I worked as a bouncer, a painter, yard worker, etc. Finally, after university, which was time well spent despite a new resulting career not had, I worked (again) for my dad's and friends moving companies and for temp agencies. These temp agencies were wonderful in that you experienced many different jobs, including two days laying a basketball court, without any long-term commitment. You could also get bits of work all over the place, including doing different jobs back-to-back to, sometimes, back. I didn't mind working long hours. I liked money.

At the risk of belabouring my resume, I worked a lot of different jobs when I was young and met a lot of different people. In one particular job, placing flyers into newspapers, I met a nice Korean guy around my age that smoked like a chimney. I recall his attitude on smoking. He said he didn't drink or do drugs but smoked a lot of cigarettes. When I questioned him about his smoking, he responded, smiling, *'it is an activity that doesn't hurt others.'* At 3 AM, trying to frantically stuff flyers into newspapers, this is what put a checkmark in the profound box. I never knew the Korean guy's name, and I worked with him for three months. We were close.

What I discovered during this career path was that most jobs working for someone else would not be activities you pursued if you were not getting paid. Beyond some website work, all of my jobs were primarily for a monetary return. As life progressed, the purpose of these jobs changed significantly, as did I. For example, living at home after university, the primary goal was to save, invest, and, given my affinity for precious metals, buy precious metals. But after meeting my wife and with a baby on the way, the nature of jobs and money evolved. Instead of working for precious metals and some aimless idea of what life might be like when you no longer have to work for someone else, marriage and kids, by definition, meant you were already working for someone else.

Moving from Mississauga (near Toronto) to Moncton, New Brunswick, eventually meant new jobs would be had. I ran a website and wrote an investment newsletter, but the niche-like charm of my bearish website, unlike gold, soon started to tarnish. I slowly adopted the attitude that I needed a steady income, health benefits, and, eventually, a pension. Thoughts of striking it filthy rich in the markets or making enough from online businesses not to work elsewhere were not completely dead, only in hibernation.

Along with running the website part-time, I started working at warehouses in New Brunswick to help pay the bills. I worked at a cold storage plant (laid off three times in two years), a paper-products warehouse, and a garbage bag manufacturer. While I made friends and had some laughs, none of these jobs were particularly good paying or overly joyous spots to spend time. Finally, and after considerable effort passing my resume out to every major business in the Moncton area, I landed a temp job at Canada Post. Canada Post was unionized, the pay was top-tier for a labour job in New Brunswick, and, as Newman once said, the mail never stops. While a layoff from Canada Post would be possible and the threat and uncertainty of privatization omnipresent, the more likely alternative, assuming I could move up from temp to full time, was that this was a job for life.

I spent the next six years at Canada Post working as a temp. There were no guaranteed hours, no benefits, and I always had another job during these years. The goal to be hired full-time was a slow-moving process, and, at times, life was work. In my last job outside of Canada Post, I drove a forklift for a company down the road from the Canada Post warehouse during the day, and if I got the call, I would go to Canada Post immediately after. If I left two minutes early, I could drive like a maniac and scan into Canada Post without missing any time. These 16+ hour shifts were tiresome but satisfying. This may sound strange, but I felt better, more connected with the world and time, after a 16-or-18-hour shift than I did after an 8-hour shift. Perhaps the body or mind, after this long of a stretch, releases some chemical that satiates or reinvigorates some part of us. I would research it, but some things are better left unknown.

I was hired! In Moncton, now with two kids and a house, Canada Post was the ultimate job I could hope for. I used to think of myself as keen and multi-faceted, and I even took the Securities Course to try and enter the financial field officially. You could say finance, the markets, and economics intrigued me immensely but, remembering my contrarian perspective, I could never be a Wall Street (or Bay Street) man. Instead of praying at the church of the diversified, I believed the OTC derivatives leveraged nonsense that the post-Glass-Steagall epoch spawned was one carry-trade blow-up away from a complete contagious implosion.

While not exactly the 'when I grow up' wish for work, Canada Post was safe and effective and absolutely a dream job. For whatever reason, warehouse work was what I excelled at and felt comfortable doing. There is something about turning your brain off, going to work, and mingling with friends and colleagues. Such an environment differed significantly from selling mutual funds with high or hidden fee structures to clients. Canada Post provided long-term security and good pay, decent health, dental and vision benefits, and, most importantly, a strong union that was supposed to represent all employees, or so I thought.

Chapter 3 - The Virus Cometh

'No one can confidently say that he will still be living tomorrow' ~
Euripides

Insomuch as we are unique, every soul on the earth knows
there is only one end: death. Despite many of us dealing with the
idea of death differently, the vast majority of people, at least on
some level, have a fear of death. At one extreme, there is the
anxiety disorder called thanatophobia, or an acute fear of death that
can negatively impact a person's life, while at the other extreme is
the innate desire of our body to fight for life. There is also a small
group of people, the tiny fringe, that likes or wants death.

Death was the first thing that many people thought about
when we were told in early January 2020 that COVID-19 had been
discovered in Wuhan, China. The odds of death, at least initially,
were thought to be low. No big deal, many in Canada thought -
those crazy rich Asian people will wear masks for a few weeks,
and this will blow over like every time before.

[What follows is my interpretation of events, forgoing
much in the way of evidence, footnotes, etc. Remembering my
contrarian moored mind, this is only my thought process during the
initial onset of COVID-19. I have since revised and re-revised my
analysis of events, and, no doubt, additional revisions could be
required in the future.]

Originally thought to be pneumonia, the World Health
Organization (WHO) told everyone it was perfectly fine to travel
in January even as China locked down domestic travel. This
contradiction didn't sit well with me - how is it possible that you
can travel anywhere in the world but the source of this mysterious
pneumonia? Why did China seem to be bracing for battle against
this invisible enemy while the rest of the world could dance the
night away? It took all of two seconds for my contrarian
inclinations to shift into the conspiratorial zone. China, whose
influence with the WHO had grown with its economic clout in the
years leading up to COVID-19, was up to something dreadful, or
so I thought.

Also, early on, we were told, in miraculous time, that the virus probably originated from rare bats. Rumours of the virus originating in snakes or jumping from a strange concoction of animals piled up on each other also circulated. It probably came from a 'wet market' - a place where numerous animals, including wild animals, are held and subsequently slaughtered for customers to buy. Soon after COVID-19 was unleashed, Chinese wet markets went into a compulsory shutdown, at least temporarily, and the sale of wild animals was banned. Those with a memory recalled that these wet markets had briefly been closed before with SARS.

To provide a brief history of the potential origins of COVID-19, two previous coronaviruses - SARS-CoV and MERS-CoV - both were said to have originated from animals. Both SARS and MERS are what the WHO calls 'zoonotic viruses,' meaning they can pass between animals and people. The origins of these coronaviruses are not precisely known, although reservoir hosts have been found in animals. SARS reportedly originated in Guangdong province, China, in 2008, and MERS was said to have come from Saudi Arabia in 2012. As COVID-19 started making the rounds, the SARS/MERS experiences had made the hunt for an animal host, or some type of connection between animal and human, urgent.

The tiny rumblings of a virus harmlessly gallivanting around the planet would not take long to become one of the most vicious periods of uncertainty many, including myself, had ever experienced. At this point in early 2020, Canada was still operating in its traditional docile ways, taking cues from the WHO and the U.S.'s CDC - two entities whose resources and reach dwarfed anything available in Canada. There was also a geographical limitation to what Canada could do, given that the proliferation of COVID-19 spread out from China and seemed to march, ala the game of Risk, in battle lines. Even if Canada were to become bombarded with COVID-19, it would probably take some time for it to arrive with any degree of force, or so the story went.

The U.S., led by the boisterous loudmouth President Donald Trump, was one of the first to ban travel to and from

China. This seemed perfectly logical as cases of this virus were spreading, and China had already, weeks earlier, banned some domestic travel. The backlash from Democrats and those that hate every fibre of Trump was, as expected, severe. As House Speaker Nancy Pelosi braved a walk in Chinatown in San Francisco, she played politics by saying Trump was stoking xenophobia. Then a shop owner coincidentally claimed business was down at his Chinatown store because people were racist.[12] Not to downplay racism in America, which clearly exists and is a problem, but a shop owner saying people were racist by not showing up to his store to buy cookies didn't pass the stink test. Were these people not racists the day before when they enjoyed the delicious-looking strawberry fortune cookies (yes, I looked the store up, and their offerings look tasty)?

Soon after Trump banned travel to China, the death counts in Italy from COVID-19 began to make the global news. The skyrocketing death count in Italy was the first moment during this ordeal that it really sunk in that this virus may not be going gently into the good night. Not only was it becoming accepted that this virus was light years more transmissible than, say, SARS, but in Italy, where we were immediately informed the elderly often live with family, entire households were reportedly being wiped out. While the flu typically kills less than 0.1% of those infected (estimates vary), the death rate of someone catching COVID-19 in March 2020 was thought by some to be as high as 2%-5%. If you looked hard enough for the radical death stats, some even claimed 10+%!

The Italy COVID-19 nightmare spread to cruise ships being stranded at sea, and as global case counts floated ever higher, eventually, the U.S. and Canada saw cases increase too. Thinking that the Italy experience might be the outlier, the MSM factually covered the buffet of misery being served up each night. In the early days, the so-called 'COVID-19 narrative' was still under construction. Nothing to see here; move along.

Also under construction was the theory that COVID-19 may have come from a lab, specifically the Wuhan Institute of

Virology. This lab was steps away from the suspected wet market and, reportedly, messing around with coronaviruses that could have created patient zero someway somehow. We were told early on, and after a while repeatedly, there had been no gain of function research taking place at this lab. We were told this with such zeal and energy, and later on unity, that it seemed suspicious at the time.

As rumours spread that a Chinese lab may have been responsible for the outbreak, strange stories suddenly emerged, including that the U.S. military, conducting drills near the lab and near the wet market, could have been responsible for the outbreak. This trend of any mention of COVID-19 starting in a lab being counteracted by fantastic claims made the news seem like little more than a non-stop nationalistic propaganda game. Perhaps the only thing that everyone agreed on, except China, was that China had undue influence over the WHO. Weeks into this mess and the WHO was praising China for its amazing leadership, seemingly oblivious or playing coy to the lab leak story. Again, suspicious.

Around this time, I watched a Joe Rogan interview with Infectious Disease Expert Michael Osterholm. During the interview, Osterholm, who afterward served on President Biden's COVID-19 advisory board, noted that COVID-19 was likely to be 10-15 times worse than the worst flu, that it was doubling every four days, and it could last up to seven months or even longer. Not many people in March 2020, not even in the crackpot corners, were calling for the type of duration and societal pains Osterholm's crystal ball was forecasting. My mind oscillated between thinking this guy was full of beans to that his logic, some of it above my level of comprehension, made perfect sense. As I worked myself into a frenzy listening to Osterholm and biding time on the elliptical, my stock market brain quickly reflexed - if more of these experts keep selling these types of tales, people will eventually start buying fear.

Notwithstanding the obvious lack of medical training and expertise I possessed, my difficulty in interpreting Osterholm's conclusions was that he was the contrarian on COVID-19 in early

March 2020. Being contrarian, which is always my first instinct, to someone that was already deeply contrarian would, in fact, net no end contrarian result. As coincidences would have it, this fleeting moment of angst ended on March 11, 2020, the day after Osterholm's interview, when the WHO declared COVID-19 a pandemic. Events were moving fast, and the situation was fluid.

Along with Osterholm throwing me for a loop, another newly acquainted face to me around this time was The Director of the National Institute of Allergy and Infectious Diseases (NIAID), Dr. Anthony Fauci. While my opinion of Fauci has materially changed since being introduced to him in 2020, I initially recall thinking that he was an eloquent, ultra-informed, and objective speaker. Fauci preached in early 2020 that COVID-19 didn't seem that serious an issue, but by March, he was onboard with mitigation efforts, including temporary lockdowns, to stem the tide of cases and death. Fauci had a charisma to him, like a wise and shrewd grandpa, and was one of the prominent figureheads of the COVID-19 response in North America. If Fauci was in favour of lockdowns and Osterholm was saying the pandemic party was just getting started, who was I to contradict? In my circles of discovery, no one was really arguing with any intelligent intensity to just let COVID-19 rip through society, at least not yet.

What made the lockdown theory compelling was that China had locked down tens of millions of people ahead of the Lunar New Year, and this was generally accepted as a success at limiting the spread. I wasn't sure how I felt about this. If COVID-19 was eradicated after a lockdown, obviously, this would be a screaming success, but what if COVID-19 wasn't done? Initial concerns aside, the lockdown platform in China was schematically, albeit tacitly, endorsed and replicated by the U.S. and Canada. There was a degree of unease expressed by policymakers at the time, and no direct correlation was initially made, but score one for communism.

Seemingly based on common sense, the two-pronged lockdown thesis, at least as I understood it, was that any actions to limit spread could provide immediate relief to a stressed healthcare system, and the lockdowns would quickly lead to a 'flattening of the curve.' When combined, these two benefits would, in turn, mean that the lockdowns were no longer required. With death and destruction being reported and COVID-19 all anyone could talk about, I generally accepted the idea that a temporary lockdown could be advantageous. These lockdowns were called various things in various places but were essentially rooted in the consensus that the greater good was served by temporarily limiting people's rights.

My gym was closed down on March 5, 2020, and I took a paid COVID-19 leave from my job on March 17, 2020, due to underlying health conditions. I handled this period well insofar as understanding why the lockdowns were happening, and with an estimated mortality rate 10-20 times that of the flu, my health conditions (auto-immune disease) warranted not going to work.

By late March, the panic phase was in full force in the U.S. and around the world. This is the time when 'two weeks to flatten the curve' became prevalent. This phrase is forever etched in the minds of those recognizing it as being the unofficial starting point of some of the most significant government policy blunders in history. 'Flattening the curve' was simplistic yet cunning, and it was a catchphrase that was readily absorbed and adopted by all education levels that could view a death chart with their eyes.

In the sense that flattening the curve meant spreading out COVID-19 cases so hospital capacity would not be overwhelmed, this was an effective 'greater good' slogan as well. Who wouldn't want to temporarily sacrifice some of their freedoms to save lives? We all remembered what had happened and was happening in Italy, and if we forgot, every news channel dutifully reminded us at every waking moment. And now, in late March, similar reports of widespread death were also being reported in Iran, the U.S., and Spain.

The other slogans around this time included *'Act like you've got it, stay home, save lives.'* Not as catchy and convincing as the flatten the curve jingle, this phrase irritated me and made me want to catch COVID-19 and run around spreading it. Yes, the transition from fluffy teddy bear that loved being squeezed by policymakers to pissed-off grizzly ready to maul happened in quick spurts for me. The attempt by some government heads to implement restrictions that threatened to contradict the justification for previous restrictions was a source of immediate irritation. The idea, people thought and were told, was life would return to normal so long as we banded together to get that dang curve flattened quickly. Why the heck does staying home save lives if all the curve-related angst had receded? Suffice to say, it was during these early days the seeds of dissent were planted, even though I was outwardly calm and my fluffy teddy bear side would ultimately return.

My gym would reopen on June 9, 2020, and I returned to work, by choice, on July 19, 2020. The reported death rate of COVID-19 in Canada peaked in June 2020 at 8.34% and then started falling. While 8.34% was a terrifyingly high number, studies were beginning to trickle in, even as early as mid-2020, suggesting there were a lot of asymptomatic cases of COVID-19 and mortality rates were likely closer to 0.5%-2%. Given my age and health situation, this math was in the acceptable range of returning to normal life activities, at least in my mind.

There was also budding statistical evidence that elderly people were at outsized risk of negative COVID-19 infections, that those with pre-existing medical conditions (comorbidities) were primarily the only segment of society dying from COVID-19, and that otherwise healthy people were not at great risk. These statistics were not conclusive, thorough, or in many peer-reviewed studies yet, but they were grab-bags of statistics produced from all over the world. The sick and elderly, much like with the flu, were the primary risk groups for COVID-19.

I will be the first to admit that my mind was not cemented to the idea that COVID-19 was over in mid-2020, only that it took me until this point to be done worrying about the risks of COVID-19 to me personally. When I returned to my dream job at Canada Post, it was based somewhat on the expectation of a little overtime pay - or money beyond what I was being paid to sit at home - but also on the expectation that COVID-19 was not going to be around in any serious way for much longer. It is through this lens, with a contrarian focus, that I viewed the COVID-19 drama as it continued to evolve and unfold in a way few were prepared for.

Around this time, the push for the vaccines took flight, with AstraZeneca having already started testing and stating that their COVID-19 vaccine could be available by October 2020. Contrarianism of a cranky variant joined with common-senseism - how in the bleep can a vaccine be ready only a few months after the discovery of the virus? I didn't know a lot about vaccines in 2020, but I thought the development timeline was years, not months.

I confirmed my suspicion by viewing Pfizer's flow chart on its website entitled *'The Four Phases of Clinical Trials.'*[13] In this chart, Pfizer said Phase 1 is 20-100 participants and takes weeks to months to complete, Phase 2 could be hundreds of participates and takes between 1-2 years to complete, Phase 3 could be thousands of participants and takes 1-4 years to complete, and Phase 4 could be thousands of participants and take years. Phase 4 is also usually, according to the former Head of Medical Affairs and Research at Pfizer, where *'the real world effectiveness of a drug as evaluated in an observational, non-interventional trial in a naturalistic setting which complements the efficacy data that emanates from a pre-marketing randomized controlled trial.'*[14] Put in laymen's terms, Phase 4 is the World Series, while Phases 1, 2, and 3 are typically batting practice.

I also knew that my new COVID-19 czar, Lord Fauci, had previously said how vaccines mature in trials before graduating into a lot of people's arms. Consider this quote from Fauci from October 29, 2019, when he was discussing how we might make the transition from traditional vaccines to 'something better':

"In order to make the transition from getting out of the tried and true, egg growing, which we know gives us results that can be beneficial. I mean, we've done well with that...to something that has to be much better. You have to prove that this works. And then

you've got to go through all of the clinical trials, Phase one, Phase two, Phase three, and then show that this particular product is going to be good over a period of years. That alone, if it works perfectly, is going to take a decade."[15]

Given that Fauci said in late 2019 that new vaccines would take at least a decade, was it really safe or even sane to think that vaccines could be used to fight COVID-19 by the end of 2020?

As I started to pay more attention to the enthralling vaccine storyline(s) taking place, it was worth remembering that these were early days, and deciphering some standard of facts, or truth, was an unachievable task. Digesting the lockdown realities required putting some blind faith in government, an idea that had historically rarely proven wise. And thinking vaccines could save the day given the deplorable track record of big pharmaceutical companies (big pharma) seemed equally unwise. Barring divine intervention, there was no feasible way to squeeze the necessary clinical trials into the time frame being discussed by AstraZeneca and others. Then again, if the government and big pharma could not be trusted to save us from COVID-19, then who?

Chapter 4 - So Many Conspiracy Theories, So Little Time

One of the most basic 'conspiracies' talked about in Canada is the unique relationship between the World Economic Forum (WEF) and Canadian politicians. For his part, Trudeau has never denied being influenced by the WEF, nor has he ever denounced WEF ideologies or pledged to fight for Canadian sovereignty against any and all outside actors. Moreover, Trudeau frequently agrees, verbatim, with the words of the WEF chair and founder Klaus Schwab, or a man that continually says the part that is supposed to be kept silent out loud.

Schwab: *"I have to say when I mention now names, like Mrs. (Angela) Merkel and even Vladimir Putin, and so on, they all have been Young Global Leaders of the World Economic Forum. But what we are very proud of now is the young generation like Prime Minister (Justin) Trudeau…We penetrate the cabinet. So yesterday, I was at a reception for Prime Minister Trudeau, and I know that half of his cabinet, or even more than half of his cabinet, are actually Young Global Leaders."*[16]

Like a skilled angler using the best test, the 'penetrate the cabinet' line is the anti-WEF bait most often thrown into the murky conspiratorial waters. For those enamoured with the idea that the WEF and Canada are one and the same, the militaristic word 'penetrate,' like *pincer movement* or *blitzkrieg*, evokes the image of bodies and annihilation. By contrast, if you are all for globalist love, population control, and stopping climate change, the penetration of new world ideas into the cabinet is as innocuous as apple pie. Ever the contrarian, I tend to see each of these extremes as being overboard, if for no other reason than 'Young Global Leaders' can, and do, change their viewpoints and attitudes. Most can also be voted out of their positions of authority as well.

We have known for a long time of the WEF/Canada connection, with the Financial Post telling us during Trudeau's first visit to Davos in 2016 that the *'Prime Minister's middle-class agenda comes straight from World Economic Forum playbook.'*[17] In the same article, a throwaway joke was added in the last paragraph. For those watching Canada today, this was oddly prophetic:

"...if Canada is looking for some rebranding, especially since peacekeeping has entirely lost its lustre: what about Climate Keepers? We can ride it all the way to increasingly-indebted economic oblivion, which, after all, was the main point of Maurice Strong's Davos "plot."

From the astonishingly high pandemic spending to most definitely vying to become one of the world's top climate keepers, Canada is, intentional or not, following Mr. Strong's plot. Incidentally, Canada's Maurice Strong was an interesting person that made his money in oil and adamantly fought for the environment, a pattern replicated by Canada itself. Strong's deep connection to the WEF was illustrated by Klauss Schwab's words following Strong's passing in 2016.

"He [Strong] was my mentor since the creation of the Forum: a great friend; an indispensable advisor; and, for many years, a member of our Foundation Board. Without him, the Forum would not have achieved its present significance."[18]

So while the conspiracy goes that the WEF is a diabolical cabal resolute on things like population control and one world government, it could also be said that there would be no WEF as we know it without the significant works of Canadians like Maurice Strong. Other Canadians, including Trudeau's former chief of staff, Gerald Butts, and current Deputy Prime Minister, Chrystia Freeland, likewise have deep ties to the WEF and could easily, if still deploying military terms, be considered WEF espionage agents. There is also an expansive list that would cover many pages, of additional agents and foot soldiers, from all political parties, races, and segments of society that are already garrisoned in Canadian politics and powerful positions in business. The question of whether the WEF is infiltrating Canada or Canada is infiltrating the WEF would not be entirely ridiculous.

But while the backroom deals made at Davos, which I am sure there are plenty, likely have some sway in global policymaking efforts and business, a direct link to a WEF control or a command structure is not readily apparent. Moreover, is it really a conspiracy if the WEF proudly promotes its globalist agenda for the whole world to see? Consider the following quote from Schwab in June 2020:

"To achieve a better outcome, the world must act jointly and swiftly to revamp all aspects of our societies and economies, from education to social contracts and working conditions. Every country, from the United States to China, must participate, and every industry, from oil and gas to tech, must be transformed. In short, we need a "Great Reset" of capitalism."[19]

Given that I am a realist and not from Schwab's fantasy island, I shall refrain from casting aspersions on words that resemble those of a cult leader. What can be said is that shortly after the publication of Schwab's 'COVID-19: The Great Reset' (this is an actual book you can buy and read), Trudeau delivered a corresponding speech with striking similarities. Below is a clip:

"...this pandemic has provided an opportunity for a reset. This is our chance to accelerate our pre-pandemic efforts to reimagine economic systems that actually address global challenges like extreme poverty, inequality, and climate change."[20]

In the context of trying to get vaccines equitably distributed, the above quote would really not be off the wall. However, three little words - 'pre-pandemic efforts' - mean that the 'reset' Trudeau was alluding to was being discussed before the pandemic. The outcry following the above speech was loud and swift - Trudeau is a puppet of the WEF! Unfortunately, this outcry was largely muzzled by the MSM and not heard by the majority of Canadians.

There are absolutely overlapping interests between the WEF and many governments, and many leaders do replicate, verbatim, the WEF's 'build back better' concepts and climate change mantras and ideologies. But do cozy relationships, groupthink, and outrageous pretenses really mean the WEF is hell-bent on global domination? In the same way the WEF lacks enforcement mechanisms to compel sovereign countries to do their bidding, global citizens lack the enforcement mechanisms to change the WEF. Isn't this alone more suggestive of impotence than omnipotence?

The WEF's annual meetings, a feature in Davos Switzerland since 1971, are where financial dealings, some devious, some not, transpire amidst a great deal of intellectual waxing. These annual jet fests with the financial and political elite do, at least in recent years, seem to be a staging area for the globalist agenda despite the limitations of enacting such an agenda.

Where the WEF has limits, the WHO does not. Quite frankly, while some of the conspiracies focus on Bill Gates, China, George Soros, or the Rothschilds to speculate that COVID-19 was pre-planned by a group of reprehensible individuals, it may be appropriate to shift the suspicious lens upon the WHO. The WHO was getting ready for something like COVID-19 as early as 2016, when then head of the Organization, Dr. Margaret Chan, was forcefully declaring that the world *'Is Not Prepared To Cope'* With Pandemics. Ms. Chan suggested modes of preparedness at the 2016 *'Address to the Sixty-ninth World Health Assembly'*. Below are some highlights:

"Let me give you a stern warning. What we are seeing now looks more and more like a dramatic resurgence of the threat from emerging and re-emerging infectious diseases. The world is not prepared to cope.

I welcome the current joint external evaluations that are looking at preparedness and response capacities in several countries. The evaluations need to continue with the utmost urgency as a tool under WHO authority and coordination.

WHO is the organization with universal legitimacy to implement the International Health Regulations. The evaluations must be accompanied by well-resourced efforts to fill the gaps. Many generous countries have promised to support 76 countries to build IHR core capacities. I urge you to keep this promise."[21]

Trying to best prepare for the next pandemic is one thing, but Dr. Chan was proposing changes to the WHO's authority and reach. She wanted the WHO to broaden its purview and adopt enforcement mechanisms that the WHO lacked, something that China would further propose during the COVID-19 pandemic. Consider some additional comments from Dr. Chan from 2016:

"The Secretariat's report gives you an overview of the design, oversight, implementation plan, and financing requirements of the new health emergencies programme.

Setting this up marks a fundamental change for WHO, in which our traditional technical and normative functions are augmented by operational capacities needed to respond to outbreaks and humanitarian emergencies."

Expanding operational capacities to respond to outbreaks sounds, maybe, reasonable. Dr. Chan added:

"The programme's design is aligned with the principles of a single programme, with one clear line of authority, one workforce, one budget, one set of rules and processes, and one set of standard performance metrics."

That the WHO was proposing 'one' set of principles and rules for member states to abide by in 2016, and is still doing so today, is where the chilling part arrives. What if these types of new authorities meant that things like vaccination, lockdowns, mandates, and even masks became enforceable by the WHO? Could the case not be made that countries would unwittingly be signing away their sovereignty to 'be safe'?

In addition to the terrifying *'one clear line of authority'* statement, there is also the possibility that certain countries, or powerful/wealthy interests, may have undue influence on the

WHO. As Dr. Chan would later state, years after her tenure at the WHO ended, money definitely plays a role. And yes, Dr. Chang said the part you are not supposed to say out loud:

"The WHO, as an organization, only 30% of my budget is predictable funds. The other 70%, I have to take a hat and go around the world to beg for money. And when they give us the money, they are highly linked to their preferences – what they like..."[22]

When people say the WHO is bought and paid for, the above quote is one of the reasons why. It does not take much imagination to speculate that rather than holding its hat out for donations, the WHO might auction policy decisions to the highest bidder. For the greater good, of course.

Getting back to 2020, the term 'with covid' is an essential phrase for people to understand, given that in April 2020, the WHO changed how countries code for COVID-19 deaths (see the WHO's *"International Guidelines For Certification and Classification (Coding) of COVID-19 as Cause of Death"*[23]). These changes included the following:

"COVID-19 should be recorded on the medical certificate of cause of death for ALL decedents where the disease caused, or is assumed to have caused, or contributed to death."

While 'assumed to have caused' is a bit peculiar, the three words 'contributed to death' is downright crackers. How or why would COVID-19 be the cause of death if it merely played a role in someone with severe illnesses? Didn't we have tools, such as tests and autopsies if necessary, to accurately determine the cause of death? The WHO report continued:

"There is increasing evidence that people with existing chronic conditions or compromised immune systems due to disability are at greater risk of death due to COVID-19. Chronic conditions may be non-communicable diseases such as coronary artery disease,

COPD, and diabetes, or disabilities. If the decedent had existing chronic conditions, such as those listed above, these should be listed in Part II of the medical certificate of cause of death."

Tying the above paragraphs together, even if COVID-19 'contributes' to a death, it can be the cause of the death, and multiple chronic conditions can be listed in Part II on the certificate of death. Needless to say, prior to April 2020, death from an illness like Alzheimer's disease vacillated in a somewhat predictable manner based upon trends like our aging population, not whether patients tested positive for a coronavirus.

* Just so there is no confusion, the WHO's coding for COVID-19 deaths document is the absolute judge and jury that Canada and most of the world adheres to:

"Deaths due to COVID-19, as displayed on Statistics Canada's website, are those for which COVID-19 was found to be the underlying cause of death (UCOD), defined by the World Health Organization."[24]

Finally, the WHO's instructions went on to add a confusing little paragraph that requires some concentration to grasp:

"A death due to COVID-19 may not be attributed to another disease (e.g., cancer) and should be counted independently of pre-existing conditions that are suspected of triggering a severe course of COVID-19."

Although wordy, the above guideline suggests that even if someone's underlying health condition(s) is the only reason a person got deathly ill, the death is due to COVID-19. It doesn't matter if someone extremely sick goes to the hospital for, say, cancer and then happens to catch COVID-19 after already being in the ICU for cancer. If a positive test occurs at any time, COVID-19 can become the cause of death.

Thanks to the newly authored decree from the WHO, the idea that someone died 'with covid' but not necessarily from COVID-19 was born. This would prove a major theme for the duration of the pandemic.

In short, there is enough dirt and speculation about the suspicious, sleazy, and potentially criminal actions of the WHO to make anything the WEF has ever done look like tiddlywinks (or some other simple childhood game). While the WEF makes for great intrigue and sensational water-cooler banter, the WHO is the force looking to, literally, take over the world's response to perceived health threats with enforceable actions. In fact, given that the WHO's death coding for COVID-19 recommendations were widely adopted, the case could be made that the WHO already operates as the world's 'one clear authority' on matters of global health. Some might counter this theory with the contention that the WHO has no actual rule over sovereign nations. Perhaps this is the case. But perhaps the unfortunate reality is that when everyone is scrambling around in the dark, like in early 2020, people will follow just about anyone who vows they are the light.

Chapter 5 - The Virus Breeds Insanity

In the latter half of 2020, the seemingly necessary 'temporary' lockdowns practised in March became twisted and contorted into a pretzel-baked psychosis. Quite frankly, as we learned more about COVID-19, the policies being implemented seemed to become more disjointed from reality. In the case of masks - of which there was scant evidence of them being effective at slowing airborne viruses before COVID-19 started - the pro-mask case weakly asked 'why wear them?' and then answered 'because the models say so.' One such model-based paper entitled *'Universal Masking is Urgent in the COVID-19 Pandemic'* used *'agent-based modelling'* with *'theoretical simulations'* to conclude that masks, even of the homemade variety, were urgently required. This paper, which was released in April 2020 and rather oddly demanded universal masking, also suggested that the public awareness slogan to sell mask mandates should be something like *'masking protects your community, not just you.'* The study wasn't exactly scientific or impartial. It did, however, try to impart the feeling that communism was warm and wonderful. I would link the study, but I worry Trudeau may charge me with spreading misinformation, which the study clearly was.

As 2020 progressed, the models and papers amassed in the muck like a haphazard military bracing to storm a beachhead. And like clouds providing cover for manoeuvres, these studies co-opted the widespread uncertainty and social fear to conceal their marching orders. One such model, devised by an assistant professor at Shaanxi Normal University in China and a Theoretical nuclear research physicist at the Cyclotron Institute in Texas, warned that Italy was sure to see mass death from COVID-19 in late 2020:

"The model predicts more than 130,000 deceased by the end of the year 2020 if no effective measures are taken. If similar measures to the March ones are quickly adopted, the number of deceased may decrease to over 50,000. The situation is extremely serious and requires collaboration from everyone starting from wearing masks and other protections when social distancing is not feasible."[25]

Far be it from me to impugn the findings of the academically gifted, but this paper was oddly specific about picking the lowest hanging fruit off of the COVID-19 death tree and throwing it into the public's face. Italy indeed logged one of the highest death rates during the first wave of COVID-19, but this was largely due to the fact that it had the oldest population in Europe and, according to a 2017 report, *'71% of over-65s [Italians] had at least two underlying health conditions'.*[26] With literally only a few months of data to expand upon, the authors of the study concluded that failing the immediate implementation of broad preventive measures - LOCKDOWNS! - up to 80,000 extra Italians would die by year-end. The lowest tally of COVID-19 deaths, even if all the restrictions were immediately implemented, was 50,000 dead. Terrifying, yes, but were these models really reliable?

The model used to arrive at the terrifying Italy death forecasts, which I would implore anyone to try and comprehend, was clearly devised by a couple of professors and can only really be deciphered by professors or the mathematic elite. Ever the contrarian, I immediately thought the very idea that severe restrictions could save so many lives was off. To me, it looked like the authors were shooting for shock value instead of scientific discovery. The restrictions and lockdowns didn't seem to work that great in March 2020, and now they must be rehashed to save 80,000 lives?

This same tandem of authors - a Chinese assistant professor and Texan physicist - had previously teamed up with an even more intentionally obscure model-based paper called *'Chaos, percolation and the coronavirus spread: a two-step model.'* In their web of convolution, apparently for the purpose of freedom castration, the authors wrote:

"The data from the 50 U.S. states are of very poor quality because of an extremely late and confused response to the pandemic, resulting unfortunately in a large number of casualties...S. Korea,

notwithstanding the high population density (511/km^2) and the closeness to China, responded best to the pandemic.''[27]

These and other statements from these two seemed oddly political, and oddly anti-America for 'science.' The assumption that 'casualties' could have been avoided if a more restrictive approach had been universally adopted was also, rather strangely, professed as gospel. While some restrictions maybe were beneficial to controlling the spread of COVID-19, the idea that one very narrow fragment of time could be picked like grapes and made into fine policy wine was, at least in my mind, patently absurd. The virus was still spreading.

Also, around this time, greater information was arriving daily, telling us exactly what type of people die from COVID-19 (or 'with covid'). Those with comorbidities, particularly *'cardiovascular comorbid conditions including hypertension or neurological disease,'* fared poorly when catching COVID-19, while healthy people seemed to handle COVID-19 fine.[28] As Osterholm had pointed out months earlier, the elderly and those who smoked had 10-times the death rates as those that did not smoke in China. This was why in China, where men smoke much more than women, the majority of deaths occurred in older men. Osterholm also postulated obesity affects the body very similarly to smoking, something a lot of us probably already knew.

Suffice to say, that the U.S. was one the most obese nations in the world seemed a key factor in understanding why their death rate may have been higher than, say, Korea. Maybe it wasn't entirely the masks and lockdowns that had the largest roles in mitigating death counts. Maybe, just maybe, the more notable factor was that Korea, at around 5%, had one of the lowest obesity rates in the world (OECD)?

That Hua Zheng, who had studied at the Wuhan University of Technology, China, was one of the authors making bold model-based claims about necessary policy decisions did, I will admit, stir up irrational nationalistic apprehensions. These fears were not related to COVID-19, as the risks here were becoming better quantified, but by the coincidental location and mighty political clouds I speculated might be hovering over Mr. Zheng. I didn't have direct evidence that Mr. Zheng was a spy or spreading misinformation for the Chinese government. Instead, given that his models seemed to produce nationalistic bias, it was difficult not to put on the conspiratorial cap. These and other studies seemed bought and paid for, by big pharma, government(s), or both. For good measure, you could also easily throw the WEF or WHO influencers into this mix.

Incidentally, where there was a nationalistic bias at play was something that the WHO called 'vaccine nationalism.' The concept here was that nations would hoard and buy vaccines for their own people first, thus making the distribution of vaccines an equity issue and, potentially, prolonging the crisis.[4] Even as Chinese President Xi Jinping and UN Secretary-General António Guterres regarded vaccines as *global public goods,'* there was this sense that a new stratum of nationalized vaccine warfare was taking place. By late 2020 there were 58 different vaccines that had been developed against COVID-19 and were in clinical trials[29], and more than 140 candidate SARS-CoV-2 vaccines in development/trials.[30] It would be naive to think all these would be vaccine-Kings were just in it for the greater good.

As for Italy, whose lockdowns in March 2020 were some of the most restrictive on the planet, the targets of the 'with covid' death model proclaimed by two academics were never reached, proving the models were, to put it delicately, hogwash. The professor tandem that screamed in November 2020 that 130,000 Italians could die from October 6, 2020, to December 31, 2020, unless the country immediately adopted some of the most restrictive measures imaginable, had been way off the mark. Italy eventually relented to the pressures of those extolling models, and on December 19, 2020, Italian President Conte stated, *'Our experts*

---

[4] If you believe, like many did, that the COVID-19 vaccines could end the pandemic, then getting these vaccines distributed to everyone in the world was essential. 'Vaccine nationalism' ran contrary to this perceived greater good.

fear that the infection curve will increase during the Christmas period. '[31] Ah yes, flattening that terrifying curve, isn't that what it is all about?

Despite holding off the lockdowns until late in the year, just over 38,000 Italians died 'with covid' during the timeframe noted in the study. This was 12,000 fewer than the lowest number of deaths the authors thought possible. The gotcha takeaway was that the model, and others like it, failed to predict the future with any degree of accuracy. The real takeaway may have been that the whole point was not to make an accurate forecast but instead to help create the fear-laden conditions necessary to instigate some variant of control. Despite the defective models and indications that COVID-19 was probably seasonal, much of the world did indeed adopt the type of draconian restrictions endorsed by the WHO, China, and the modellers.

The academics advocating man-made models had become the antigen to widespread social fear and, perhaps more extraneously, the solution to policy guilt. Policymakers treading softly on societal infringement grounds needed justification to push or pull Chinese-style lockdown tactics out of their tool belts, and the models became the key blunt instrument. The taking and granting of freedoms thrust people into some twisted Pavlov's dog COVID-19 experiment. Strange or not, in 2020, we all started watching the models, perhaps for reasons, we can't be entirely sure of. This was both fascinating and scary.

Like a snowball acquiring size as it rolls down a hill, the freshly powdered models synchronized and solidified brainwaves that said closing businesses saved lives, masking saved lives, and, eventually, vaccines would save lives. Models from mathematicians and physicists were temporarily helping dictate COVID-19 policies, and it would not be long until models from dullards, doctors, and political figures would also join in the fun. Canada was not immune to the charms of the models and quickly patched together a site labelled *'Math saves lives: How scientists use modelling to guide COVID-19 decision-making'.* Canada, as always under Trudeau, was up to speed on the latest fashionable trend:

"Models create projections for the future based on past and present data and help decision makers to evaluate and, if need be, adjust public health measures to control the spread of COVID-19. These models help answer complicated questions such as the most favourable time to reopen after a lockdown, how long to maintain individual precautions like physical distancing, and the risk associated with different gathering sizes. Decision makers at various jurisdictional levels use a combination of results from different models to inform public health actions in order to reduce the burden on our hospitals and help save lives."[32]

What the modelling-craze in 2020 did was turn doctors and academia into COVID-19 prophet-tellers. Like complex economic models that always seem to fail in predicting market crises, these COVID-19 models used select data and select variables to deliver select forecasts within a select range(s). But who exactly was selecting or deciphering these complicated organism-like models, and what were their intentions? To quickly jump ahead, on June 25, 2021 - when hyping vaccines was a government goal - hidden in the notes of a very scary model-based paper from the Public Health Agency of Canada (PHAC) was *'Key model assumptions include: The vaccine is 60% effective at preventing infection.'*[33] The Canadian government was plugging in a 60% vaccine efficacy rate to make their scary charts while, at the same time, the bosses of the modellers (i.e., Trudeau) were claiming the vaccines were highly effective (i.e., 95+%). You can't make this stuff up.

Don't get me wrong, generally speaking, I think models can provide insights and wisdom that not be available from studying real-time data. Nevertheless, in 2020 my gym - which I consider to be a great stress reliever and health provider - was closed and reopened on three separate occasions for a total of 72 days due, in large part, to the COVID-19 models. These models were being deciphered by New Brunswick's Minister of Health, Dorothy Shephard, who had no medical training and, before being named top health czar in New Brunswick, ran a paint store. This lady telling people they could not work out because it was for their own safety while at the same time saying they could buy all the liquor and marijuana they wanted was rich. It was the scary models that made her do it.[5]

The models were providing the cover for capricious and entirely unscientific policy decisions, even though the models themselves usually did not recommend such policy decisions. Think about it - the models warned covid-Armageddon was coming, so closing local businesses and keeping Walmart open had to be done for the greater good? The models said cases were going to push upward, and the hospitals may be overwhelmed, so travelling is banned, Plexiglass will be installed everywhere, and all restaurants must be closed except for big chains like McDonalds? These types of actual occurrences, which of course, were ludicrous, seemed to be inspired by big business and politics. And the models helped provide the cover, the justification, and, most importantly, the unwarranted fear.

In Canada, most were so consumed with the idea that COVID-19 was causing untold death and despair they went along with it. Those that asked if the extreme measures made sense were either ignored or softly overpowered, and it was even suggested, very quietly at first, that those questioning policies didn't care about others. It will all be over soon, the story went, just follow the government's recommendations.

It didn't make sense that something that had only been circulating for less than a year could coalesce in such entrenched and all-encompassing policy actions. It didn't make sense at all, except perhaps when you remember the economic adage that demand creates its own supply. The demand for answers, solutions, ideas, and a path out of COVID-19 was so strong that policymakers latched onto whatever they could to convey the appearance of predictability. I criticize Shephard and others because I truly believe people like her caused undue harm to

---

[5] Ms. Shephard did not respond to multiple requests for comment.

citizens (they could also be paid off; I don't know). But it should also be acknowledged that, at least in 2020, Shephard would have been out of a job if she said to let COVID-19 rip through society and told people to make their own personal health choices. Actions, no matter how preposterous, ruled the day.

The quandary is that after innocently doing the wrong things so often to appease widespread uncertainty and fear, the models and maniacal policies were incapable of building an off-ramp. If two weeks to flatten the curve and a handful of closures didn't appease the model gods, surely a month of lockdowns and closing almost everything would work, wouldn't it? Moreover, in the case of masking requirements, business closures, lockdowns, etc., there was the smell of a gambler's fallacy taking place: policymakers doubled, tripled, and quadrupled down, hoping, eventually, this would help put an end to the pandemic. In describing the overriding theme of 2020, Osterholm said it best:

"Science, when done well, can be messy, imperfect, and slower than we wish. And it's ever-evolving. Unfortunately, in the time of a pandemic, we wish this weren't the case, as we all want and need immediate answers."[34]

With the only immediate answer being there was no answer, there was this almost obsession compulsive policymaking disorder. Those idle and not demanding dramatic action were somehow not paying attention - people were dying!

While not exactly ensconced in a dystopia nightmare, at least not yet, 2020 did provide the first taste of unbridled political power that would prove alluring to would-be dictators. If the WEF faithful were really looking to spread their wings, the winds were happily in agreement that now was the time. Resetting the minds of Canadians didn't require deep mind control CIA tactics. Quite frankly, you could have done whatever the hell you wanted to Canadians, and most would have complied. The virus had made much of the world population heavily malleable and amiable to whatever the nonsense. It was all somewhat depressing and made me want to reach out for my mask.

In short, the story in 2020 was that lockdowns, restrictions, mandates, masks - whatever - were effortlessly justified, at least until the vaccines arrived. Guiding these policy decisions were states of emergency, declared by every Canadian province in 2020, and widespread fear honed perfectly by the 'with covid' death models. Also in the background, like magical wind-chimes spreading peace and love, were the real-world examples of success in stifling COVID-19 in places like China and Korea. Follow China's example, everyone, they know the way!?

Some asked, very quietly at first, if these odd alleged cures might be worse than the disease. Shhh! The models say it could get worse, and people are dying...

Chapter 6 - The "Vaccines" Cometh

"Herd immunity occurs when a large portion of a community (the herd) becomes immune to a disease." ~ Mayo Clinic[35]

While 2020 was strange and ended with screwy policy decisions threatening to become the flint for fiery frustration, 2021 was, in all likelihood and god willing, the worst year for me mentally. I had managed to go nearly five decades in this life without actually being so disgusted and disturbed that I felt like murdering someone. 2021 ended this streak.

Before jumping into it, allow me to clarify what I mean by "murder" - something I didn't honestly believe I would actually do in 2021 but thought about from time to time. At one point, I started to fill out forms for a gun licence, while at another, I half-heartedly and half-joking negotiated the purchase of illegal firearms from a friend. My logic being if you are going to commit murder anyways, why not do it with an untraceable gun? These events were about as close to a plotted murder as I had ever been (and if someone in the government is reading this, please realize these were thoughts, not actions). My other mentally-off tendency was to vent, usually swearing and cursing, about how I would like to pummel certain politicians or policymakers if I ever met them. This venting served the purpose of opening a flue in a fire that was at threat of burning out of control. I made no actual attempt to position myself for the opportunity of pummelling anyone.

The angry thoughts and venting sessions were uncharacteristic attributes for me. At the risk of self-diagnosis, I wasn't sleeping, I was under a great deal of stress, likely depressed, and by late 2021 there seemed to be no end in sight. I never went on any medications but perhaps should have. The sole conversation I had with a mental health counsellor - through my workplace program - the first question they asked was if I had any violent thoughts. I paused lengthily and, honestly, couldn't answer as the question itself raised violent thoughts.

My mental issues aside, for those thinking that COVID-19 was becoming a preordained pile of WEF, WHO, or China-sanctioned bullpucky, 2021 initially offered the potential for some respite. The 'vaccines' were, per Mighty Mouse, coming to save the day (incidentally, and contrary to the conspiracy theories that no animals were used to test these new mRNA vaccines or that all the animals died during testing, mice were used in testing.[36] Where there is confusion is that animal testing occurred simultaneously with human testing.[37] This was, we were told, to get the vaccines to market faster for 'our' safety. We were also told to please ignore that researchers 'killed the test animals shortly after vaccination' in all 3-major vaccine studies.38)

One of the first vaccines to arrive in Canada in quantity was made by AstraZeneca, a company that in 2011 had paid out $647 million to settle 28,461 lawsuits that contended the drug maker failed to warn the public that one of its products could cause diabetes.[39] Keeping its legal troubles in mind, one of AstraZeneca's business slogans was *We push the boundaries of science to deliver life-changing medicines.* The contrarian comeback was maybe the company should leave these boundaries in place! Thankfully, for AstraZeneca shareholders, indemnification agreements with Canada meant that they could not be charged for any side effects of their COVID-19 vaccine.

Having not studied indemnification clauses intensely and also having a generally blasé interest in legalese, I can't speak to the ironcladness of said agreements. What can be said is that in late 2020-early 2021, if you wanted COVID-19 vaccines, you needed to sign indemnification clauses. No signature, no vaccine. Canadian Procurement Minister Anita Anand eventually acquiesced to media 'pressure' and noted that *indemnification clauses in vaccine contracts are standard.* Apparently, living under the thumb of vaccine manufacturers that many governments, including the U.S.[40], gave large sums of money to was simply the way business had to be done. After all, the major COVID-19 vaccine makers were publically traded, and there were shareholders to think about. Ms. Anand added:

"To prevent delays in release of the vaccine at time of pandemic, the pandemic vaccine supply contract stipulates that the Government of Canada will indemnify the manufacturer against any claims or lawsuits brought against it by third parties."[41]

With the comprehensive results from the completed clinical studies not available (due to the fact long-term Phase 3 trials take years, not months), the Canadian government threw caution to the wind and, in the process, *'agreed to assume liability for injuries or deaths as a condition in its contracts with vaccine suppliers.'*[42] After 'a months-long review,' Health Canada approved AstraZeneca's vaccine on February 26, 2021.[43] The release brought hope to those that were told the only way out of the pandemic was to take a vaccine.

February 26, 2021 - Regulatory Decision Summary - AstraZeneca COVID-19 Vaccine - Health Canada[44]
"There were no life-threatening AEs or deaths related to the vaccine. Based on the available data, the vaccine at the indicated dose was considered safe and well-tolerated."

As AstraZeneca started to make its way into Canadian arms, some negative side effects started to appear immediately, including death. The month-long review from the Canadian government concluded no adverse events (AEs) from the vaccine. Were the data and studies on the AstraZeneca COVID-19 vaccine rushed for the supposed greater good?

At this point, in the eyes of lawyers and policymakers, the Canadian government was in a box. The option of admitting the launch was rushed and these deaths could have been avoided would be horrific. Likewise, saying nothing and continuing to push AstraZeneca's concoction into more arms could be an equally poor move. With options limited and time of the essence, the Canadian government was in indistinct wait-and-see mode.

April 27, 2021 - Health Canada stands behind AstraZeneca COVID-19 shot after 1st blood clot death reported[45]

"The woman's death linked to a cerebral blood clot - which Quebec public health assured is extremely rare, a one out of 100,000 chance - is Canada's first death linked to a COVID-19 vaccination."

Remembering that AstraZeneca's vaccine was still in clinical trials, how the heck did Quebec, headed by WEF acolyte Premier François Legault and Minister of Health Christian Dubé, know that there was only a one out of 100,000 chance of blood clots? As an aside, shortly after the news of blood clots from AstraZeneca's vaccine, one of my big bosses at work asked a group of us if he should take AstraZeneca or wait for the mRNA vaccines (a question many Canadians were facing). Not extremely fond of this man who seemed to have a curious penchant for trying to fire people, I looked him straight in the eyes and said, 'you should take the AstraZeneca vaccine.' I am not sure he caught my ominous joke, but within weeks he absolutely would have. Below is part of the AstraZeneca timeline:

May 5, 2021 - Alberta confirms first death linked to AstraZeneca vaccine[46]

May 6, 2021 - BC reports 1st case of rare blood-clotting disorder in woman who received AstraZeneca vaccine[47]

May 11, 2021 - 'Very little excuse' to continue to use AstraZeneca in Canada: infectious diseases specialist[48]
The risk of VITT - vaccine-induced thrombotic thrombocytopenia - now sits at one in 60,000 doses, based on Ontario data.

May 12, 2021 - Future of AstraZeneca COVID-19 vaccine in question in Canada over blood clots...[49]
Risk of blood clots tied to AstraZeneca shot now estimated at 1 in 55,000 in Canada

May 21, 2021 - New Brunswick reports 2nd AstraZeneca-related death[50]

May 25, 2021 - Ontario confirms first blood clot death in man who received AstraZeneca COVID-19 vaccine[51]

August 12, 2021 - Blood clots associated with AstraZeneca vaccine are 'rare but devastating,' study says[52]

Along with the shocking death side effect, what stands out from the abbreviated trail of misery is how quickly the odds of serious blood clots and/or related injuries materially increased. The best available information available to Health Canada in February 2021 was proven, based upon the best available information weeks later, to be wildly inaccurate. Rare or not, the vaccine was killing people and not only the unhealthy or elderly. AstraZeneca's Phase 3 clinical trial was not expected to be completed until February 24, 2023.[53] When the final results are disseminated, it is doubtful it will be mentioned by the MSM in Canada.

Due to the reported deaths, the AstraZeneca saga was pretty much over by May 2021, or when *'several provinces...paused the rollout and administration of the first doses of the AstraZeneca vaccine, citing safety and supply concerns.'*[54] Canada's National Advisory Committee on Immunization (NACI), which has similarities to the U.S.'s CDC,[6] then caused a mini-panic when on May 22, 2021, it recommended the *'vaccine series be completed with the same COVID-19 vaccine product when possible.'*[55] There were more than 2 million Canadians with one dose of AstraZeneca waiting for answers. Canada's Chief Public Health Officer, Dr. Theresa Tam, arrived on the scene to say that *'ongoing studies,'* none of which were published yet, said mixing vaccines would be fine.[56] NACI, despite logging concerns, complied. It was a good ol' fashion Catalina Vaccine Mixer.

As AstraZeneca slid off the vaccine injection casino boat, the mRNA vaccines, which we were told had different safety profiles, climbed aboard. While Health Canada stated that all

---

[6] NACI's vaccine recommendations have been provided directly to the Canadian Government since 1964. NACI's recommendations are also published in vaccine-specific chapters of the Canadian Immunization Guide.

approved COVID-19 vaccines are safe and effective, even after the deaths, they also provided a special note for the mRNA vaccines:

"Myocarditis and pericarditis seem to be occurring more often than expected in some populations and situations."[57]

The above quote was taken directly from the Government of Canada on November 26, 2021. A brief timeline on the subject of heart inflammation from the mRNA vaccines is below. It reads much like the AstraZeneca trend - or from 'not that bad' to 'look the fuck out':

June 1, 2021 - The side effect [myocarditis] is considered important but uncommon - arising in about 12.6 cases per million second doses administered[58]

June 25, 2021 - *"...the FDA is announcing revisions to the patient and provider fact sheets for the Moderna and Pfizer-BioNTech COVID-19 vaccines regarding the suggested increased risks of myocarditis (inflammation of the heart muscle) and pericarditis (inflammation of the tissue surrounding the heart) following vaccination."*[59]

September 1, 2021 - Symptomatic Acute Myocarditis in 7 Adolescents After Pfizer-BioNTech COVID-19 Vaccination[60] *Systemic reactogenicity occurred more commonly in younger patients and after the second dose of the vaccine.*

October 8, 2021 - Two studies from Israel quantify the risk of myocarditis following the Pfizer-BioNTech shot, with one suggesting the chance of developing the condition is about one in 50,000.[61]

November 21, 2021 - CDC and its partners are actively monitoring reports of myocarditis and pericarditis after COVID-19 vaccination.[62]

December 4, 2021 - 1 in 2680 young men develop acute

myocarditis/pericarditis in adolescents following Comirnaty
[Pfizer] vaccination in Hong Kong[63]

While the above trends were extremely alarming, please
remember that the Moderna and Pfizer vaccines were still in Phase
3 clinical trials until December 29, 2022, and February 8, 2024,
respectively. Quite frankly, until these studies are completed and
all the data is collected and released, the odds of an mRNA vaccine
triggering things like heart inflammation, bell's palsy, or death by
cardiac arrest are simply not fully known.

This said, the obvious danger if the Hong Kong study was
accurate (1 in 2,680) was that thousands of young people in
Canada could get myocarditis or something similar if they were
vaccinated. Doing damage control, some 'experts' concluded the
vast majority of myocarditis cases were not that bad and were
readily treatable. Other doctors noted, more convincingly, that all
cases of heart inflammation in otherwise healthy young people are
serious. What these experts neglected to mention is that young
people, by and large, handled COVID-19 without any problems
whatsoever.

As the mRNA vaccines took the spotlight, there was the
matter of which vaccine injuries were being reported and which
were not. In the U.S., there is the VAERS[64] system, and in Canada,
there is Adverse Events Following Immunization (or AEFI
Reports.)[65] Despite there being a general consensus before
COVID-19 that VAERS dramatically underreported vaccine
injuries, a lot less was known about Canada's reporting system.
Upon investigation, it can be said that AEFI reports are
cumbersome and time-consuming to fill out, and there is reason to
speculate that a lot of vaccine injuries never make it into AEFI
reports. For example, in the case of Alberta, which fired doctors
for speaking out against the vaccines and forced nurses and doctors
onto Leave Without Pay (LWOP) for not taking the shots, the
province noted that all AEFI reports must be filed within *three
days of the health practitioner determining or being informed that
a patient has had an AEFI.*'[66] We were told hospitals and ICUs

were being overrun and that medical staff was working non-stop doubles to keep people from dying. It seems an obvious observation that a lot of AEFIs probably got shelved simply due to time management limitations.

Despite the side effects sometimes being reported, the path to full vaccine distribution was done in record time,[67,68] and the response after a few months of dosing as fast as possible was, we were told, absolutely stellar. The initial clinical trials for both mRNA vaccines showed around 95% efficacy, and in the real world the data was, we were told, just super terrific. Here is what Fauci had to say in May 2021:

"Now, usually, as many of you know, the effectiveness in the real world is often not as good as the efficacy in the pristine conditions of a clinical trial. We have found just the opposite with COVID-19 vaccines, where effectiveness is easily as good, if not better, in the real world setting."[69]

Thanks for the positive news, Fauci! Damn those rare side effects. The race to vaccinate and reach herd immunity was on.

Chapter 7 Is (Not) Brought to You by Pfizer

"It's funny how big pharma is so evil, until now. What's it, $200 a pill? Yeah, that's good, that's fine, I'll take it. Give me all you got"
~ Norm MacDonald[70]

Despite side effects like myocarditis or even death, people promoted the new COVID-19 vaccine slogan 'safe and effective' with such zeal and conviction it was like they had been indoctrinated into a cult. Even if your math led to the conclusion that the rare side effects from the shots were dwarfed by the risks of catching COVID-19, a risk/benefit analysis should have been provided and openly discussed. Instead, if you questioned the veracity of the vaccines you were stigmatized, likely banned from social media platforms, and, eventually, would be treated like human garbage. Were Canadians aware that the average age of someone dying from COVID-19 in 2020 was 83.8 years old versus our national life expectancy of 82.1?[71] Was stating that COVID-19 had a 99.5+% survival rate for anyone below the age of 70 really 'misinformation'?

Those in 2021 who contended the vaccines were not great at limiting spread were, in the minds of some in the Canadian government, awfully close to committing a crime. And if you were a doctor in Canada questioning the conclusions of Public Health, you could end up disciplined or even fired. The science changes all the time, we were told, but the remarkably safe and effective mRNA vaccines would never change and were bulletproof from reproach.

While the vaccines were causing harm, and the media was screaming how wonderful they were, Pfizer was paying for an independent study that showed mRNA vaccine efficacy started to wane immediately and was below 50% within a few months. Just to be clear: this study was from the same Pfizer that in 2009 then paid the largest healthcare fraud settlement in U.S. history.[72] While the 'kickback'-related schemes that Pfizer deployed can be complicated and have many moving parts, the statute Pfizer previously broke was more concise:

"The Anti-Kickback Statute, 42 U.S.C. § 1320a-7b, prohibits pharmaceutical companies from paying remuneration to induce Medicare beneficiaries to purchase, or their physicians to prescribe, drugs that are reimbursed by Medicare."

Paying out kickbacks, or put more delicately incentives, is something companies like Pfizer do, and sometimes paying massive settlements or fines can be said to be the cost of doing business. This isn't to suggest all payments to doctors are a crime, only that doctors tend to provide more of a drug if they receive compensation from a pharmaceutical company and that this situation is a potentially slippery slope.[73] Pay a doctor's travel expenses, feed them, and throw in a $2,000 speaking fee at a conference, and chances are they will speak very kindly about your product.

In the funded by Pfizer study released on October 3, 2021,[74] the authors were in the thick of Pfizer's web. Of the many contributors, seven were *'employees of and hold stock and stock options in Pfizer,'* and eight contributors in total *'received research support from Pfizer.'* Suffice to say, if ever there was a study that was going to be juiced up to promote high vaccine efficacy, this was it! This was one of the largest and longest studies ever conducted on COVID-19 vaccine efficacy, and, in my mind, it obliterated any and all doubt that these vaccines were effective. If Pfizer was saying their vaccines were not as efficacious as originally touted, this meant every 'news' report lauding the mRNA jabs as the pathway to endemic salvation was reporting misinformation.

While the correlation has not been made, this study, in my mind, was the reason why the CDC changed the definition of a 'vaccine' on September 1, 2021, or less than a month after the Pfizer study was released. Consider the definition changes from the CDC.[75]

Vaccination (pre-2015): *Injection of a killed or weakened infectious organism in order to prevent the disease.*

Vaccination (2015-2021): *The act of introducing a vaccine into the body to produce immunity to a specific disease.*
Vaccination (September 2021): *The act of introducing a vaccine into the body to produce protection from a specific disease.*

Along with changing the definition of 'vaccination,' shortly after the Pfizer study, the CDC changed the definition of a 'vaccine' from *'A product that stimulates a person's immune system to produce immunity to a specific disease'* to *'a preparation that is used to stimulate the body's immune response against diseases.'*[76] The justification given for this change, which entirely transformed the notion of what a vaccine is, was that since no vaccine is ever 100% effective, the definitions required tweaking. Adding to this pathetic explanation was a CDC spokesperson, which said that along with being safe and effective, COVID-19 *'vaccines and the act of vaccination has prevented millions of illnesses and saved countless lives.'*[77] This statement was curious given that the virus was still spreading and the long-term Phase 3 studies of the 'vaccines' were not yet completed.

As Fauci had taught me in 2020, vaccines are not vaccines if their efficacy rates are below 50%. Pfizer's vaccine was below this mark in five months or less, and this was according to the Pfizer-funded study (which, let's be honest conspiratorial buddies, was almost surely rigged in some manner).

Not to be outdone, soon after the CDC massaged its 'vaccine' definition, Merriam-Webster dictionary followed suit. As the conspiracy corners of the internet lit up and threatened to hit tilt, the trusty fact-checkers at USA Today dropped an amusing and likely heavily massaged fact check:

"Merriam-Webster revised its "vaccine" definition to replace "immunity" with "immune response." The change also addresses the new technology of mRNA vaccines in light of the COVID-19 pandemic."[78]

You read that correctly - given that the mRNA shots failed to live up to what a 'vaccine' has been ever since Edward Jenner released a smallpox vaccine in 1796, the definition of a vaccine must be changed. Anyone with common sense knew, instantly, that if you have to take an injection of something every few months this is not, by any intellectually honest characterization, a 'vaccine.'

The pro-new-vaccine-definition crowd countered logic by arguing that no vaccine is perfect, that the mRNA shots were limiting death and hospitalization, and that, per the CDC's new definition of a vaccine, the shots *'stimulated the body's immune response against'* the virus. This group could also say that an mRNA vaccine is a vaccine because it *'contributes to immune defense by supporting various cellular functions of both the innate and adaptive immune system.'* Finally, they could also add that the mRNA vaccine *'has been shown to enhance differentiation and proliferation of B- and T-cells, likely due to its gene regulating effects'* and that mRNA vaccines are a *'a cofactor for the hydroxylase enzymes involved in the synthesis of catecholamine hormones, e.g., norepinephrine, and amidated peptide hormones, e.g., vasopressin, which are central to the cardiovascular response to severe infection.'* I'll be the first to admit that I have no idea what some of the words mean in that last quote, but what I do know is all of the quotes in this paragraph relate to taking vitamin C, not the mRNA 'vaccines.' According to the new definition of vaccine adopted by the CDC, vitamin C is also a vaccine?

While effective, like many things, at priming a person's immune system for battle, at least temporally, any serious interrogation of the data and studies starting to arrive in 2021 proved these mRNA shots were not capable of ending COVID-19. The headline from Pfizer and Moderna, and repeated by Fauci and every major politician purchasing these vaccines, was that efficacy was 90%-95%. Even if these estimates were valid, and there are ample indications to contradict them, efficacy against transmission began to drop precipitously shortly after the second injection, and the vaccines were considerably less effective with the new delta strain.

The failure of the vaccines to attain and maintain high rates of efficacy is the reason why the Pfizer-funded study strenuously pushed the idea that these shots could limit hospitalization and reduce your chance of dying if you caught COVID-19. This ability to quickly avert the focus from shots that could end COVID-19 to shots that will have to be taken repeatedly to prime your immune system or replenish your antibodies had to be handled delicately by Pfizer and the press. With its vaccine operating under the FDA's Emergency Use Authorization (EUA), Pfizer was not permitted to advertise its COVID-19 shots to the consumer directly. The company found a neat way to circumvent these restrictions by focusing on name-only sponsorship. From an excellent montage on YouTube, below are some of the programs Pfizer sponsored.[79]

- Good Morning America was brought to you by Pfizer
- CBS Healthwatch, sponsored by Pfizer
- Anderson Cooper 360. Brought to you by Pfizer
- ABC's Nightline, brought to you by Pfizer
- Early Start, brought to you by Pfizer
- CNN tonight, brought to you by Pfizer
- Friday night on Erin Burnett out front, brought to you by Pfizer
- This Week with George Stephanopoulos is brought to you by Pfizer.
- This weather report brought to you by Pfizer
- Today's countdown to the royal wedding is brought to you by Pfizer
- And now, CBS Sports Update brought to you by Pfizer
- Meet the Press data download, brought to by Pfizer
- This portion of CBS This Morning sponsored by Pfizer
- On how to find the hidden sugars in the American family diet (60 minutes), sponsored by Pfizer

That the media was accepting funds from Pfizer and then charged with interrogating and reporting on the vaccination campaign was, to the laypeople, a direct conflict of interest. But what the average person didn't understand was that Pfizer had more than a $2 billion annual advertising budget and the producers of the above media loved money! Those quick to rush to judgement need only remember that Jack Daniels isn't promoting its booze when it sponsors Alcoholics Anonymous meetings, and Pfizer wasn't promoting a EUA vaccine when it threw money at those talking about vaccines. Get your mind out of the gutter.

Pfizer would get full FDA approval in late 2021 and was able to finally advertise its COVID-19 product that no one on the planet had not already heard about. As Pfizer aligned the best in the business to 'softly' promote their miraculous COVID-19 boosters, their first promotion was to thank the 5-11-year-old kids that helped with their trials. One of the first ads/videos with a superhero theme caused a stir as it seemed to insinuate that taking the vaccine would make kids superheroes.[80] Pfizer later clarified the kids themselves were the heroes for participating in the trials. This was the exact same story told a year earlier, but since Pfizer couldn't tell this story due to EUA limitations, ABC[81] and numerous other media outlets did. Kids were the heroes in the awesome new Pfizer study,[82] we were told, repetitively, almost a year before Pfizer was officially permitted to advertise their vaccine.

Pfizer was contacted and given a chance to refute statements made in this chapter. They were also provided the opportunity to sponsor the chapter by way of a charitable donation to the IWK Children's Hospital. This was done for a half lark, but also, like jumping on a forklift you can't drive, a flippant leap to see if I was meant for philanthropy (Bill Gates seems to be ~~profiting from~~ enjoying it). Pfizer Corporate Affairs Canada kindly took the time to respond.

"Thank you for reaching out to Pfizer with this update and with your suggestion. At this time, we must decline any opportunity to be involved in your book."

Apparently, with booster season nearing and those pesky anti-vaxxers still spreading misinformation, Pfizer's advertising and goodwill dollars have all been accounted for. And, just to be clear, booster season is every season.

In short, as the media and Public Health officials ignored the October 3, 2021 study sponsored by Pfizer, my stress level quickly doubled. Remember that on August 13, 2021, Trudeau forever changed Canada with his vaccine mandate. The new Pfizer study, and many others like it, should have meant any mandates be discarded. Instead, with the vaccines failing to limit transmission materially, this meant the government was vying to dictate personal health choices and coerce otherwise healthy or young people into taking a medical procedure they simply did not need. I started to hedge the possible effects of a complete meltdown and tried to curb the insomnia with nighttime sips of Whisky. Whisky used to be medicine, just like 'vaccines' used to work in limiting transmission. My logic was sound.

As the cornucopia of misinformation and outright lies from policymakers piled ever higher, the word Pfizer had suddenly become ubiquitous. My mom, God bless her heart, didn't know how to use her cell phone or sometimes turn the television on, but she knew Pfizer would help her beat covid.

Chapter 8 - "Never let a good crisis go to waste"*

"I really believe COVID has created a window of political opportunity..."
~ Canadian Deputy Prime Minister, Chrystia Freeland[83]

By October 2021, we knew from the most recent studies and real-world statistics that the COVID-19 vaccines would not be able to limit transmission greatly. It is at this point that those who questioned the pro-vaccination narrative went from wearing a healthy open-mindedness to a headstrong rejection of the pervasive COVID-19 orthodoxy. Also at this point, the escalating attacks on the unvaccinated should have ceased. They did not.

Still clinging to the COVID-19 narrative was the majority of Canadians, most of which, in 2021, were vaccinated by choice. Many in this crowd used catchy jingles like the 'pandemic of the unvaccinated' to feed their unnatural egotism toward the unjabbed. Instead of seeing the inadequacies within most government reports, they were satiated, even entranced, by the headlines. To use a quick example, on October 21, 2021, Alberta Health noted that *'COVID-19 vaccine studies show that vaccinated people are well protected from infection. They are 20 times less likely to get COVID-19 illness.'*[84] The MSM lapped up this story like a thirsty dog. What they didn't do, however, was actually read the study, which, down in the notes, acknowledged *'These findings pertain mainly to non-Delta COVID-19 transmission.'* Delta had taken over as the dominant strain in Canada in July 2021. Why were our top Alberta Health experts spreading old and useless information months later?

To get an inkling of how quickly and deeply the tide was about to turn in 2021, remember that those arguing against vaccine mandates by the end of the year would be censored and wished dead by some Canadians and the media. But before this happened, Trudeau was the one who started warning about 'fairness and justice' in March 2021 as he railed *against* the idea of vaccine mandates:

"The idea of certificates of vaccination for domestic use does bring in questions of equity. There are questions of fairness and justice. There could be discrimination."[85]

After questioning the rationale of vaccine mandates in March 2021, Trudeau followed this up in May 2021, making it crystal clear the Canadian way:

"We're not a country that makes vaccination mandatory."[86]

In this quote, Trudeau is absolutely right. Before COVID-19 Canada did not mandate vaccines or immunizations. Moreover, in the two provinces where immunization proof for schooling was required, if parents chose not to vaccinate their kids there were grounds, medical or ideological, to get an exemption.

Trudeau, in early 2021, like my former naive pre-COVID-19 self, seemed indifferent to the very idea of vaccines. Trudeau definitely saw the utility in the shots within the context of the pandemic - which is why he ordered more in early January 2021 than any sane person would - but he wasn't exactly pushy about it. If you don't want one of these products to fight COVID-19, don't take it. Makes sense to me.

After championing vaccine choice, something happened in the summer of 2021 to dramatically alter Trudeau's opinion of mandates. This is, I admit and acknowledge, where your WEF conspiratorial angle(s) flicker into focus. The change in Trudeau and, subsequently, Canadian policy was so profound and started to run so extremely hot in opposition to the scientific data that something was seriously amiss. There is no way the often listless and go-with-the-woke-flow Trudeau suddenly came up with the idea to punish anyone who dared not take the shots. Even if Trudeau's Foundation was raking in sleazy funds from vaccine purchase orders, as some wildly alleged, he would have made a lot of money without the mandates. Canadians, generally easy-going, and government-conforming, were already taking up the vaccines *by choice* in massive numbers.

It is possible that through some domino of logic effect, or monkey see monkey do, that Trudeau adapted his path and started to mimic trends taking place across the planet. Even so, the impetus behind the global push, and Trudeau's push, to mandate vaccines was well beyond any twisted measure relating to public health. Was this groundswell of change the WEF finally activating the chips in world leaders' heads and telling them to adopt vaccine mandates or risk annihilation? Was it big pharma doing what big pharma usually does and squeezing a final round of record profits before their vaccine-like products were exposed? Or maybe it was China, a country that simply held some citizens down and forced injections into them[87,88] finally winning the model war and watering the seeds of communism wherever the weak-minded resided? Whatever the case, it was absolutely not for the health or the greater good of citizens in Canada. And this is where my contrarian but usually logical and objective mind began to fracture, leading to a Creedence-Clearwater-Revival of conspiracy inclinations. Let's take a run through the jungle.

Even before Trudeau started dancing like a vaccine-mandate-puppet in late 2021, the rest of the world was toying with mandates and vaccine passports, and guiding this charge was Israel. Israel's leader, Benjamin Netanyahu, was the longest serving Israeli Prime Minister in history (2009-2021), and he had a long and illustrious history of involvement with the WEF. Below is a lengthy but essential quote from Netanyahu, delivered at Davos in early 2021:

"Actually, we have vaccinated 82% of our above about six years, it's not enough. We have to vaccinate...at least of 95%, which is a big task...I intend to get it up there further. If you ask what's the challenge, we're in an arms race, except it's not an arms race. It's a race between vaccination mutations and mutations, especially the British mutation. But there'll be more mutations. There are limitations. There'll be more mutations in the future, that means that we have to race as fast as we can to vaccinate first the risk

*groups of the population and then everyone else in order to give
immunity and then probably expect the companies that are
producing the vaccines at this point to modify their vaccines to
accommodate the mutations that they don't cover now as they
develop, and then we'll have to purchase them. That's going to be
our life. For the coming years. I don't think that we're going to
evade that. But we can overcome."* [89]

A true visionary, Netanyahu said the vaccine mandates
were necessary to beat COVID-19 or to reach 'immunity,' but that
additional shots, likely for years, would also be required. This was
either an admission that Netanyahu had no idea what he was
talking about, or he was privy to the fact that these vaccines waned
rapidly and boosters would be required. In either case, that
Netanyahu said the shots needed to get into 95+% of arms was an
outrageous statement when contrasted against most herd immunity
estimates, including Canada's estimate, from Dr. Tam, of
approximately 75%. Netanyahu added:

*"The reason we did well in Israel is one because we purchased a
lot fast. We didn't quibble about the price. I personally got
involved, and I said just basically to the bureaucrats whatever, I
want to be diplomatic, so cut the C word...This is ridiculous. You
know, you'll pay a few more dollars for those now, and tomorrow
everybody will be paying 10 times that much..."*

The takeaway was that wealthy nations, with direct lines to
vaccine producers, would fight for their own interests first. Don't
get me wrong, I am a capitalist/free market spirit, and I abhor the
idea that great gobs of socialism or dabs of communism can solve
the world's woes, but when it comes to healthcare, to these
vaccines, the hypocrisy was too profound not to notice. If the only
way out of the pandemic was to get everyone vaccinated, as most
leaders clearly stated, then hoarding vaccines was a terrible thing
to do. The WTO, in a report entitled *'The Tragedy of Vaccine
Nationalism,'* warned exactly of what Israel was doing:

*"Vaccine nationalism is not just morally and ethically
reprehensible: it is contrary to every country's economic,*

strategic, and health interests. If rich, powerful countries choose that path, there will be no winners - ultimately, every country will be a loser."[90]

When Netanyahu stated that *'tomorrow everybody will be paying 10 times'* what Israel paid, he neglected to mention that many countries simply could not afford to enter a bidding war for COVID-19 vaccines. With wealthy nations pining for vaccine supply and companies like Pfizer exploiting the fact that countries were fighting to throw money at them, vaccine nationalism had merged with corporate greed. The toxic result was that Pfizer could, per Public Citizen's look at the secretive contracts, *'silence governments, throttle supply, shift risk and maximize profits in the worst public health crisis in a century.'*[91]

Finally, the Israeli leader, who was acting like a dictator, spoke about why his country was working with Pfizer to track all Israeli citizens. Once again, this seemed to be the part that was not supposed to be said out loud:

"I actually was on the phone with the President, the CEO of Pfizer, and I think at two o'clock in the morning as an advisor or a legal adviser... So you need personal leadership to move it [vaccine contracts/deliveries]. And basically, the selling point was a real one turns out to be true, that Israel could serve as a world laboratory for herd immunity or something approaching herd immunity very quickly...98% of our citizens have digital records in these HMOs that go back 20 years, and we offer to share that with Pfizer and with all humanity to understand what the effects of mass inoculations are on subgroups..."

In a concluding gush of honesty, the admission that his population was going through an experiment (but of a good variety) is what, at the root, fuels the flames of distrust directed at the WEF. Even though it was less than a year since the genetic sequence of COVID-19 was shared by China, and the vaccines were only in trials for months, Netanyahu wanted to vaccinate all

Israelis. Before COVID-19, such talk would have been reserved for madmen.

There is no doubt that Israel was the leader in developing and implementing not only the most aggressive vaccine acquisition efforts but the strict mandates that seemed to follow naturally. Israel's 'green pass,' which limited access to parts of society for the unvaccinated, started in March 2021. Beyond communist China, which was doing whatever it wanted to citizens whenever it wanted to, few countries in the world were as restrictive as Israel in March 2021.

Israel's vaccination and mandate tactics meant it was both guinea pig and boldly going where no one else had ever gone. People marvelled and watched the show, and soon after Netanyahu's January vaccine supply victory speech, world leaders wanted to be like Israel. Whether through sheer laziness or waiting for delayed vaccine supplies to show up, Trudeau was indifferent early in the year, even after he first spoke with Netanyahu on January 28, 2021:

"From fighting the virus to rolling out vaccines, Prime Minister Netanyahu and I focused on COVID-19 when we spoke on the phone today."[92]

The next month Trudeau again spoke to Netanyahu. The topic was all COVID-19:

"Prime Minister Trudeau and Prime Minister Netanyahu discussed the measures in place in Canada and Israel to limit the spread of the COVID-19 virus, save lives, and support people. They agreed on the vital role of safe and effective vaccines to protect people and end the pandemic around the world."[93]

You could speculate that Netanyahu was grooming Trudeau to be a vaccination czar or that maybe it was Trudeau digging for answers to why Israel was so far ahead of the curve that every policymaker was looking to flatten. What was known was that these WEF buddies had grown savvier at concealing their discussions since their 2018 *what happens in Davos stays at Davos* moment.

2018: *"Prime Minister Justin Trudeau downplayed that he was planning to have a brief meeting with Israeli Prime Minister Benjamin Netanyahu Wednesday at the World Economic Forum, leaving several Canadian journalists travelling with him in Davos questioning why."*[94]

Yes, CTV did question, from time to time, the motivations of Trudeau.

As Netanyahu basked in his vaccine hoarding glory, the sombre stories relating to Trudeau's vaccine activities were piling up. In late 2020 Trudeau threw $173 million at Medicago, a Canadian start-up looking to make plant-based vaccines. Then there were reports that Trudeau 'wasted millions' trying to make a deal with CanSino Biologics in Tianjin, China.[95] The Canadian government wouldn't reveal how much money it wagered in its CanSino scheme, even after the deal fell apart in late 2020.[96] These failed efforts had sent Canada to the back of the vaccine line.

"If the Canadian vaccine is contributing to this success, there won't be any dividends coming this way anytime soon. And because Trudeau pinned so many hopes on the deal, his government was late to sign contracts with bona fide Western pharmaceutical companies, which likely contributed to our current shortages."[97]

That Trudeau was spending money like a drunken sailor to try and combat the pandemic wasn't the real issue. That he was gambling on a Chinese solution, and throwing hundreds of millions of dollars at a Quebec company with no product was. Chinese-based CanSino Biologics is a direct competitor to Pfizer, and Medicago could be a direct competitor to Pfizer one day. Channels like this could have been explored more discretely or with an off-hand government approach. Instead, Trudeau gave himself a pat on

the back for his investment in Medicago and cheered that he had
*"signed an agreement with Medicago to secure up to 76 million
doses of their COVID-19 vaccine candidate, enough to vaccinate
38 million people."*[98] And when, exactly, are these 76 million
doses expected, Mr. Prime Minister?

The game Trudeau was playing was not unlike the one
former President Obama tried with loans to Solyndra, a solar
energy company that would go bankrupt less than two years after
accepting Obama's funds. It wasn't really Obama's money, of
course, but when you visit the plant for photo ops and make
Solyndra the *'first recipient of an energy loan guarantee to the
tune of $535 million',* your name will forever be tied to the loan
default.[99] The correlation is that if Obama believed he could pick a
solar power winner and Trudeau believed he had the acumen to
pick a start-up vaccine maker, why not shut the hell up and just do
it? Politics is all too often about hyping the effort rather than
allowing the results to speak for themselves.

To many Canadians, it was deeply disturbing that places
like Israel and U.S. were getting a lot more vaccines than Canada.
The reality was Israel and the U.S. were getting the most shots
because they paid up and played ball early and didn't dilly-dally
with China's CanSino Biologics or start-ups like Medicago. The
tension over vaccine supply in early 2021 had gotten so heated that
CTV News reporter Don Martin observed, *'Ordering millions
more vaccines than we need is one thing. When they'll be delivered
for injection is another question altogether.'*[100] Trudeau panicking
and ordering enormous amounts of vaccines was an admission that
he failed to execute a cohesive vaccine plan.

Suffice to say, Trudeau was late to the vaccine acquisition
party just as he would be late to the vaccine mandate after-party.
He was also, even after more vaccine supply started filtering in,
falling behind the pace being set by many of his WEF buddies with
regards to passports and, more generally, an open disdain of the
unvaccinated (which seemed a prerequisite for all WEF-influenced
world leaders). Remember, Emperor Netanyahu demanded a 95+%

vaccination rate in January! Trudeau seemed blithely unaware of what was going on four months later:

May 12, 2021 - *"On Tuesday, Prime Minister Justin Trudeau said restrictions need to stay in place until at least 75 percent of the population has at least a first shot."*[101]

As Trudeau probably surfed and took much time off in the summer, as he usually does, his indifference was not being mirrored by others. By the time a tanned Trudeau returned on the scene, much of the free and not so free world had already enacted passport-like plans or vaccine mandates, including most EU countries, the U.S., New Zealand, Australia, and France:

"During the summer of 2021, French authorities implemented a health pass, or passe sanitaire, requiring everyone aged 12 and older to present proof of vaccination or a negative test for SARS-CoV-2 to access a wide array of public spaces, including bars, libraries, and hospitals."[102]

As French President Emmanuel Macron and others were implementing an aggressive two-pronged vaccine and mandate attack, declarations out of Israel heralded that the country had achieved herd immunity. You read that correctly - as early as May 2021, it was generally accepted that Israel, following one of the most aggressive vaccination and restriction-based programs on the planet, had already reached herd immunity. With barely any cases of the COVID-19 left in the country, Israel's 'green pass,' one of the first of its kind, was scrapped. In Israel, COVID-19 was over. Prof. Dror Mevorach, a senior physician from Hadassah-University Medical Center, said, *'If you look at the reality in Israel, we have achieved actual herd immunity.'*[103]

Israel was so successful, it was thought, that there was really no need to vaccinate kids. The thinking in May 2021 was with some data showing that more than 30% of school kids had antibodies to COVID-19 and cases plummeting in response to the meticulously executed vaccination/restrictions strategy, the heavy lifting was finished. Despite these speculations all turning out to be utter horsecrap, in the summer of 2021, Israel was the envy of a world seeking freedom from COVID-19.

With Trudeau's schemes to try and capitalize on vaccine alternatives dashed, his late vaccine shipments placing Canada slightly behind the relative vaccination curve, and all his WEF buddies way ahead of him in cracking unvaccinated skulls, something finally snapped. Sometime between Israel declaring herd immunity and places like Australia and France showing open hostility against the unvaccinated, the pendulum started to swing in the opposite direction.

Maybe Trudeau remembered Winston Churchill's famous words*, or that Freeland had said COVID-19 was a 'political opportunity,'[104] or maybe he even recollected that he read a speech in 2020 where he had said COVID-19 was an 'opportunity.' Whatever the case, Trudeau finally woke up, read the sinister script, memorized his lines, and bolted into action. Having suffered a Hamletesque period of hesitation and contemplation, the directive was now clearly in front of Trudeau - 'dead for a ducat' or annihilate the unvaccinated!

Chapter 9 - Trudeau's Big Lie

"Make the lie big. Make it simple. Keep saying it, and eventually, people will believe it." ~ Adolf Hitler

In an attempt to justify their vaccine mandate Trudeau's government repeatedly claimed that the shots were capable of stopping the spread of COVID-19. From official quotes and statements to the widespread media coverage that dependably followed, claims that mRNA vaccines were able to *'finish the fight against COVID-19'* were disseminated in all mediums. The speculation that the vaccines were capable of getting us to herd immunity may have made sense in early 2021, but the data was wholly contradicting this faith when on August 13, 2021, the Canadian government stated the following:

"Today's announcement comes in recognition of the dynamic public health situation in Canada. Since the start of the vaccination campaign in mid-December, less than 1% of COVID-19 cases have been among those who were fully protected by the vaccine."[105]

As my saddened, contrarian mind pondered the eight months prior - which involved vaccine deaths that were hardly safe or effective - I interrogated this *'less than 1%'* statistic mercilessly. After all, it was the notion that breakthrough cases[7] rarely, if ever, happened that made the government's mandate digestible to many people. In conducting my analysis, I didn't rely on models and political or geographical biases. Instead, I used the government's own statistical releases.

To my surprise, the >1% statistic could not be verified when studying any government database. The jackrabbit conclusion was that the breakthrough case stat had either been misreported in error or fabricated by the Canadian government. With my dream job threatening to expel me on November 26,

---

[7] A 'breakthrough case' is when a person tests positive for COVID-19 after beign fully vaccinated.

2021, it was essential to understand the minutia to pen precise grievances and win at arbitration, or so I thought.

The first step was to track government case counts in which breakthrough cases were trending higher with each passing day. As of October 9, 2021, the Canadian government reported that 6.0% of total COVID-19 cases were fully vaccinated, 6.4% of the cases were partially vaccinated, and 5.8% *'were not yet protected by the vaccine.'* This meant that 85% of the cases (and 78% of the deaths) had occurred in the unvaccinated. This didn't seem out of line, given that the vaccines had just begun to be put into arms, and before the vaccines, all COVID-19 deaths were unvaccinated.

While the stats up until October 9, 2021 meant little on their own, remember that the Canadian government, on August 13, 2021, advertised that *'less than 1% of COVID-19 cases have been among those who were fully protected by the vaccine.'* How is it possible that *less than 1%* of the total COVID-19 cases were from vaccinated individuals on August 13, 2021, but as of October 9, 2021, total cases from the vaccinated were at 6.0%?

Assuming the statistics from our government are accurate, one of the only things that could explain the reported rise in vaccinated COVID-19 cases from August 13, 2021, to October 9, 2021, is an enormous/unbelievable amount of breakthrough cases. The other possible scenario, which is considerably more nefarious, is that the government simply made up a vaccinated breakthrough case number to make their flimsy vaccine mandate appear more robust. Whatever the case, for the fully vaccinated rate of infection in Canada to rise from less than 1% to 6% over a mere 56-day period, this would require total breakthrough cases to have risen from *less than* 16,591 to at least 99,544.[106] This would mean that vaccinated cases of COVID-19 skyrocketed by more than 500% at the same time total COVID-19 cases increased by only 14% (Aug 13-Oct 9). There is no data that can be gleaned to support that this happened. Emails and telephone calls to Public Health officials went either unanswered or sent up the never-ending food chain of nonsense.

On October 3, 2021, Canada Post announced its vaccine mandate because the Federal government said it would help stop COVID-19. Canada Post reiterated that '*Vaccination has been shown to be effective in reducing the transmission of COVID-19*'. The news was disappointing, although not unexpected. Despite the corrupt data from the federal government, the increase in breakthrough cases alone was compelling enough to build a strong cease and desist case against Canada Post. A quick survey of the provinces before writing grievances in late October would suffice, or so I thought. The idea that breakthrough cases were running at less than 1% was utterly absurd.

October 29, 2021 - Of the reported 141 new cases (October 29, 2021, 12:30 PM), Manitoba reported that *"97 were unvaccinated, 7 were partially vaccinated, and 37 were fully vaccinated."*[107]

October 28, 2021 - *"About 35.6 percent of COVID-19 infections in Ontario over the past two weeks have been in individuals that were fully vaccinated against the disease..."*[108]

October 28, 2021 - Of the reported 511 new cases (see chart on link), Quebec reported that *"327 (63.9%) were unvaccinated, 14 (2.7%) were partially vaccinated, and 170 (33.2%) were fully vaccinated."*[109]

October 27, 2021 - In New Brunswick on October 27, 2021: *"Of the new cases, 24 - or 42.1 percent - are unvaccinated, seven - or 12.3 percent - are partially vaccinated, and 26 - or 45.6 percent - are fully vaccinated."*[110]

October 28, 2021- In British Columbia, for the week ending October 24, 2021 COVID-19 cases were: *"Not vaccinated: 2,377 (56.9%), Partially vaccinated: 300 (7.2%), and Fully vaccinated: 1,504 (36.0%)."*[111]

While statistical transparency can vary from province to province (as can PCR cycle thresholds which impact case totals), the fact is that no province was reporting anything remotely close to less than 1% of cases coming from the vaccinated. Even

Alberta, which provided fewer detailed daily insights, reported that more than 15% of cases had been from fully vaccinated people since January 1, 2021. This statistic alone tells us that Alberta - except for a few days or weeks when vaccination began - had *never* been at less than 1% of vaccinated cases.

October 28, 2021- Alberta reports that *"84.3% of cases (185,251/219,726) since Jan 1, 2021, were unvaccinated or diagnosed within two weeks from the first dose immunization date."*[112]

Even more troubling than the sharp increase in vaccinated people catching and spreading COVID-19 was the fact that many prominent doctors were warning that this trend would continue to intensify going forward.[113] Some doctors from reputable groups like Johns Hopkins and even *some* at the CDC had gone from the idea that *'breakthrough cases are rare'* in early 2021 to the following by September 2021:

"It's likely that everybody will probably get infected with COVID-19 [at some point] because it's an endemic respiratory virus." Amesh Adalja, a doctor and infectious disease specialist at Johns Hopkins Center for Health Security.[114]

To highlight just how stunning the change had been, the CDC previously stopped tracking breakthrough cases in May 2021 due, in part, to the fact that so many scientists believed there were not that many cases to be tracked.[115] It took considerable pressure for the CDC to start even looking at breakthrough cases more seriously. On July 19, 2021, Dr. Scott Gottlieb stated:

"There are breakthrough infections occurring in vaccinated people. I don't think it is an overwhelming number. But we are not tracking it here in the United States, that's the bottom line, we should be tracking it."[116]

With no national body tracking breakthrough cases in the U.S., perhaps by design, how could anyone trust statements from

CDC's Rochelle Walensky and President Joe Biden when they said respectively that, *'vaccinated people do not carry the virus'*[117] and *'You're not going to get Covid if you have these vaccinations.'*[118] If two of the top U.S. COVID-19 policymakers were spreading falsehoods, what hope did the average person have in making informed COVID-19 choices? More importantly, was Trudeau just as misguided as Walensky and WEF Agenda Contributor Biden?

What the government didn't know, or wasn't paying attention to, was that by September, Israel, which through brute force had reportedly reached herd immunity in May, was now getting almost 11,000 cases per day. Israel's initially glorious management of the pandemic played a part in convincing Trudeau to spurn his mandatory vaccination misgivings, and now Israel had *"the highest 7-day rolling average of new daily coronavirus cases per million people."*[119] This should have been another wake-up call that these vaccines were doing a terrible job limiting transmission, even before the omicron variant arrived.[8]

But what should happen doesn't always transpire in this imperfect world, at least not when we expect it to. On July 23, 2021, PHAC noted that 'over 80% of people aged 12 years or older have received at least one dose of COVID-19 vaccine.'120 This was well above the benchmarks for freedom set by Tam and Trudeau throughout the pandemic, including the 75% mark discussed only weeks before. These encouraging statistics would not be enough to stop Trudeau's election power grab and his warm embrace of mandates. It didn't matter to the strategists that a big lie about breakthrough cases was told (please prove me wrong); this was merely one component of a much larger story or plan. The strings pulling Trudeau to-and-fro were tightening. How would he respond?

---

[8] Israel hit nearly 11,000 COVID-19 cases per day in September 2021. When omicron arrived daily case counts peaked at more than 20 times this amount!

Chapter 10 - Now You See Vaccine Injuries Now You Don't

"Public statements from physicians that contradict public health orders and guidance are confusing and potentially harmful to patients. Those who put the public at risk with misinformation may face an investigation by the College, and if warranted, regulatory action." ~ Dr. Heidi Oetter, Registrar and CEO of the College of Physicians and Surgeons of BC[121]

After the big breakthrough lie, nothing would ever be the same. How quickly the changes happened was remarkable and, at the same time, terrifying. In early 2021 the Ontario Science Table (a very pro-vaccination body) openly discussed vaccine-induced immune thrombotic thrombocytopenia (VITT) and other vaccine injuries, trying to provide the best data as it became available.[122] Also, back then, the media reported vaccine deaths and injuries, often even before such injuries could be finalized in AEFI reports. But shortly before the big lie, vaccine injuries and deaths, which while rare were still happening, seemed to vanish. The COVID-19 cases and 'with covid' deaths were still extensively reported on a daily basis by policymakers and the media. The 'after vaccination' deaths and injuries were not.

Part of the unofficial media blackout on vaccine injuries may have been connected to the government taking on greater vaccine-related liabilities. To wit, in June 2021, Canada finalized its first national vaccine injury compensation program,[123] and in August, it was confirmed that *'Burial costs will now be covered by Ottawa for individuals killed by federally approved vaccines.'*[124] If you believed that the government influenced the media, which it sponsors, it is reasonable that Trudeau's launch of the Vaccine Injury Support Program (VISP) and the upcoming mandates changed the direction and tone of COVID-19 news in Canada. Those that think this sounds conspiratorial need only look at the finances of, say, CBC, which in 2020 had less than $200 million from advertising revenues versus $1.3 billion in government subsidies.[125] The reality is CBC does not exist without Trudeau's guiding hand.

Another explanation for the shift in focus was that many media bosses, personalities, and journalists believed that vaccination and mandates were essential for stopping COVID-19. Given that in August 2021, more than 50% of vaccinated Canadians were already 'unsympathetic' if the unvaccinated caught COVID-19,[126] it would not take much for these sentiments to be leveraged and, in some cases, radicalized. As cases of COVID-19 started increasing at the same time Trudeau pledged strict vaccine mandates, the unvaccinated were being blamed for cancelled cancer screenings, delayed operations, and, in effect, for prolonging the pandemic. Under these circumstances, if the greater good could be served by ignoring vaccine side effects, why not overlook a rare vaccine injury or three? The stirring feeling, like an ominous dew in the air, was that if those damn unvaccinated would just take the damn shots, we could end COVID-19, or so the story went.

The only thing more remarkable than how quickly most Canadians started blaming the unvaccinated for many societal ills was how quickly vaccine injuries vanished from view. In May 2021, the government said there were 5,989 reports of AEs in Canada following a COVID-19 vaccine, of which 1,126 were considered serious.[127] We read about many of the AstraZeneca-induced blood clots and deaths, and even some legacy media in Canada sometimes picked up the news about side effects from Johnson and Johnson's Janssen vaccine being announced globally. Then, as Trudeau's August mandate day neared, the volume of negative vaccine news coverage abruptly declined; some might even say it crashed. This didn't make any sense in the context of rising vaccine injuries. After all, the 1,126 'serious' injuries reported by May 2021 would jump, according to our government, by nearly 750% over the next 12 months![128] Where was all the news coverage of these serious injuries? Anyone? In New Brunswick, vaccine deaths were one day on the province's counter, and weeks later, the death by vaccine category was simply erased off the COVID-19 dashboard.[9] Was it out of sight, out of mind?

------

[9] Dr. Russell was asked via email and telephone why vaccine deaths and injuries stopped being updated daily. Per the trend, she did not respond.

At the same time the big lie and anti-unvaccinated campaign were set in motion, Sweden and Denmark paused the use of Moderna in younger people due to *'possible rare cardiovascular side effects.'*[129] At the same time Trudeau was dreaming up schemes to punish the unvaccinated the *'National Institutes of Health awarded grants totaling $1.67 million to five institutions to explore potential links between COVID-19 vaccination and menstrual changes.'*[130] And at the same time the Liberals promised $1 billion to provinces enacting vaccine passports,[131] Iceland suspended Moderna's vaccines completely,[132] and France and Germany limited the use of Moderna in younger people.[133] Apparently, safe and effective meant different things in different areas.

Armed with whatever amount of money the federal government wished to conjure, there was a seemingly well-engineered plan - that Trudeau wanted to be adopted at every level of government and by every major political party - to punish the unvaccinated until they bent the knee. Before the big lie, there were many provincial leaders and Premiers that didn't want to coerce their citizens into taking vaccines or join a crusade to crush those in society who cherished medical choice or privacy. Consider what Alberta Premier Jason Kenney said as recently as July 2021:

"We've been very clear from the beginning that we will not facilitate or accept vaccine passports...I believe they would, in principle, contravene the Health Information Act and also possibly the Freedom of Information and Protection of Privacy Act. These folks who are concerned about mandatory vaccines have nothing to be concerned about."[134]

In the case of New Brunswick, Premier Higgs also didn't want mandates, but business was business. Supported by the COVID-19 influx of federal funds and Trudeau's promise for more, Higgs would parlay a projected record deficit in 2021 into a massive surplus. Like many unscrupulous politicians flip-flopping for federal funding, Higgs was hoping no one would remember what he said on July 23, 2021, literally only weeks before Trudeau's big lie:

"We have surpassed our goal of 75 percent of the eligible population with their first vaccine and are now at 81 percent. By the end of next week, the percentage of eligible New Brunswickers vaccinated with the second dose will be high enough to balance out many of the risks of living with COVID-19...we believe we are safe to take this next step and learn to live with COVID-19 without the mandatory order."[135]

It didn't matter that more than 80% of citizens were voluntarily taking the shots, and likely many more would. To cash another cheque, Higgs had to read the script, mandate vaccines, and announce a vaccine passport in New Brunswick right before the election. So he did.

Eventually, all the provinces, to varying degrees, adopted mandates and vax-passes, with Quebec starting on September 1, 2021, BC on September 13, 2021, and Ontario on September 22, 2021, to name three. With many polls saying the public was vehemently against mandates in Alberta - which some compared to the freedom-loving U.S. State of Florida - the province was reluctant to comply. Nevertheless, Premier Kenney, less than a month after pledging *'folks who are concerned about mandatory vaccines have nothing to be concerned about,'* still read the script, mandated the vaccines, and established a vaccine passport that started on the day of the election.

As deeply disconcerting as the lack of information about vaccine injuries was, the ominous extension of Trudeau's grasp around the provinces added to the sense that the battle lines between unvaccinated and vaccinated could become even more entrenched. Quite frankly, the mandates left an indelible rip in the social fabric of Canada in ways that were completely inconceivable only weeks before, and there was the sense that repairs would not be imminent. To use a quick example, 50-year-old cardiologist Dr. Sohrab Lutchmedial was so upset by the unvaccinated that he lashed out at them on social media, arguing he wanted to punch some of the unvaccinated in the face and that he would not shed a tear if they died.[136] This was a man of science, supposedly intelligent and, per the job, compassionate. Not surprisingly, when Mr. Lutchmedial died three weeks after his third shot of the vaccine, the response from some was vile and merciless. There was no evidence that Mr. Lutchmedial's 'sudden death'[137] was related to the vaccines, but those that were hurt by Mr. Lutchmedial's insensitive comments, those damaged mentally or financially after being persecuted for their medical choices, screamed karma and retribution sentiments. Still more blamed Trudeau for allowing this deplorable state of affairs to happen in the first place by sanctioning division and hate.

What was lost in this landslide of rage-inspired unruliness was the honest and important question - did Mr. Lutchmedial die from a vaccine injury? Asking the question meant you were insensitive, probably an 'anti-vaxxer,' and not showing enough concern following a young man's death. Conversely, not asking this question, or at least not taking an honest look at vaccine injuries, may have meant you blindly trusted these new vaccines with a sense of naive obedience. Trudeau often said, *the science is settled'* when discussing vaccines. After hearing this so many times, like a form of hypnotism, were some people starting to believe this in their bones?

It wasn't that the unvaccinated were right and the vaccinated were wrong. Like everything in life, there was context, nuance, and the insight that no one on either side of the vaccination spectrum had ownership of absolute wisdom. But many of the emotionally charged vaccination crusaders behaved as if their defences could never be dropped until every last person on earth took the shots. This position that no one was safe until everyone took the shots was off-the-wall bizarre. Many Canadians had already had three shots of mRNA, and Israel was about to start doling out shot number four. Was there a point where the number of boosters becomes ridiculous, and if so, where exactly was this point? Likewise, was there a number of vaccine injuries or deaths when the mandates should be reversed, and if so, what were these numbers?

By December 2021, there were more AEs reported from the vaccines in Canada than there were deaths 'with covid'. This fact remains a constant until this day. And by December 3, 2021, shortly after Canada Post's vaccination mandate kicked in, there were already 6,581 serious AEs from the vaccines officially reported,[138] and likely many more that were never reported. Along with anecdotal information and my firsthand experiences (of watching those injured by the vaccines not being able to get AEFI reports filed), the AEFI numbers seemed to be an anomaly compared to the higher rates of vaccine injuries being logged in the U.S. VAERs system and other countries. For example, while Canada reported 28,825 COVID-19 vaccine AEs as of December 3, 2021, Australia, with 10 million fewer people vaccinated than Canada, had already reported nearly 80,000 AEs.[139] How is it possible that Australia was reporting AEs at more than four times the rate of Canada?

Canada was well known, legally speaking, to be one of the most challenging places to fight vaccine injuries in the courts. In 2009 a five year old girl took an H1N1 vaccine, and five days later, her heart stopped. The judge ruled *'The only proven relationship between the vaccine and Amina's death was time,'* and Ontario's chief forensic pathologist said *'Amina may have died from Sudden Arrhythmic Death Syndrome (SADS).'*[140] Despite no definitive cause of death, the judge added that *'plaintiffs must prove both general causation (whether a vaccine could cause the alleged injury) and specific causation (whether it actually did so).'*[141] From what I can discern, zero otherwise healthy five year olds die each year in Canada because their hearts just stop. The overriding point is getting a vaccine injury declared a vaccine injury in Canada was difficult, and getting any vaccine injury affirmed in the courts was next to impossible. It wasn't coincidental that Canada had some of the lowest rates of reported AEs. It was how vaccine injuries were scrutinized and, in most cases, ignored.

The coincidences were also being pulled out of hats elsewhere in the world, including Canada's neighbour to the south. As Steve Kirsch wrote in his popular and thought-provoking blog, *'something changed around July 2021 when the NIH abruptly stopped responding to the vaccine injured.* '[142] Why would the U.S., around the same time as Canada, curtail efforts to investigate and document vaccine injuries timely? Ah yes, I almost forgot:

July 27, 2022 - Biden White House readies a vaccine mandate for federal workers[143]

With much of its MSM pretty much one giant corporate ad already, that the U.S. was reducing efforts to shine a light on vaccine injuries was not surprising. The basic theme, also playing out in other countries and purely by coincidence, was that the unvaccinated must be penalized until they take the shots. This goal is so crucial there is nothing untoward with any actions or inactions that serve to diminish the significance of vaccine injuries. This story continued that the crisis was the fourth wave of cases, and the unvaccinated hooligans were putting a strain on healthcare, not the ultra-rare vaccine boo-boo!

If you were really nuts enough to believe herd immunity was still attainable in late 2021, the logic of avoiding mention or coverage of vaccine injuries was sound. After all, the pressure via mandates and passports was being applied now; more and more people were getting vaccinated now, so why not worry about recognizing, updating, or paying out people for vaccine injuries later?

For the greater good or not, holding this iron curtain up against vaccine injuries produced nocuous effects, including further dividing people across the country by vaccination status. As those vaccinated parroted 'safe and effective,' the unvaccinated raged the vaccines were not very safe and not at all effective. And as the unvaccinated protested, 'my body my choice,' the vaccinated said the unjabbed should not be allowed to work or go out and be with any vaccinated person in society. Whether you wanted to play in this game or not, the mandates were going to throw you on a team, and you were going to be told to fight, and fight most did.

Dr. Lutchmedial, who died too young, believed so strongly that some unvaccinated people were spreading misinformation and scaring others not to vaccinate that he lashed out. Although I disagreed with his conclusions, and he may have chosen his words unwisely, in a strange way, the doctor's heart was in the right place. Similarly, many unvaccinated people believed so strongly that people like Dr. Lutchmedial were part of the problem that they propelled any ammunition they could to attack him professionally and tarnish his memory. This tit-for-tat trend escalated until people were so frazzled and frustrated on both sides that watching the extremes became heartbreaking. By late 2021 a vaccine death, verified or not, was hailed as victory and vindication to some that chose not to take the jab, and, conversely, anything that punished the unvaccinated, no matter how cruel, was a victory for those that made the 'right' choice in taking the jab. We all may be good enough as we are, jabbed or not jabbed, yet in this narrow fragment of time in late 2021, suspicion and paranoia festered and blinded people. The quarrel between the vaccinated and unvaccinated threatened to become a blood sport. It was a brutal moment in time that was partly inspired by King Trudeau's brutal policies and words.

During these dark days, the provinces would update their daily statistics with things like COVID-19 hospitalizations, ICU, and death counts. We were informed that the main story on most days was that more unvaccinated people died than vaccinated, and for this reason, the unvaccinated were selfish. What we were rarely reminded of was what the National Institute of Health (NIH) and others had been telling us for more than a year:

"...30% of these [COVID-19] hospitalizations were attributable to obesity, 26% to hypertension, 21% to diabetes, and 12% to heart failure. These people would still have been infected with COVID-19 but likely would not have been sick enough to need hospitalization."[144]

Did being unvaccinated and catching COVID-19 exacerbate underlying medical conditions like those noted above? In many cases, yes. Could the vaccines have saved the lives of some of the sick people that died from COVID-19 in 2021? Absolutely yes! And lastly, were healthy people below the age of 65 clogging up hospitals and dying 'with covid'? No. No, they were not.

What the deeply flawed and completely sickening hospital data (discussed later) didn't tell us was that the vast majority of people in hospitals or dying from COVID-19 were already sick and unhealthy. Vaccines do not magically make people healthy.

If trees start falling in a protected forest, the first instinct is to query who is cutting them down. Seemingly healthy people like Dr. Lutchmedial sadly suffered cardiac-related injuries shortly after being vaccinated, and some were even dying. It didn't make you a bad person to ask if the vaccines were the cause. It didn't make you selfish to wonder why the Ontario Science Table was updating vaccine injuries at a snail's pace, if at all.

When information and transparency become the enemy for the supposed greater good, as was the case in Canada in 2021, seldom have the results provided a long-term benefit to the general public. The country of Eritrea wears the unenviable crown of having the most jailed journalists, and CPJ notes that *'even those working for the heavily censored state press live in constant fear of arrest for any report perceived as critical to the ruling party, or on suspicion that they leaked information outside the country.'*[145] As Trudeau and his companion, Jagmeet Singh, refused to answer questions from the far right 'Rebel News' during the election campaign and Liberals talked tough about new laws to censor 'misinformation', you could not help but cringe. A month after announcing extreme mandates and calling one segment of society hurtful names Trudeau, our dictator, blamed Rebel News for a polarized Canada:

"The reality is organizations, organizations like yours, that continue to spread misinformation and disinformation on the science around vaccines, around how we're going to actually get through this pandemic, and be there for each other and keep our

kids safe, is part of why we're seeing such unfortunate anger and lack of understanding of basic science, and quite frankly...your group of individuals need to take accountability for some of the polarization that we're seeing in this country... "[146]

As the vaccine injury information was being overlooked, delayed, or likely willfully suppressed, Trudeau injected the type of despotically charged rhetoric that only a dictator would. It's not about whether Rebel News is right or wrong on the variety of subject matter they investigate and report. It is about the fact if you don't like Rebel News, you don't have to watch and read Rebel News.

Angry that people didn't believe him when he said Canadians were so dearly distraught because they didn't know how to turn Rebel News off, Trudeau's RCMP security detail would later, coincidentally, assault Rebel reporter David Menzies.[147] The misinformation-filled video that included Mr. Menzies getting roughed up was, much like vaccine injuries in late 2021, not covered by the MSM.

Chapter 11 - The Mandates Cometh

"In 1918, at the recommendation of the Surgeon General of Public Health Service, entire States reportedly shut down public gatherings of any kind, including funerals. The American Public Health Association agreed that "[n]onessential gatherings should be prohibited." Laws "regulating coughing and sneezing" were also deemed desirable. Huge signs on New York streets warned, "It is unlawful to cough and sneeze." Within days more than 500 New Yorkers were hauled into court..." ~ Michael Greger, M.D., FACLM. How To Survive A Pandemic

Trudeau didn't seem to care or perhaps didn't know that in Israel, one of the most vaccinated places on earth, COVID-19 cases were skyrocketing in September 2021. Rather, with some of his vaccine policy mandates announced and the election weeks away, there was no putting the genie back in the bottle. Leading up to the election on September 20, 2021, Trudeau lashed out against Canadians demanding medical privacy, choosing not to take an mRNA shot for legitimate reasons, or simply protesting mandates. Trudeau lumped this diverse collection of Canadians all under the 'anti-vaxx' umbrella. His verbal attacks and lies levied against this group were, per Mein Kampf, *'so colossal that no one would believe that someone could have the impudence to distort the truth so infamously.'*[148] Here are two of them:

September 1, 2021 - *"The folks out there tonight shouting, the anti-vaxxers, they're wrong. They are wrong about how we get through this pandemic. And more than just being wrong, because everyone is entitled to their opinion, they are putting at risk their own kids, and they are putting at risk our kids as well...Everyone needs to get vaccinated, and those people are putting us all at risk."*[149]

September 17, 2021 - *"Yes, we will get out of this pandemic by vaccination. We all know people who are a little bit hesitant. We will continue to try and convince them, but there are also people who are fiercely against vaccination. They are extremists who don't believe in science, and they're often misogynists also often racists...This leads us, as a leader and as a country, to make a choice: Do we tolerate these people? "*[150]

The anti-vaxxers were wrong? The anti-vaxxers were racist and misogynistic? Trudeau obviously didn't know or care that according to a poll reported in Maclean's, the *'Typical 'vaccine hesitant' person is a 42-year-old Ontario woman who votes Liberal.'*[151] He didn't care about this because his primary election foe, Progressive Conservatives leader, Erin O'Toole, was a wet fish on the topic of vaccine mandates. Not exactly an electoral genius Trudeau nonetheless had some savvy, and he recognized that O'Toole's floppy take on vaccine mandates was a weakness worth exposing at every possible moment. Many Canadians still demanded someone that would cherry-pick models, espouse easy mantras, and shout that COVID-19 was the enemy soon to be vanquished by the vaccine weaponry. O'Toole was for vaccines but had been wishy-washy on mandates and draconian pandemic restrictions. It didn't matter that O'Toole was more rounded and judicious on the topic of vaccinations, the mandates were coming down the track, and a lot of Canadians wanted to climb on board.

During his election campaign, Trudeau was often heckled, verbally harassed, and once had small rocks tossed at him. The government was capable of tracking every Canadian during the pandemic without telling them,[152] but apparently, this pebble thrower was somehow never found. The story that Trudeau was the victim and the rock thrower didn't believe in science played for a day. Maybe said thrower was a plant, I thought. After all, and not to make an inappropriate comment, but if I were nuts enough to toss some tiny rocks at Trudeau during broad daylight, the rocks would be much larger, and they wouldn't have stopped being hurled until I was cuffed. Along with rocks and yelling, a lot of yelling, a few venues had to be cancelled as those raging against his mandates were raging a little too much. Protesters in Trudeau's presence needed to conduct themselves with suitable decorum, lest they be ignored and not tolerated like Rebel News.

While a smidgen of leeway can be given to Trudeau for making mindless statements and intentionally stirring up hate during the election campaign, that he continued to play the role after the election was more than a little irksome. As Trudeau stayed in Hitleresque character - yes, these comparisons were already starting to fly - more data relating to the Phase 3 clinical trials of the mRNA vaccines began to trickle in. Released on September 30, 2021, one major report was entitled *'Increases in COVID-19 are unrelated to levels of vaccination across 68 countries and 2947 counties in the United States.'*[153] Published shortly before the Pfizer-sponsored study that said the vaccines don't limit transmission, the study was a direct assault on prevailing attitudes. If you were to read one study, this would be the one to read.

"At the country-level, there appears to be no discernable relationship between percentage of population fully vaccinated and new COVID-19 cases in the last 7 days. In fact, the trend line suggests a marginally positive association such that countries with higher percentage of population fully vaccinated have higher COVID-19 cases per 1 million people."

With the notable exception of fraudulent data, it didn't seem possible that this study, which was the largest of its kind, produced fallacious results. The verdict was abundantly clear: the vaccines may limit severe outcomes in certain groups of people, but they are not capable of limiting transmission. Counteracting the steady inflow of reports telling everyone to get vaccinated because the shots limit hospitalization and death, this massive study also made an ominous recommendation:

"The sole reliance on vaccination as a primary strategy to mitigate COVID-19 and its adverse consequences needs to be re-examined, especially considering the Delta (B.1.617.2) variant and the likelihood of future variants."

Unlike the statistics coming out of Canada and its leader that never discussed actual COVID-19 facts with any degree of objectivity, the study even accounted for the key variable of efficacy lag. The conclusion was much the same - vaccination does not influence case counts!

"Since full immunity from the vaccine is believed to take about 2 weeks after the second dose, we conducted sensitivity analyses by using a 1-month lag on the percentage population fully vaccinated for countries and U.S. counties. The above findings of no discernable association between COVID-19 cases and levels of fully vaccinated was also observed when we considered a 1-month lag on the levels of fully vaccinated."

Shortly after this ground-breaking study was released, Trudeau announced, on October 6, 2021,[154] that another vaccine mandate for all transportation employees and travellers would commence on October 30, 2021. Having barely won a pointless election two weeks earlier - where the Liberals merely maintained their minority role - the implementation of more mandates and more tough rhetoric was a strange path. The contrarian mind fluttered and flexed that maybe this wasn't just an election issue and that maybe, just maybe, this moron believed the nonsense he was saying. The alternative was that the WEF (or similar type of unnatural force) was pulling Trudeau's strings, that he lost a bet, or he was somehow profiting from each dose delivered.

On October 25, 2021, another study, this time out of Sweden, stated that *'seven months post-vaccination, the Pfizer and AstraZeneca vaccines had no detectable effectiveness at preventing infection.'*[155] Given that the majority of Canadians were already more than seven months removed from their vaccinations, this study was important. The MSM and the government-friendly doctors they regularly aired ignored this study entirely. Then, like raindrops falling, studies from all over the world confirmed that the vaccines were not working to limit transmission and that their efficacy rapidly waned even before the omicron variant arrived on the scene. The studies were telling us things like the *'humoral response was substantially decreased'*[156] and *'BNT162b2-induced protection against SARS-CoV-2 infection appeared to wane rapidly following its peak after the second dose'*[157] and that *'Natural immunity was 27 times more effective than vaccinated immunity in preventing symptomatic infections'*. We also knew, as Trudeau pounded his fists and seemed to be leading a charge to complete mandatory vaccination in Canada, that there was *'no significant difference in cycle threshold values between vaccinated and unvaccinated, asymptomatic and symptomatic groups infected with SARS-CoV-2 Delta.'*[158] Even Sir Fauci agreed viral loads were similar in the vaccinated and unvaccinated. Few in Canada cared.

That there was no real difference in viral load between the unvaccinated and vaccinated was important! That natural immunity was stronger and lasted longer than two doses of vaccines was important (and much, much later confirmed by the CDC)![159] These studies and the real-world data out of Israel informed us, beyond any doubt, that there was absolutely no way these vaccines were going to end COVID-19. Why the hell was Canada about to force more people to take these injections?

Then, finally, a large study out of the UK, a country usually weeks ahead of Canada in the COVID-19 game, was released. It was a doozy entitled *'Community transmission and viral load kinetics of the SARS-CoV-2 delta (B.1.617.2) variant in vaccinated and unvaccinated individuals in the UK: a prospective, longitudinal, cohort study'.*[160] The takeaway from the UK study was that those vaccinated were just as likely to spread COVID-19 to those in their household as those that were unvaccinated. This was a mic drop study barely covered by the MSM.

The problem wasn't that Trudeau couldn't understand the data and the studies - with a little effort, anyone could - but that he was either being kept from it or didn't care. Equally concerning was that the majority of Canadians didn't care either. When discussing the upcoming mandates at my work, a lady puffing a cigarette who had just been vaccinated said in her group, *'they [meaning the anti-vaxxers] should just take the vaccine.'* When I calmly interrupted and asked why she thought taking the vaccines was a good idea, she said it was the 'science.' That's it. One word. Science.

There were rising breakthrough cases almost every day in Canada, rising vaccinated deaths on an absolute or relative basis, and all this was taking place as there was a massive push worldwide for the booster shot(s) to start increasing. Instead of spreading the lie that vaccination could end COVID-19, the government should have accepted the reality that even if a 100% vaccination rate could be immediately achieved, COVID-19 would still continue to exist and spread. Sometimes this truth eked out in the heavily biased Canadian press, but not often.

Dr. Dale Kalina: *"If 100 percent of the people were vaccinated here in Ontario, then 100 percent of the cases would also be in vaccinated individuals."*[161]

With the Government of Canada and Canada Post having failed or never even really attempted to demonstrate that the vaccines were absolutely necessary, the mandates should have been scrapped. Forcing individual health decisions on employees would set a terrible policy and precedent.

My gym started asking for vaccine passports on September 21, 2021, which would persist until February 28, 2022. A few days before this happened, while on the treadmill, I heard the owner say to another person that *'they're the reason why this is happening [referring to the unvaccinated].'* I kept quiet, knowing I would never return. In the early days, these lockdowns or restrictions were sold as necessary to break the curve that would overwhelm our healthcare system. Now the message was to blame the unvaccinated because they are selfish sons-of-bitches. At what point were Canadians going to wake up and see that it wasn't the unvaccinated, or those with the flu, or the obese, or smokers breaking the healthcare system, but the policymakers that had proven over time incapable of fixing the healthcare crisis?

This blame game had been played before. Consider what happened 13 years ago with the H1N1 vaccine in a Globe and Mail article entitled *'Refusing to get vaccinated is selfish.'*[162]

While the above words may have sounded convincing 13 years ago, they were nonetheless based almost entirely upon fear. As it would turn out, only 41% of Canadians got the H1N1 vaccine, and the healthcare resources of Canada were never close to being 'depleted.'[163] You would think that after writing such ridiculous forecasts, the authors would bury their heads in shame. On the contrary, the same co-authors of the above hot air - Associate Professor Juliet Guichon and University of Calgary's Ian Mitchell - were back floating more wild theories in November 2021 with *'10 reasons to book a COVID-19 vaccination appointment for your child.'*[164] Be it perpetuating undefined 'long covid' fears or stating unscientifically that kids 'have died,' it was actually difficult to read the complete article without getting upset.

"Vaccinating your child will help other people because vaccinated people rarely infect others."

The above-unmitigated falsehood was unleashed on November 24, 2021. I tried contacting both authors for an explanation. No response. I believe that Guichon and Mitchell are little more than two deranged lunatics.

The same devices Guichon and Mitchell used to make their hay in 2009 and 2021 were being co-opted by Trudeau and his gang, along with the notable addition of one new wrinkle being added to the dictatorial fold. The Canadian Federal vaccine mandate started on October 30, 2021. Trudeau wasn't bluffing.

* Contextual Interlude Activated *

Before proceeding on the journey, it would be prudent to emphasize that I am not boldly claiming every study I comment on is 100% infallible. Quite frankly, I lack the expertise to make such a determination. What's more, I cannot say that I have somehow miraculously distilled the most critical elements of what constitutes the COVID-19 'science'. As Dr. Peter McCullough notes:

"On PUBMED, there are 27,901 papers in a search for "Spike Protein." This is not good news for those who have taken 1, 2, 3, 4 injections of the genetic code for Spike. The protein damages the human body and causes a wide array of symptoms, disease, disability, and sadly death."[165]

Most people in the medical field, much less ordinary citizens, do not have the time to read 27,901 papers or comb through the minutia and either agree or disagree with the viewpoints of doctors like McCullough. What people should do, in my humble opinion, is be critical of all information at all times.

This said, when the lead author from the UK paper in the previous chapter, Annelies Wilder-Smith, wrote a summary of her team's study, it struck me as an effective way to highlight my thought process. Professor Wilder-Smith is almost as world-renowned as Dr. Fauci, and she has ties to both the WHO and WEF. Consider the following:

"Infectiousness of breakthrough infections can be measured by viral densities. Higher SARS-CoV-2 viral density in the upper airways of people infected with the virus is thought to increase transmission to household members. If vaccines reduce viral density in those who do become infected despite vaccination, it would probably lead to lower infectiousness and less onward transmission. Hence, the authors compared the viral kinetics in breakthrough delta variant infections in vaccinated people with delta variant infections in unvaccinated people. They report that peak viral loads showed a faster decline in vaccinated compared

with unvaccinated people, although peak viral loads were similar for unvaccinated and vaccinated people.

Although preventing severe disease and deaths remains the primary public health goal in the acute phase of the pandemic and is still being achieved by available COVID-19 vaccines despite the emergence of the delta variant, addressing SARS-CoV-2 transmission is a crucial additional consideration. Reducing transmission is necessary to reduce virus circulation, reach herd immunity and end this tragic pandemic. This study confirms that COVID-19 vaccination reduces the risk of delta variant infection and also accelerates viral clearance in the context of the delta variant. However, this study unfortunately also highlights that the vaccine effect on reducing transmission is minimal in the context of delta variant circulation. "[166]

Now, when the MSM puts a doctor on the news, they see a study like this to make a case for vaccination. There is enough source material to absolutely promote the vaccines as providing certain benefits. But when I look at this study, I see one consequential sentence - *'the vaccine effect on reducing transmission is minimal.'* In the context of mandating someone to take these injections, potentially for an extended period or maybe even for life, this is the only line in my mind that matters.

- Do I care that *'peak viral loads showed a faster decline in vaccinated compared with unvaccinated'*? I would if this led to a notable reduction in rates of transmission, but according to the study, they did not.
- Do I care that some people believe that *'preventing severe disease and deaths remains the primary public health goal'*? No. I care if these shots notably reduce transmission, which they do not.

Some might say I am being heartless and that preventing disease and death should be a major concern for all. My response is, please make your own personal health decisions, and please refrain from trying to influence mine. To use a comedic quote to explain my position, Ron Swanson from the television show Parks and Recreation will suffice:

"The whole point of this country is if you want to eat garbage, balloon up to 600 pounds, and die of a heart attack at 43, you can! You are free to do so. To me, that's beautiful."

Similarly, if you choose to take a vaccine or not to take a vaccine, I think the act itself, or the choice, is the beautiful part.

The prime reason for the lengthy quote is that deciphering the spirit in which information is being imparted to the world can sometimes be immensely more fascinating than the information itself. The authors of the UK study wanted their theories relating to *infectiousness* and *onward transmission* to succeed, and they absolutely believed in the efficacy of the vaccines, but in the end, they begrudgingly had to acknowledge no notable reduction in transmission. I trust this study's conclusion.

I also trust, as mentioned, the October 3, 2021, Pfizer study and will endlessly find this study fascinating. Does anyone really believe that Pfizer would pay for and then rig a study to say that its COVID-19 vaccine sucked at limiting transmission? Anybody?

Conversely, what I don't have much confidence in are COVID-19 studies that preach policies instead of plainly covering the facts, and studies that appear bought and paid for by special interests. Case in point, a massive Israeli study released on May 5, 2021, covered the January 24 to April 3, 2021 period to tell us the Pfizer vaccine was working wonderfully. Less prominently displayed in the study was the fact that eight of the authors held *'stock and stock options in Pfizer'* and that despite no direct 'funding,' the study was in the complete control of Israel's Ministry of Health and Pfizer:

"MoH and Pfizer were involved in the study design and writing of the report and approved the decision to submit for publication."[167]

Netanyahu paid more than everybody to purchase Pfizer's vaccines faster, and in early 2021 on a *'doses per 100 population'* metric, Israel was vaccinating at a rate more than three times that of any other country in the world.[168] It didn't take a conspiratorial leap to assume Israel and Pfizer had a vested interest in ensuring everything was awesome with this vaccination program, even if they suspected in a few months' time, everything might fall apart. Like actors doing a media tour for a subpar movie, Netanyahu and Pfizer still had to put on a brave face and smile.

The high efficacy 'studies' out of Israel seemed to ignore waning vaccine strength by simply not looking at it. You may recall that Netanyahu said Israel and Pfizer were going to treat the Israeli people like they were in a laboratory and intensely study the vaccinations so that the world might benefit from this new knowledge. This didn't appear to be what was happening:

"With nearly 7 weeks of follow-up after the second dose, our study has the longest follow-up reported so far, although longer-term data on effectiveness are needed."

We were told by Netanyahu in Davos that 98% of health records were digitized, and money was no object to purchasing, administering, and monitoring the greatest vaccination campaign in history. If this were true, applauding the seven-week 'follow-up' as some type of splendid achievement was really pathetic, given that the vaccines had been aggressively administered for more than 18 weeks by the time the study was released. Did all the data and information, which one would think would be near instantaneous, somehow get caught up in an unknown tech buffering cloud? Or maybe it was Israel's MoH and Pfizer using extra cautious hands to edit, limit, and redact? The other less likely alternative was that technologically unmatched Israel was unable to test, trace, and correlate positive COVID-19 results with those that had the shots.

---

[10] Mr. Kennedy Jr's amazing book is entitled *The Real Anthony Fauci: Bill Gates, Big Pharma, and the Global War on Democracy and Public Health'*. It is a must read for those interested in the subject matter.

Despite most of these real-world studies shyly looking at efficacy for less than seven weeks, these were the types of studies regularly mentioned by Fauci and other vaccine salespeople in early 2021. I don't spend a great deal of time criticizing Fauci, given that Robert F. Kennedy, Jr. did an amazing job already,[10] but in an effort to provide context to why I disparage Fauci, a quick look will suffice.

To begin with, Fauci knew at least as early as July 6, 2021,[169] that vaccine strength could be waning, and on July 18, 2021, Israel's Ministry of Health[170] confirmed that the vaccines were *just 39% effective as delta spreads.'*[171] With this knowledge in hand and fully aware that the delta variant already made up more than 80% of the cases in America,[172] Fauci still went on television and stated the following:

"These vaccines work well against this virus, including the Delta variant. We just need to get more and more people vaccinated."[173]

With the help of the always trustworthy Pfizer lawyers, Israel had been cooking up happy-rainbow vaccine efficacy studies for months; now, the actual raw statistics, not an interpretation thereof, were saying efficacy waned dramatically. The kicker was that the July 18, 2021 statistical release made a point of stating it used the exact same methodology as the limited May 5, 2021, Pfizer report. The window for ignoring waning efficacy was starting to close.

Despite all of this, Fauci, who since February 2021 had been mentioning the preliminary Israeli data as often as possible because the vaccines were tremendous,[174] still went on countless television programs saying the vaccines were good against delta. And even when talk of waning immunity brought the topic of boosters into focus, Fauci stressed the vaccines were totally awesome on July 13, 2021:

"This [the boosters] has absolutely nothing to do with the effectiveness of the vaccine. These vaccines are highly, highly

effective, both in the clinical trials and the real world effectiveness studies."[175]

Like the CDC changing the definition of the word, 'vaccine,' Fauci was trying to tweak the definition of the word 'effective.' This man had no shame. The definition of effective is: *successful in producing a desired or intended result.* People that took these vaccines desired not to catch COVID-19 because they were repeatedly told by every major policymaker, Fauci included, that the vaccines were 90+% effective at stopping transmission. The purpose of the vaccines wasn't so that your body would make memory B cells or to boost your immune system - the vaccines were supposed to reduce transmission, help get us to herd immunity, and end COVID-19! To this end, when Pfizer told us the vaccines were still effective at reducing transmission after 6-months on April 1, 2021,[176] Fauci practically had a parade to celebrate. Now faced with conflicting data, Fauci was struggling to conceive how the vaccines could still be construed as being highly effective. As Fauci delved deeper into his tunnel of folly, he strained to keep a straight face:

"This [the need for boosters] isn't a question of whether the vaccine is effective or not. It has to do with the durability of the protection. So there really is nothing wrong if, in fact, and I don't know whether it's going to happen or not, but if there will be a necessity to maintain a high level of effectiveness by having a booster sometime down the pipe that that be that a year or two..."

The very idea that Fauci's sanctimonious wordplay could somehow negate the fact that durability and efficacy were intrinsically related was contemptible. The U.S. booster campaign that Fauci said may start in a 'year or two' on July 13, 2021, would actually commence only weeks later. These 'highly effective' vaccines were the least 'durable' in history.

During the key weeks when the Israeli data threatened the entire COVID-19 vaccine edifice, Fauci was extra curt, cantankerous, and lying his ass off all over television and media.

The increasingly smug and openly combative Fauci quickly went from being the charming old man to the psychotic screaming, 'I am the science!' The reason for the overly defensive stance was that Fauci was the first prominent American figure, one of the first in the world, in fact, who was trying to delicately articulate that the vaccines were so ineffective at blocking transmission we should just switch our focus entirely and look to hospitalization and death prevention instead. The repercussions of suggesting this change in focus without careful discernment could mean, obviously, that many could be turned off completely to the vaccines.

Whether this tactical change was adopted for the purpose of some greater good or something entirely more wicked, it was nonetheless clear that Fauci was a bullshit artist. The very idea that Fauci was intimately aware of all Israeli data from February to June 2021 but then suddenly acquired amnesia when this data stream started telling a different story in July 2021 is malarkey. If I was following most major reports out of Israel, rest assured, Fauci was too.

By August 12, 2021, approximately seven weeks after we first started hearing vaccine efficacy was rapidly waning, Fauci finally acknowledged that everyone would eventually need a booster.[177] And by August 30, 2021, Israel had become much quicker at compiling and releasing data as a nationwide study on all PCR positive test results from July 11-31, 2021, was released.[178] It would take until the Pfizer study on October 3, 2021, before the Israeli data would be confirmed by a trustworthy source (and to reiterate, this is when any thought of mandates should have expired). During this time, I began to see Fauci as little more than a punchline that one day, with any hope, would be reprimanded for his gain of function and other shenanigans.

Next, there is a vital consideration when I, or anyone else for that matter, discusses things such as case counts, hospitalization rates, ICU rates, or COVID-19 deaths. The idea isn't to trust Canada because it used to be a nice country and not trust China because it is, well, a communist hellhole when it comes to reliable data, but to not trust any country's statistics. To use a quick example, COVID-19 hospitalization cases in Canada started out with those that went to the hospital suffering from COVID-19 registering as a hospitalization. Then, once hospitals started screening and testing all patients for COVID-19, any positive test for the virus immediately became a COVID-19 hospitalization. Even if you went to the hospital with a broken leg, if you happened to test positive for COVID-19, you were a COVID-19 hospitalization. Only in 2022 (spoiler alert) did they start telling us that a lot of the cases of COVID-19 hospitalization had shown up to the hospital for other reasons and just happened to test positive for COVID-19. Moreover, from hospital to hospital, province to province, and country to country, when exactly these types of statistical changes took place is impossible to track.

Along with not trusting the statistics due to geographical incongruities, government influence, or perhaps insufficient resources, there was also the question of undue monetary influences. No more prominent was this the case than in the U.S., where a COVID-19 patient netted a hospital an additional $13,000, and a COVID-19 patient on a ventilator bumped this amount to $39,000. I have watched some creepy videos where doctors say influenza was misdiagnosed as COVID-19 and the government-enforced treatment protocols almost killed the patient. It is not my place to judge the veracity of these claims, but I will say that when you financially incentivize the identification of a COVID-19 patient and the standards used to verify a COVID-19 patient are extraordinarily lax, it would not be surprising if some COVID-19 hospitalizations tallies were embellished. Sen. Scott Jensen, R-Minn., a physician in Minnesota, said it best:

"Hospital administrators might well want to see COVID-19 attached to a discharge summary or a death certificate. Why? Because if it's a straightforward, garden-variety pneumonia that a person is admitted to the hospital for - if they're Medicare - typically, the diagnosis-related group lump sum payment would be $5,000. But if it's COVID-19 pneumonia, then it's $13,000..."[179]

Next, mortality rates are difficult to pin down, and I, like many people playing armchair COVID-19 quarterback, will make speculations that are not backed by hard evidence. This is done because there is no science that tells us precisely how many cases there have been due to things like asymptomatic cases, false positive tests, lack of testing, etc. If someone acting smarmy asks if you are a doctor when it comes to mortality rates, understand that no doctor, anywhere, has the exact mortality numbers.

Also, to note, some quotes contained within are exceptionally long. This is usually done to provide full context or because the original source material is sometimes deleted or revised without accreditation.

Finally, after much ado, there is the topic of ivermectin. I have purposely refrained from mentioning ivermectin because the implications of the word are amazingly polarizing. Ivermectin is both the conspiracy artist's ultimate muse and the simplest word used to call someone a crackpot. My advice is if you want to go down the ivermectin rabbit hole, by all means, please do, but set a hard date and time when you will exit. Then after exiting and contemplating all that you have seen and read, write down your honest opinion, seal it, burn it, and move on.

[My opinion only] - I believe ivermectin is an extremely safe anti-parasitic drug that was used by some countries to *maybe* treat COVID-19 successfully. I also believe ivermectin has been unceremoniously bashed because, *maybe*, the only way drug manufacturers could get EUA for their vaccines was if there were no treatments for COVID-19. I further believe that Merck, whose patent on ivermectin expired in 1996, attacked its own inexpensive and low-margin drug[180] because more money could be made from bringing Molnupiravir to market. In short, and to be perfectly blunt, if someone is sick with COVID-19 and wants to take ivermectin, what the hell is the harm? Reprimanding or even arresting doctors for prescribing ivermectin is one of the ghastlier acts undertaken during the pandemic. The best conspiracies are rooted not only in the land of plausibility but in the lingering weeds of deep thoughts. Why would the FDA care so dearly that a doctor was giving a COVID-19 patient ivermectin?

In summary, when I reference studies or ballyhoo medical information, please keep in mind how I personally gather, interpret, and value information. I am not a doctor writing a prescription, Pfizer refused to pay me off, and I try my best not to be a Fauci.

With the above in mind, end interlude.

Chapter 12 - Grievances, Activism, and EI, Oh My

Following the August 13, 2021, declaration of war against the unvaccinated, Trudeau's government pledged to meet with stakeholders (i.e., unions) to discuss how to implement the vaccine mandates. Canada Post Corp., a Crown Corporation, wasn't directly mandated to follow the Federal government's policy but was expected to follow it. Long story short, and after some legal semantics, Canada Post and every other Crown Corp. were picking up weapons and fighting against the evil anti-vaxxers.

The first problem with The Canadian Union of Postal Workers (CUPW) meeting with Canada Post to discuss mandatory medical procedures for all employees is that employees were not consulted. Of the numerous articles in our collective bargaining agreement, which supersedes Canadian law in some cases, none came close to suggesting a handful of CUPW leaders could meet with a handful of Canada Post lawyers and decide on the best health choices for all members. The very idea that CUPW would agree members must be vaccinated or sent home without pay was so astonishingly bizarre I couldn't believe it. Unions are supposed to fight for the rights of all members, not simply the ones acting with an irrational fear of dying from something that was highly unlikely to harm them.

At this point, I quickly did the math using the latest government statistics available at the time. Of the 16,333 'excess deaths' that occurred in 2020, COVID-19 accounted for 14,140 of these deaths, and if you take out the deaths of those 65 years of age or higher, the excess deaths from COVID-19 number dropped from 14,140 to approximately 707. Needless to say, the vast majority of Canada Post employees were below the age of 65.

More shocking than the excess COVID-19 related deaths were overdose deaths in Canada, which, according to the Canadian Vital Statistics Death Database, had skyrocketed during the COVID-19 pandemic: *'there were 5,535 more deaths than expected in those younger than 65 from the end of March 2020 to the beginning of April 2021.'*[181] When contrasted against the 707 excess deaths from COVID-19 in people below the age of 65, the 5,535 excess deaths from overdose in this same age group were outrageous. You could state that when speaking of excess death, people less than 65 years of age were almost eight times more likely to die from an overdose than from COVID-19. Why was Canada Post trying to force all employees to take a vaccine when far greater benefit to employees could be achieved by directing these mandate-related resources into mental health and addiction treatment modalities?

I then looked at healthy people below the age of 65 or those that did not have any known comorbidities. Using the government's math, I arrived at 73 'healthy' people that had died below the age of 65 from COVID-19 since March 2020. The overriding point was that an extremely low number of people under the age of 65 had died from COVID-19, and a low number of otherwise healthy people of any age had died from COVID-19. When contrasted against approximately 4,000 people in Canada dying every year from suicide[182] and another 4,000 from poisoning,[183] COVID-19 deaths in otherwise healthy people were a preposterously small number.

These types of statistics and the complete lie the federal mandate was based on (>1%) begged the question: why wasn't our union standing up and fighting for member rights? Why were our leaders meeting behind closed doors discussing coercing medical procedures? Many members I worked with were equally dismayed. And so began the resistance.

Our local leadership, try as they might, was uninterested in rocking the boat. They were of the mind that this was the way society was going and that it wasn't illegal to have mandates since we were in a pandemic. At the time, many of us were obviously exceptionally frustrated, but the thinking was our local wasn't paid off so much as haplessly ambivalent. They were, as when I was a child, simply of the mind that people sometimes have to take vaccines.

At our local, we were more than 400 members, with approximately 70 on my shift. In less than a half hour, the majority of members on my shift (more than 40) signed a document demanding medical privacy. These people were not all 'anti-vaxx,' against the government, or in a sleeping cell of terrorists looking to hop in a truck and park it in Ottawa. Rather they were hardworking people (who would likely laugh as I use the words 'hardworking') that simply wanted to keep their medical choices private. Some of the most ardent vaccine supporters on our shift, the members that wore masks alone in their cars and would do long jumps to keep their distance from everyone, actually signed the petition because they, per the petition, *preferred not to disclose their personal health information (PHI) to Canada Post or CUPW.'* Simple. Elegant. The majority! There was a faint hope we might stop the mandates from being enacted yet.

To be fair, there were also members disgusted by the mere sight of the petition. These people believed unvaccinated people were a burden on society, that they were selfish, and a tiny minority of them wished ill will toward the unvaccinated. Arguing or debating with these hard-core members had to be handled delicately. For example, saying the vaccinated could still catch and spread COVID-19 was apparently no match for the sophisticated comeback - *'this is a pandemic of the unvaccinated!'* And when these individuals contended that the hospitals were overflowing, offering to drive by the two main hospitals in Moncton to see if this was true wasn't considered polite. Like precious snowflakes quick to become rabid wolves, this tiny group softly believed that anyone questioning the 'science,' or anything the government said for that matter, should be immediately fired and then banished from society. They knew this in their hearts to be true.

Leading up to LWOP day, I never really had a major issue with anyone on either side of the issue, but when challenged, I absolutely stood my ground and tried to state facts. If people wished to argue or debate, that was wonderful, although most of the indoctrinated scoffed at the mere thought they would ever catch COVID-19. Instead of telling these people that everyone was highly likely to catch COVID-19, you would have more luck convincing them the moon was made out of cheese. It has been said that between first contact and the first desire to leave a cult takes approximately 22 months. We were less than 12 months into the vaccination campaign, and it had been 19 months since COVID-19 started. No one was leaving the anti-unvaccinated cult quite yet.

The petition was sent to our local. No response. It was also sent to our National President inside a 23-page document outlining member concerns with the ongoing discussions between Canada Post and CUPW. These packages of information and questions were sent in late September, or just over one month after Trudeau announced his vaccine mandate plan. Plenty of time for member concerns and questions to be researched, analyzed, and hopefully, answered. Our National leadership didn't respond. A follow-up email on October 10, 2021, also was ghosted. Apparently, our President and National Executive were too busy discussing how best to mandate members to take vaccines.

The Canada Post vaccine practice was to start on November 26, 2021, or about a month after the general Federal mandate went live. The reason for the delay was that Canada Post and CUPW were working on a testing option for those that would not get vaccinated. The deal to allow unvaccinated employees the testing option was extremely far advanced, and a CUPW October 7, 2021 press release outlined this agreed-to option:

"Canada Post will announce its plans to comply with the vaccination requirements for federal workers to the membership next week...By choosing the rapid test option, you will be required to self-test twice (2x) a week prior to entering your workplace".

A couple of weeks after being posted, the above press release from CUPW was deleted from CUPW's website. The deal was off. Canada Post's vaccine policy would force all employees out of their jobs if they did not comply with the mandate by November 26, 2021, and the option to test was completely gone. All emails and calls to CUPW National leadership were unanswered. No one at my local could answer why the press release was deleted from the CUPW website. You could say the fix was in, and many did. The hum from someone somewhere was unmistakable - those damn anti-vaxxers deserve what they get!

As our union tried to shift the blame to Canada Post, the story told by facts spoke differently. Had our union leaders simply refused to negotiate forced medical procedures on members, there is no way the mandates would have happened. Instead, our leaders went into meetings thinking they would negotiate a vaccine mandate that had a testing option, and the company scrapped the testing component of the deal completely. The union was left rudderless and didn't know what to do. So, as is often the case, union leaders blamed the company for backing out of the original deal. Canada Post could counter they only backed out of part of this deal. What no one at CUPW did was acknowledge that the mistake was going into the room with the company in the first place.

As if these developments were not bad enough, CUPW's cease and desist order was denied on November 25, 2021[184], and the union proceeded to call up Colin Furness as an expert witness in the first arbitration case. Colin Furness was an academic that had never treated a patient and constantly made the rounds on MSM, praising how wonderful the vaccines were. Furness didn't believe in medical exemptions but was a strong proponent for mandates, or the very thing members wanted to fight against! From this moment on, I did not doubt anyone who said our union was corrupt or incompetent. Our leaders had asked, down the entire chain of command, for members to file individual grievances. The content of these grievances was completely disregarded in favour of basically agreeing that vaccines were necessary to stop the spread. This was backstabbing for the ages.

All the union demanded was that the testing option be brought back. While this demand is fine on its own, why the hell did it have to be lumped in with CUPW agreeing that the vaccine's limited spread? The Colin Furness debacle was and is a soreness that lingers until this day. It would take until June 25, 2022, before I finally spoke with President Jan Simpson and found out why Mr. Furness was selected as our witness. The reason will surprise you. All horrifically idiotic things come to those who wait.

Shortly before our LWOP day, there was a protest in Moncton over the mandates. The Canadian Frontline Nurses started the protest, and some of us from work decided to show support. Beyond the strikes I had been involved in, this was the first real protest I had attended. It was a happy event. We held signs and waved at cars as they passed by and honked. Just as some pro-vaccination people had found unity with others that had made the 'right choice' to take the shots, this protest was about unifying and bonding with those that believed 'choice' should not be weaponized for political or powerful ends. Many at the protest were vaccinated, including some nurses who came out of the hospital to show support. All wanted Canada to maintain the status quo - no mandates!

As LWOP day arrived, Employment Minister Carla Qualtrough (Carla) argued that those being forced out of their jobs for not taking the shots would not be eligible for Employment Insurance (EI):

"It's a condition of employment that hasn't been met...And the employer choosing to terminate someone for that reason would make that person ineligible for EI. I can tell you that's the advice I'm getting, and that's the advice I'll move forward with."[185]

That Carla, to who I sent multiple emails and telephone requests to (no response), had the audacity to go on television and threaten Canadians based on the 'advice' she was getting was appalling. Carla's threats were at the behest of her boss Trudeau and arrived before re-writing the EI Act or having consulted those charged with the EI benefits mechanism. At the time, I hoped this was a toothless scare tactic. With Trudeau and others peddling craziness all the time, that didn't mean the rules surrounding EI were going to be changed to punish those who failed to disclose their medical information, did it?

As the EI threats were being dropped like bombs on the unprotected, the war of opinions that Trudeau had started continued to rage ever hotter. Having been forced out of work on LWOP, the grievances filed, and the maybe pointless EI claim sent in, it was time to turn the brain off in December. How does one do this exactly?

Chapter 13 - The South Africa Swindle

On November 26, 2021, I was forced out of my job for not disclosing my vaccination status, and I entered December 2021 with no severance, no EI, and a union that was, almost openly, gunning for these mandates to stick. To say that these were stressful times - something I thought I usually handled very well - would be an understatement.

My position made speaking with others sometimes painful and heated. In the case of my mom, on the phone, when discussing that I was off work on LWOP due to the mandates, she said, 'why don't you just take the vaccine?' I started to answer calmly that I didn't want to take any of the current vaccines, and I was only on leave right now, when she interrupted me and stated something like, 'well, you can't lose your job!?' My mind went black as I screamed something to the effect that it was none of her business, and if Trudeau wanted me to take his crap, he better bring guns. My mother and I didn't speak for more than a week. She was thinking about my kids, of course, as was I, but irrationality begets irrationality. I started to realize my level of stubbornness was elevated and that I would immediately grow irritated with anyone, including my mother, delving into my choices.

As December progressed, I drank a bit more and, at least a couple of times a week, would completely lose it on the phone with someone. Living in New Brunswick, the usual suspects for people like me to vent, rage, and ask questions to were Premiere Higgs, Doctor Russell, Shephard, and, surprisingly enough, Education Minister Dominic Cardy. While the Three Stooges - Higgs, Russell, and Shephard - were never available to comment on their policies, this left secretaries, assistants, and voice mail to pass messages along. As for Cardy, we had multiple conversations, many of which I cursed loudly at him. To his credit, he did not hang up (he seemed to like it, actually). Cardy was a witty, smart, but also fanatical figure whose COVID-19 hit list was widely followed and panned in New Brunswick and around the world. The velocity at which Cardy would deploy insulting and assaultive language, without the threat of exaggeration, rivalled that of anyone on the planet. Consider Cardy at his most ludicrous:

"Parent: How can you say it's alright to vaccinate our children? It's our children, not yours.
Cardy: No. They are our province's children."[186]

Yes, Cardy, who does not have children, said the province owned kids, and he said this out loud and on camera. The uproar across Canada and parts of the world was fantastic. Here are some of Cardy's other controversial statements:

August 27, 2021 - *"These folks [the unvaccinated] are going to get worse until they are confronted and beaten by regular people who see them as a threat to our (imperfect) institutions as they are."*[11]

August 29, 2021 - SD: *"A lot of kids will be staying home if Mr. Mandatory Vaccine Cardy gets his way!"*
Cardy: *"please keep your plague kids away..."*[11]

September 13, 2021 - *"At some point, we have to call this pandemic what it is. The pandemic of the unvaccinated spread by unvaccinated to innocent others."*[187]

September 13, 2021 - *"At some point, we have to say there is going to be a response by the vaccinated. By the enormous majority who've done the right thing, and there is going to be a decline in tolerance for those, for whatever reason, endanger the lives of the people around them. That's about where I am right now."*[188]

October 19, 2021 - *"We'll be keeping the unvaccinated people out of schools, out of hospitals, out of our government offices."*[189]

Following a couple of these and other reckless comments, I would call Cardy's office and complain. Although part of me

---

[11] Mr. Cardy made these comments in response to tweets. A screenshot was taken. The tweets are no longer available online.

realized this was likely wasted energy, it was a compulsion when reading the latest news that I could not control. Once I called late at night with the intention of getting his answering machine, and a voice picked up and said hello. I said is Mr. Cardy there and the voice responded with 'speaking.' After a couple of minutes of debate about COVID-19 child mortality rates, which Cardy equivocated on, he told me people were threatening him and sending him a barrage of hate mail. Fascinated, I asked him point blank: *'Are you really surprised by the reaction to some of the crazy shit that you have been saying?'* He said he didn't see it this way. We argued a bit more. It was like talking to a wall.

In many respects, Cardy was like Furness in that discussing facts, and debating these facts, was not his forte. Instead, Cardy preferred to ruminate on things like long covid or the threat of kids spreading COVID-19 to grandma to justify his pre-contrived conclusion that there should be mandatory child vaccination. By contrast, I wanted Cardy to admit that the individual risk to kids from COVID-19 was basically zero and that the risks from the vaccines to kids were not zero. Neither Cardy nor Furness would ever acknowledge or quantify these facts.

The next eruption phase arrived when reading the 'news' in the middle of December. The quote from Cardy that sent me into a tizzy was:

December 15, 2021 - *"The preliminary information that we're receiving around the Omicron variant is that it is significantly more risky for children compared to the previous editions."*[190]

I picked up the phone to complain and, once again, Cardy picked up. I asked what the hell he was thinking about making such an outlandish statement. Cardy didn't think the quote made it into the papers, given that he was not in an interview at the time. I informed him that it did and read him the quote. He contended the information was based on a South African study. Having been watching the hot sheets on omicron intently, I said he was full of shit and asked if he would recant and apologize. He refused and said his comment was based on the study. He was cocky, as usual, and my mood was deteriorating, so I then asked him if he would apologize for the blood on his hands for the AstraZeneca deaths earlier in the year. His silence spoke volumes. This was a slime ball, know-it-all that didn't quite know it all.

By way of a recap, in May 2021, Cardy, who is not a doctor, said people should take the first vaccine that comes in their direction. He also said don't listen to NACI recommendations. A least two people died in New Brunswick from AstraZeneca. This wasn't a VAERs-like conspiracy or potentially fake filings. These vaccine-induced deaths were reported in the mainstream press. With a population of 800,000 and the AstraZeneca vaccine just being released, two deaths were exceptionally notable and terrifying. Below are Cardy's words, reported in the news in a May 4, 2021 article entitled *'N.B. minister says to 'ignore' federal vaccine panel, accept first vaccine offered.'*[191]

"Ignore NACI, ignore anti-maskers, ignore the people undermining faith in science, and do your part for New Brunswick."[192]

Remembering that NACI was Canada's CDC, how is it possible Cardy got away with saying 'ignore NACI'? Perhaps because he also mentioned that people *'ignore anti-maskers'* - words that warmed the cockles of many a Canadian heart in 2021.

Beyond his 'I stand by my comments,' Cardy refused to add a comment to the AstraZeneca deaths. As for the South African study, Cardy acted like a petulant child hiding a rare dinky car when I asked if he could share the link. He said I would be able to find it. I hung up. With thoughts of strangling the bastard running through my head (briefly and with love Canadian thought police), I eventually did track the study down, and I started to interrogate the veracity of his claim. It was called *"Discovery Health, South Africa's largest private health insurance administrator, releases at-scale, real-world analysis of Omicron outbreak based on 211 000 COVID-19 test results in South Africa..."*[193] Here are the opening highlights:

"Children: Despite very low absolute incidence, preliminary data suggests that children have a 20% higher risk of hospital admission in Omicron-led fourth wave in South Africa, relative to the D614G-led first wave."

The above statement seemed to suggest Cardy wasn't full of beans. However, as the study continued, the innards quickly turned rotten:

"It is important to note that these insights relate to data from the first three weeks of the Omicron-driven wave in South Africa. Therefore, the insights should be considered preliminary since they may change as the wave progresses."

The above words provided the wind-up. Then came the fastball:

"Anecdotal reports from hospitals in South Africa indicate that most COVID-19 diagnoses in children admitted to hospital are co-incidental - many children who are admitted for non-COVID-19-related conditions and who are not experiencing COVID-19 complications test positive for COVID-19 on routine screening tests."

That routine screening tests could be responsible for 'most' of the children testing positive for COVID-19 meant the study, insofar as child hospitalization rates, was completely unreliable. As for the word 'anecdotal' - if you don't have the actual data and you are not disclosing when, exactly, full screening began, what the hell is the good of any kid-related information in the study? The study went on to add:

"Children were 51% less likely to test positive for COVID-19 relative to adults in the Omicron period and, overall, the risk of children being admitted to hospital for COVID-19 complications remains low."

Cardy had stated that omicron was *'significantly more risky for children.'* The above statement was saying the exact opposite of this. Days after the South African study, even Dr. Eric Topol, who often exhibited extremely biased pro-vaccination carolling, had a moment of perfect clarity:

"It's a peculiarity that hasn't been explained," Topol said of the high rate of hospital admissions for children [in South Africa]. "It hasn't yet been seen in the United Kingdom, Denmark, Norway, and other places hard hit by omicron."[194]

The reported high rates of hospitalization for kids in South Africa had not been explained or confirmed because it was not happening. If Cardy and Topol had read the entire South African study, they would have known this. On LWOP and curious, it seems that I had the time while they did not.

It turns out this wasn't an isolated incidence. Incomplete or fraudulent data and conclusions were making the rounds with each new variant. On this topic, Russell Viner, Professor of Child and Adolescent Health, UCL, stated the following:

"Regarding the suggestion of higher hospitalisation rates in children for Omicron, it is essential to recognise that these are incomplete and partial data. For each previous variant, we saw early claims that children were more affected, which turned out later not to be true. In November 2020, we saw claims that the alpha variant affected children more, and in May-June 2021, we saw similar claims about delta. Each of these were the result of early partial data, and neither turned out to be correct. This emphasises the importance of being careful about extrapolation from very limited data."[195]

Cardy wasn't even extrapolating limited data; he was simply taking one sentence of a report and making a harebrained fear-laden statement that was entirely inaccurate. It was like saying *'the dog ran by the mailman'* and concluding that the mailman was safe, while the real story was *'the dog ran by the mailman and then came back and mauled him.'* Cardy didn't read the whole study; he didn't realize that hospitalizations for kids were up due to skyrocketing cases from omicron and a substantial increase in 'incidental' hospital visits. He also didn't read that, compared to adults, kid cases of COVID-19 were actually down with the arrival of omicron. This wasn't simply a case of cherry-picking; it was the erroneous adoption of a proliferation of fiction.

When the UK Standard covered the South African report, they used the headline *'Children may be more at risk from Omicron, experts warn,'* and when thehill.com used early South African data on omicron, they came up with the headline *'Top South African expert says omicron is surging among children under 5 years old'.* Panicky headlines may sell clicks or attract eyeballs - and convince someone like Cardy to make dangerous claims - but it was completely counterproductive to intelligent discussion.

With the South African study clearly debunked, I emailed Cardy. No reply and no recant or apology for his false statement. I would never speak to this appalling man again. Part of me wished him harm, an eye for an eye, and another part of me felt sorry for him. Cardy was saying outlandish and intentionally false things. Karma was coming for him, I thought.

Unfortunately, this Cardy experience was replicated in other arenas in December 2021, many of which I am not proud of. As more evidence that kids handled COVID-19 just fine continued to arrive, somehow, the push to vaccinate kids was given renewed powers by the misinterpretation of statistics out of places like South Africa. This push to vaccinate kids, without even a mention of the natural immunity many kids already had, was, in my mind bordering on abuse.

In late December, I got a call from an RCMP officer asking if I had been harassing a pediatrician. I asked the officer what I had done, and he said nothing serious but inquired if I had left the pediatrician a message. I almost asked the officer which pediatrician but quickly surmised this might not be the best question to ask. Being evasive and surprised that my exploits had risen to this level, I acknowledged I asked questions on Facebook to a pediatrician, and they were there for all to see. I then inquired what the message on the pediatrician's machine stated. The officer said the message was a little aggressive, and they thought they should call it in. I responded that any pediatrician stating 'your child could die' from COVID-19 was being more than a little aggressive, and if any doctor makes such a claim, they should absolutely produce the risks associated not only with catching COVID-19 but also the vaccines.

I knew or thought I had done nothing illegal given that the pediatrician had on their webpage contact if you have any questions. Moreover, I had not used foul language or threatened anyone on Facebook or in the telephone message. But I was quite firm in asking, 'since you mentioned kids could die, what is the risk of death for kids in Canada from COVID-19?' The officer, somewhat amused by my evasiveness but not really, simply asked that if I did make the call, not to make anymore. I concurred using a Pfizer-like 'without admitting or denying making the call' statement. I politely informed the officer that if these mandates kept going, he might have to make a choice of which side he wanted to be on. He quietly chuckled and paused. He knew I was serious. We parted ways.

Immediately following this call, I knew that if the mandates, vaccines, and boosters kept going into perpetuity as the studies and facts continued to tell us the vaccines didn't work, I would be amassing weapons and preparing for battle. I'll be the first to admit that sounds a little nuts, but there was a stirring feeling that I would rather die than live in a Trudeau-dictated WEF-related, communist-leaning hellscape. In China, there were reports of overzealous officials forcibly pinning citizens to the ground and injecting them with the vaccine. Low odds or not, I would not be getting pinned to the ground to take an injection of something that doesn't work, not so long as I had breath left in my body.

There are those reading this that may surmise I was over-exaggerating events. The ominous reality may have been that I was under-exaggerating. The lockdowns were initially about containing case spread until the vaccines arrived, and now, with vaccination rates above any herd immunity estimate provided by Dr. Tam, the lockdowns were about what exactly? Those that said the government wanted vaccine passports in 2020 were deemed crackpots, so why was Trudeau, even as vaccine efficacy was confirmed to be terrible, now openly talking about a national and international vaccine passport system? We knew that the risk COVID-19 posed to kids was comparable to that of the flu,[196] so why did kids need to take the shots to play sports, go to dances, and attend once-in-a-lifetime grad events? There is no way to overstate that the policy overreach, brought to Canada by Trudeau, was absolutely not about public health. You could argue, and many would in 2022, that these policies were actually anti-public health.

As the month of anger sessions and sipping whisky would help illuminate, it wasn't that the mandates were unlawful that was really irking me. It was the fact that they didn't work, and, risking hubris, I absolutely knew they would never work. The very idea that 70% wasn't enough for herd immunity, 80% wasn't enough, and then somehow 90+% might be enough was logic based upon a mountain of lies.

There was no longer much nuance or open-mindedness to my contrarian viewpoint. Instead, I adopted a scorched earth mandate. To those with differing opinions that wished to dance, they had better bring facts to the floor. When combatants denied facts, I resorted to questioning their intelligence or demeaning them. In this sense, I was threatening to become that which I loathed, or a person exhibiting cult-like fanaticism for their respective group ideology. I reckoned since I was right, I wasn't really allowing my biases to cloud judgement. Yet, the rare concoction of chemical stimuli coursing through my body sometimes made me question just how level-headed I really was.

In the introduction, I alluded to providing more information on my mental health situation. The anxiety build-up in December 2021 was the pinnacle of my most neurotic behaviour. I could not stop thinking about the mandates, the threat of losing my job, my kids losing their health coverage, or even the threat of losing the house. In my mind, I was under attack, and the ammunition I thought best to strike back with was ignored by my union and ignored by those mandating me to take the shots. This wasn't a simple incentivizing program to take a vaccine. This was coercion, assault, and torture. Until my last breath, an unshakable part of my mind believed this to be true.

Feeling desperate, lost, and devoid of the tools for remedy, I put the call in with two Moncton psychologists. Do you know what it feels like to leave messages with psychologists and not get a call back? The profession I had ridiculed as hokum before was too busy to give me the time of day. Karma, it seemed, was laughing at me. There were rumours that Trudeau's government was putting retainers out to lawyers across Canada to limit anti-mandate lawsuits. Was Trudeau also somehow limiting access to psychologists to punish the unvaccinated into taking the shots? Were Trudeau's goons telling all mandated companies and agencies to ignore any questions relating to vaccine efficacy and safety?

The word for my rambling was paranoia, or *the irrational and persistent feeling that people are 'out to get you.'* My mind during these days sometimes lacked the ability to decipher real versus imaginary threats. On buses in Ontario, there were banners with pictures of a child in a hospital bed with the ad reading 'Kids have strokes too.' Jesus, I thought - there were mounting reports of young athletes around the world dropping with cardiac episodes after being vaccinated; now, this? Eventually, everything in my cosmos was lighting up COVID-19 this or vaccine that, and the wattage was blinding. Apophenia was drawing connections and parallels that were not there. I wondered if my intense and sometimes compulsive association tendencies would become pathological or remain relatively sporadic or passive. I also wondered if I was the right person to be making such a determination.

Confirming every instantaneous thought of something being amiss in the insanely mandated and overly China-friendly world being dictated by King Trudeau went beyond my reasonable purview. The idea wasn't too many rabbit holes, not enough time, but that too many compulsive brainstorms had rendered time an extinct species. Part of me knew the correlations were mostly fantastic derivatives of memes circulating around the internet that, if you somehow conjured the objective inclination, you could probably debunk. But then again, psychologists were listening to my telephone messages and not calling me back, and Cardy and many others, using a South African swindle, were permitted to say whatever the hell they wanted.

Given that the big lie and a constant diet of misinformation were the primary ingredients used as justification for the mandates, I now understood why the other side, at the extreme, battled using similar weaponry. Stories that 5G amplified COVID-19 into a killer, that the virus and the vaccines were engineered bioweapons, or that Bill Gates was a murderer that also wanted to starve the world by purchasing all the farmland were the popular extreme notions passed around by the 'anti-vaxxers.' Less popular were the esoteric studies about vaccine efficacy.

The idea that any means necessary may be required to win this war vibrated within me. I saw a glimpse of how diving into radicalism or extremism might be necessary evils for glorious victory. At the same time, my contrarian instincts bedevilled me from leaping freely into the pool. If it took misinformation, misdirection, and the straight-faced spreading of pure fiction, could I really partake? Did I have the mental fortitude to throw my sense of fairness to the wind? Did I have the stamina to be effective in this type of slimy warzone? For a moment, the eerily evilness of those using a South African swindle for their ends jaded my character and marooned my moral compass. It had been some time since I had a good night's sleep.

As my mind raced, paced, and rattled around sometimes aimlessly, I recalled that Cardy was called a 'virus whisperer' back in May 2021 by the National Post.[197] It turns out his predilection for making dire predictions, spreading lies, and attacking the unvaccinated may have all been part of an act to promote his long-held goal to force all kids to take vaccines.[198] I pitied Cardy, and the best part of me knew I didn't want to be like him.

Chapter 14 - Finding My Hill to Die On

Shortly before LWOP day, there was another protest in Moncton. We marched downtown listening to Twisted Sister's 'Were not going to take it.' The crowd, much larger than the nurses' rally, was still very peaceful. One impatient driver skinned a protester driving through the crowd. He was later arrested. It did not ruin the day.

Next, there was a new bridge opening in Riverview that Trudeau was anticipated to attend. At the bridge opening/protest, there was an elderly couple standing next to our group, and the lady was visibly upset that she couldn't get closer to the ribbon-cutting ceremony. Standing right beside her, I sincerely tried to be nice and jokingly interjected, 'well, it's still a free country, I guess.' The lady became irate, and her husband lunged at me with his fists up, ready to hit me. In a shocked pause, I kind of laughed but then realized he was deadly serious. He stood still for a moment with his arm cocked.

I calmly informed the old man if he touched the women, I would beat the crap out of him (this wasn't meant to be misogynistic as I happened to be at the protest with a group of all women, including my daughter. I try to respect both men and women, or whatever gender you happen to believe you are, equally). Save the remote possibility of severe mental illness, this older man wanting to punch me for literally no reason was my first encounter with an agent provocateur. My theory was that this older fella and his wife or accomplice came to the protest that Trudeau was expected to attend, looking to cause a scene. The story would read – *an elderly gentleman just wanted to watch the ribbon cutting at the new bridge opening when he was viciously attacked by an 'anti-vaxxer.'*

Was I being overly paranoid? Perhaps. But moments after trying to goad me into hitting him, the older man was calling a younger kid holding a flag an idiot and raising his fists again. Either this guy was the most passionate bridge ribbon-cutting aficionado in the world, or he wanted to get punched. The kid didn't budge and laughed off the old man's aggressiveness, as no doubt most at this protest would. Security arrived, and as quickly as the insanity started, the elderly couple was escorted away.

Trudeau never showed, and the bridge opening was cut short as hundreds of protesters drowned out the speakers. Despite pushing up the bridge opening by two weeks to align with when Trudeau would be swinging by, the 'media' (CBC) reported that internet rumours falsely said that Trudeau would be at the bridge opening. This seemed like a taste of psychological warfare, meant to make the protesters feel like they were wasting their time. Regardless, there was no violence, no arrests, and, thankfully, none of the peaceful protesters were charged with mischief.

After the protests, I was getting all hooked up on the covert media destinations, and I was speaking with like-minded people who wanted to do more than hold signs and march. This crowd wanted, for lack of a better way of putting it, to break some shit. Still hoping for a late-hour reversal of the crumbling vaccine mandate, I was reticent to climb aboard the crazy train in October and November, but we were now into December 2021. The vaccines were not and would never be able to stop COVID-19. The mandates had to go, and the pattern of tormenting and torturing private medical choices had to be stopped.

The eureka moment arrived when Higgs announced his 'Winter Action Plan' on December 3, 2021.[12] Within the plan was the option that grocery stores could require proof of vaccination instead of enforcing physical distancing and strict capacity limits. Even in the face of vaccine passports becoming commonplace across Canada for things like restaurants, entertainment events, and gyms, the idea of limiting access to food from the unvaccinated had never been done. Food, obviously, was essential.

____

[12] New Brunswick's 'Winter Plan' was released on December 3, 2021. During COVID-19 Higgs and company sometimes changed wording of press releases without acknowledging these changes.

Needless to say, this took an already tense and depressing situation and threatened to make it much, much worse. With many people freshly unemployed and not able to go anyplace, denying access to food would surely spark violence. Meeting with friends on protest pages, we joked about how it was unlikely any major grocer would ever commit to banning people from food because of their medical choice. But the majority of us nonetheless concurred, quite seriously, that they would act if this happened. Like kids doing virtual pinky swears, the oath was put out in our space of cyber - if Superstore bans the unvaccinated from their stores, every fucking window they have at every location they have is being busted for a start. I was absolutely prepared to go to jail if grocery stores started asking for vaccine status, and I absolutely knew that I would.

The likelihood of a large grocer demanding vaccination was quite low, and Sobey's was quick to come out and say that they would not be limiting people to the essential service they provide. Nevertheless, and I don't care if the actual evidence is light, New Brunswick was being used as a test case to see if Canadians already under some type of mass-psychosis spell would comply with the next step of the operation. Canada already was one of the highest vaccinated countries in the world, and the province of New Brunswick had the highest rate of vaccination in the entire country. This was not about COVID-19 or people's health. It was about control. Just because the impetus behind this control wasn't readily identifiable does not mean it didn't exist.

The secretive goals may have been a mix of Trudeau or his owners demanding a 100% vaccination rate, a universal vaccine passport, and, perhaps longer-term, a social credit system similar to China's. Whatever the case, variants of these types of control had been and were being openly discussed in Canadian society. This was no longer conspiratorial. There was also the obvious fact that the lackadaisical Premier Higgs and inert Minister of Health Dorothy Shephard didn't suddenly have an epiphany one evening and say let's take food away from the unvaccinated. This wasn't being done anywhere else in Canada. It was completely off-character and off-brand. Clearly, someone above anyone in New Brunswick was pulling the strings.

Then, on December 9, 2021, the bomb was dropped by Boyce Farmers Market, which stated on Twitter, *'As per Public Health guidelines, proof of vaccination will be required to enter the market building for everyone 12+. Please have your proof of vaccination and eligible ID card ready when you arrive...'*[199] It didn't matter that Boyce was a small market not really crucial to the nourishment needs of New Brunswickers. They were, by definition, a grocer or a food provider about to deny access to people because of their medical choice. The shit was about to get real.

After discovering the news, I went to social media to see the lay of the land. The upheaval was unlike anything I had seen before. Of the non-cancelled Facebook groups I frequented, people were saying what time they would arrive at Boyce on December 18, 2021, and what materials they needed to make a human chain surrounding the building. The consensus from some of the larger groups was that this chain would be erected around the entire building, and come hell or high water, it would not be broken. Some in the group seemed to be waffling and suggested letting peaceful patrons in, while others were basically set on the fact that this was a must go to jail moment.

As I read more, I did so with the solemn reservation I was going to jail. There is no way police would be breaking up a chain of people protesting human rights and fighting for an end to these illegal and insane mandates with me not plowing some cops over. It had been a long time since I read Thoreau, and I was fairly certain my thoughts didn't quite fit underneath his 'civil disobedience' umbrella. I reckoned I would have lots of time for reading in prison.

At anti-lockdown protests in Australia a week earlier, protesters ran through police barricades, and one man, who had been coined Jason Bourne after the movie super-agent, was running over cops, close-lining cops, and, literally, causing complete chaos[200]. Not to romanticize violence, but I pictured myself doing something similar in Fredericton on December 18, 2021. I also imagined being cuffed by the officer who called me about leaving aggressive messages to a pediatrician - *'I told you it would come to this.'*

After the Facebook session, I acquired the courage to venture into other realms of discussion not monitored (at least not as closely) as Facebook. The talk was scary. I didn't really care much for torching the whole building or some of the more radical ideas being bantered about, and I didn't participate in the bartering of violence and destruction. The problem, I rationed, is that if you burn the buildings down, you could not only be charged with arson, you could hurt people. The vendors in Boyce Market probably didn't do anything that warranted violence against them or their inventories. I wasn't exactly sure of the best avenue for protest. What I did know is Fredericton was two hours away, and I was going.

The fuel rattling around my noggin to instill the sense of resoluteness was headlined by the fact that Trudeau had said the unvaccinated were taking up space and wondered if Canadians should 'tolerate' them. It is these types of aggressive words that had people, myself included, fired up. My response to being treated like a second-class citizen, by being labelled selfish, was to going to be plowing over cops (they could take it). There would be no fists flying toward heads or any weapons used to risk getting shot, just plowing over cops and seeing how many I could get to the ground. I speculated that with a surprise bull-rush, I could drop at least two cops. I may have been just south of 50 and lacking in the endurance department, but I was also 6'3, 210lbs, with some quickness and power. I also speculated that the cops left standing would likely be a little pissed and take some extra time and effort cracking me. I would not take it personally.

The 'Justice Centre for Constitutional Freedoms' was a collection of lawyers doing pro bono work to *'defend citizens' fundamental freedoms under the Canadian Charter of Rights and Freedoms.'* These were the good guys, and they had previously taken up fights for doctors that had lost their jobs because they believed in informed consent and for people that had been arrested for *'disobeying public health orders.'* The Justice Centre began supporting our fight in New Brunswick with a demand letter to the Minister of Justice of New Brunswick on December 7, 2021,[201] and another demand letter sent to the City of Fredericton on December 15, 2021.[202] Shortly after the second demand later, in a sudden change of heart, Higgs' government said New Brunswick would not be the first place in Canada to officially deny people access to food based upon medical status. The test was over. It failed. The Justice Centre commented:

"This Order which served to segregate citizens, was a very concerning development in Canada. It would have been the first attempt by a government to deny essential services and food to Canadians who decide against receiving a Covid vaccine, as is their constitutional right."[203]

The food fiasco in New Brunswick, like the Cardy phenomenon, made Canada-wide and world news. It went to show the extent of psychological warfare the government was conducting to achieve its ambitions. And while some might say Higgs backing down was not a major victory, it is worth remembering that every marathon starts with one step and this, hopefully, was the first step. The momentum could be changing, or so I thought. Go long, freedom!

As for Boyce Farmers Market, amidst all the commotion, what was almost missed was that Boyce was purchased by the New Brunswick government in 2009.[204] This provided a degree of solace against often feeling isolated and reviled. No company or collection of New Brunswickers tried to ban the unvaccinated from food. Only the government did.

Chapter 15 - Omicron Cometh

"For unvaccinated, we are looking at a winter of severe illness and death - if you're unvaccinated - for themselves, their families, and the hospitals they'll soon overwhelm." ~ U.S. President Biden. December 16, 2021[205]

After omicron's arrival in South Africa, we quickly learned that it was way more contagious than the delta variant, it was milder across all age groups, and the vaccinated, statistically speaking, had less severe outcomes compared to the unvaccinated. From the context of mandates, omicron was a blessing as it completely and quickly shattered the myth that these shots would get us to herd immunity. Omicron did the work I believed delta would have eventually done, but instead of taking the scenic route to reach endemic island, omicron was clear-cutting through the forest with napalm. I honestly believe if anyone or any power was 'evil,' they shed a tear as omicron ripped through the population. Natural immunity was free and a massive threat to big pharma profits.

What omicron did was take some of the smartest 'contrarian' opinions and obliterate them. Case in point, Dr. Peter McCullough, who had surmised the worst of COVID-19 had passed before omicron, had this to say shortly before the South African variant took over:

"There's a general recognition through May that 40% of children have already had COVID-19. That's through May [2021]. That's before the Delta outbreak. The Delta outbreak was huge in the United States. You know what it was two-thirds of the peak of our pre-vaccination peak...And so my estimate would be...80% of children now that are in the discussion for vaccination have already had COVID. And now, the CDC, in the last week, has acknowledged that they don't have a single case of someone who has recovered from COVID getting it a second time and passing it to anyone. So it's basically over with. We have now the CDC estimates are generally for the United States 148 million

*Americans who are immune that they actually have had COVID-19
and they have natural immunity that's now supported by over 120
studies, that's been, by the way, accumulated on the Broadstone
Institute website. 120 studies supporting natural immunity is one
and done phenomenon. "*[206]

As much as I think Dr. McCullough is brilliant and helped
millions understand COVID-19 better than they otherwise would,
omicron was quickly proving that he had reached in calling for the
end to COVID-19. Within a couple of weeks of being brought into
this world, omicron was found in 77 different countries. The
vaccines were entirely incapable of stopping the spread, and rates
of reinfection, while still low, were above anything seen with delta.

Fully vaccinated people had hugged omicron and flown in
synthetic birds to spread it everywhere. The relatively slow
January 2020 dispersal of COVID-19 spread like molasses and
took until March to be labelled pandemic. Omicron had arrived in
Canada on November 28, 2021, and it would soon be coming to a
theatre near you - within days, not weeks! Please do have your
proof of vaccination card ready if you would like to watch and join
the show.

To get an idea of how crazy and quickly the omicron
phenomenon would go-go juice bonkers, on December 18, 2021,
free COVID-19 rapid tests were being made available throughout
Canada, and the Canadian government updated its website so that
companies could freely order test kits for their employees. Offering
free COVID-19 tests to any Canadian that wanted them
represented a significant switch in government policy, and it
rendered the 'pandemic of the unvaccinated' mantra obsolete. As
for those still destitute on LWOP, they laughed and cried all at
once. Think about it: if fully vaccinated employees could obtain
free tests because they might spread COVID-19 to other fully
vaccinated employees, why couldn't unvaccinated employees also
be tested and return to work?

At the time, I failed to find a Cardy-like villain to trash. My question of the day was, is catching COVID-19 from someone that is fully vaccinated somehow different than catching it from someone that is unvaccinated? I emailed the company to ask, I emailed and called our union leadership, and I called Health Canada, the Labour Board, the Treasury Board Secretariat (TBS), Transport Canada, etc. Not a single person could answer why tests were freely given to fully vaccinated Canadians and why the mandates remained.

Despite the fact that only the fully vaccinated could travel on trains, planes, etc., on December 18, 2021, the Canadian government enacted new tougher travel restrictions. In response to this news, WestJet CEO Harry Taylor said the government's new policies would create an *'unnecessary disruption and chaos'* and that *"Fully vaccinated Canadians should not be singled out for choosing to take part in a safe activity [flying]."*[207] That the 'fully vaccinated' were being unceremoniously unrewarded for their previously gallant act of vaccination nobility, I'll admit, on some level, was very gratifying. This satisfaction made me recall a poem by John Clare called 'The Badger.' I don't necessarily live with vindictiveness in my heart, but if you corner me, I'll lash out and, like the calm badger turning vicious, attack with unrelenting force. In my mind, I had been cornered since August 13, 2021, and now, to salvage some form of sanity, it was indeed the time to lash out and revel as the once upon a time virtuously vaccinated got huffy.

Also, in mid-December, policymakers across Canada began limiting capacity at restaurants, gyms, and entertainment centres - or places that only fully vaccinated people had been able to visit for some time. Again, this was unkindly satisfying. Finally, in Quebec, even though they could only be attended by the fully vaccinated, the bars, theatres, arenas, etc., were going to be forced to close.[208] If the vaccines provided any noteworthy effectiveness, these places would not be shut down. The 2020 lockdown models were being dusted off by the same policymakers that told people life could return to normal because they made the 'right choice' and took the shots. Clearly, the shots had failed.

The evidence of omicron changing the game was too vast to quantify. No study, not even the delta ones I was a fan of, accounted for the COVID-19 case count carnage that was happening now. Moreover, no model forecasted such a surge in cases relative to no corresponding surge in hospitalizations and death. On December 16, 2021, '31 out of 32 attendees'[209] at a private party in a Quebec restaurant got infected with COVID-19. All attendees were fully vaccinated. In mid-December, unprecedented COVID-19 outbreaks occurred in the NHL, NBA, and NFL, or sports leagues that were 99+%, 97%, and 94% fully vaccinated, respectively.[210] Lastly, U.S. politicians Elizabeth Warren, Cory Booker, Jason Crow,[211] Larry Hogman,[212] Tim Walz (+wife),[213] Toronto Raptors President Masai Ujiri,[214] as well as TV personality Jim Cramer (+wife),[215] and Queen guitarist Brian May[216] all tested positive for COVID-19. These individuals were not only double vaccinated but also 'boosted.' Apparently, three doses were no match against omicron.

At the risk of belabouring (the above list could continue to hundreds of pages), what many of the largest peer-review studies had been telling us for some time should have been common knowledge by now: the vaccines do not stop the spread of COVID-19. At this point, unemployed and sometimes sipping whisky, I sincerely believed that anyone who could not see this reality was either brain-dead, part of a cult, or the devil. I won't expand greatly on this for the obvious reason that I am ranting, but how much evidence would it take for people to understand that their vaccines would never stop COVID-19?

Even amidst omicron, a hellish month, and arguments on the phones, I tried to keep up with the hot sheets. The recent big gun stated, *'a mRNA vacs dramatically increase inflammation on the endothelium and T cell infiltration of cardiac muscle and may account for the observations of increased thrombosis, cardiomyopathy, and other vascular events following vaccination.'*[217][*See also correction to this abstract.*[218]] That the vaccines caused inflammation, generally known by all at this point, wasn't what irritated those attacking this study. That Dr. Gundry was suggesting *'three of the inflammatory markers...in all of our patients consecutively receiving these vaccines'* and this increased risk of *'a new Acute Coronary Syndrome'* over the next five years was. Gundy's study was sloppy and not very convincing, but as he was mercilessly attacked, some nuggets of information trickled through. Consider Dr. Luigi Adamo, the director for cardiac immunology in the Johns Hopkins University Division of Cardiology, who thought the study's testing made some sense, although he disagreed with the conclusions. Dr. Adamo wrote:

"Vaccination is designed to induce a controlled inflammatory response with the goal of preparing the body to 'fight' the targeted pathogen. It is therefore expected that administration of a vaccine induces a transient increase in inflammatory mediators in the serum. However, this cannot be automatically interpreted as an increase in the risk of having a heart attack. Even if the mRNA vaccines caused a sustained elevation of specific serum biomarkers of inflammation, the prognostic value of this change in terms of risk of heart attacks would need to be validated with population data."[219]

The big question, obviously, was just how 'transient' was the increase in inflammation following mRNA vaccination? The even bigger question was, what if this inflammation in some people was not transient? Central bankers had habitually told us for more than thirty years that inflationary pressures were transient, and for 30+ years, they were right. That didn't preclude them from being wrong about inflation not being transient in 2021-2022. With any luck, Dr. Adamo's transient inflammatory concept will be fully known and quantified sometime in 2023 or 2024 or when the Phase 3 clinical trial data is expected.

Amidst the inflammation debate, I continued to watch Novavax and Medicago. Novavax was a sub-unit protein-based vaccine (more traditional than mRNA), and Medicago was the plant-based vaccine that Trudeau had thrown $173 million at. Novavax had applied for approval in Canada on November 1, 2021, and Medicago applied on December 16, 2021. While I sincerely doubted these vaccines would be effective versus omicron, my fingers were crossed that their risk profile might be lower than the mRNA offerings. A boy can dream. After all, before the COVID-19 vaccines were rushed to market, the number of injuries from the approved vaccines being offered by Canada was reportedly infinitesimally small.

"...millions of people vaccinated in Canada every year, a handful - likely fewer than 10 - will sustain a permanent, serious injury."[220]

Along with watching and waiting, I was also committed to the idea that I would be catching omicron. Almost gleefully, I awaited it to infect my upper respiratory tract, thankful that, unlike the delta variant, omicron typically didn't nest in the lungs. I was also grateful that compared to delta, my upcoming omicron infection would see me have an even closer to zero chance of being hospitalized or dying and that the duration of my illness would likely be shorter. Like a kid craving a candy, I had elevated levels of vitamin C, D, and Zinc flowing through me, awaiting the sweet kiss of omicron. Let's go!

With omicron and inflammation inspections hogging the limelight, it was almost forgotten that the FDA had a court case. Previously the FDA had made the outrageous request for 55 years (not a typo) to release the data it had on Pfizer's COVID-19 vaccine, and on December 6, 2021, it raised this estimate to 2096. That the FDA required 75 years to release all of the data it had on Pfizer's vaccine was, obviously, completely preposterous. The Plaintiffs had cheekily asked the judge that the FDA disclose all the data within 108 days, or the same amount of time the FDA took to approve Pfizer's vaccine.[221] Made sense to me. Not only did the FDA promise full transparency with these vaccine approvals[222], but if the FDA really read and scrutinized the data, why couldn't they re-read and share this information in the same timeframe?

For whatever reasons (Trudeau's and Pfizer's money?), the Canadian MSM wasn't quick to cover the FDA's outlandish request. Instead, the contrarian conspiracists were left to read the FDA's Advisory Panel Member, Dr. Eric Rubin, words, knowing they would be coming after the kids with these shots next:

"We're never gonna learn about how safe the vaccine is until we start giving it. That's just the way it goes."[223]

Is it possible that Dr. Rubin, like many FDA gang members before him, will coincidentally find an excellent position or payday with a top-notch big pharma company in the not-too-distant future? Vaccination needles crossed.

Chapter 16 - Early Bird Catches the EI

With no income, no severance pay, and part of my family's health benefits about to be axed, I started calling EI. Having spent a month staggering wildly from fight to fight without gaining much traction, I had the epiphany to refocus my energy and try to get EI. The brief whisky soaked pity-party that the constant government and employer bullying induced was still a fresh form of trauma. It would have to be stored in the cellar while I pursued my greater good. The grey skies were starting to clear up.

I started the quest on December 30, 2021, which I reckoned was ample time for the initial filing to have been processed. My demeanour was cheery and pleasant (put on a happy face), and I wrote in an Excel file who I spoke with on each occasion. I tried to use their name as the conversation progressed, hoping familiarity might elicit some EI-insider trading information. Acquiring information, as the EI rules were literally being rewritten, was like obtaining on-the-ground intelligence behind enemy lines. I was taking this very seriously. I had paid into EI since Rubbermaid when I was 13 - why shouldn't I be eligible given that I have done nothing wrong?

Rather than play Mr. Know-it-all trying to drop legalese and demanding to speak to managers, I opted for I know nothing at all. This is to say, I planned to be as honest as possible and use the lack of information provided by the company, the union, the government, and my next-door neighbour to describe what I had gone through. My goal was never to admit, even if befallen by telephone water torture, that I would not take a vaccine. In part, this was true as I never attested to anything, and I absolutely never would. My decision was grounded in Canada's Personal Health Information Protection Act, The Canadian Charter of Rights and Freedom, and New Brunswick's Personal Health Information Privacy and Access Act. My PHI was private, period.

Some of the very devout at my work tried the religious exemption route, and others tried the ole justice of peace scheme (i.e., guilty of not taking the vaccine, but I have an explanation). What all these people had done, unwittingly in my mind, is 'attest' that they had understood the four options Canada Post had presented, and they selected that which was most applicable to them. None were applicable to me. I didn't understand anything.

This dumb defence was first set in motion when the company had the first meeting to announce its vaccine practice in October. In front of many witnesses, I and others asked a string of non-stop questions, partly to avoid going to work but also because we had genuine concerns. One of my questions was if any of the four government-approved vaccines could be taken. My boss said yes. At the next meeting with a bigger boss, I asked the same question and added what if certain vaccines were not available yet? At the time, I knew the Johnson & Johnson's (Janssen) one-shot virus vector vaccine was unavailable in New Brunswick. Where AstraZeneca had rare cases of deadly blood clots, and the mRNA's were renowned for triggering heart inflammation, Janssen's claim to shame was the rare side effect of Guillain-Barré syndrome. GBS is a disorder where the immune system damages nerves, which can include a host of problems, including paralysis and even death. In July 2021, the FDA, standing up for its sponsors, was quick to dismiss the incidences of GBS from the vaccines as not only rare but perhaps not even linked:

"Although the available evidence suggests an association between the Janssen vaccine and increased risk of GBS, it is insufficient to establish a causal relationship."[224]

This term 'causal relationship' and the legal wiggle room it generates is the reason that, to my knowledge, no vaccine injury court case has ever been successful in Canada.

Knowing why or when the Janssen vaccine would be available in New Brunswick was above my boss's pay grade, but on both of these occasions, in front of witnesses, they promised to come back with answers to these questions. They failed to come back.

I and others also forwarded questions in printed and digital form to the appropriate parties that had pledged to answer any and all questions employees had relating to the upcoming vaccine policy. These questions were left entirely unanswered because, the company informed us, too many people were asking them. Below is an actual response from the person(s) in charge of answering questions relating to my company's vaccine practice. No names or dates are included:

"These questions are quite commonly recycled across the country. We have similar lists and exactly the same questions with the same precise wording and order of questions from numerous individuals and locations."

Completely stunned, I responded that the questions forwarded were authentic and from employees in the plant, and that it was deeply concerning that all of our questions and concerns remained unaddressed. I also added that I didn't see the relevance of why related questions being asked across Canada automatically meant that no answer would ever be provided. No response. I was being ghosted, and every question we asked was answered. Why have a vaccine hotline if you refuse to answer questions of those utilizing said hotline?

To see if it was the topical matter that got our group barred from asking questions about the vaccines, I emailed a simple and more neutral question. The response was immediate - literally, one minute later! The conversation went as follows:

My Question: *Can we choose which Health Canada-approved vaccine we want? Thanks!*
Answer: *"Absolutely, as long as there is availability at your vaccination clinic. Depending on where you live, you may be able to find out ahead of time what vaccines different clinics have and book your appointment accordingly. Some clinics may also take "walk-in" clients. If you go by and see people coming out, ask if they are willing to tell you what vaccines were available. Have a good weekend."*

As thrilling a prospect of driving around town asking strangers coming out of clinics if they just got their COVID-19 shots, I took one word and ran with it - 'absolutely'. I had a third source that said employees could take any approved vaccine. Next, I called the New Brunswick COVID-19 information line and inquired when Janssen's vaccine would be available in New Brunswick. The lady on the phone said not until at least the New Year. More ammunition in the vault.

Part of me felt bad for management at Canada Post. For all of the woke and politically correct hoops the company was charged with jumping through, forcing vaccinates on employees was by far the most questionable and intrusive. This wasn't about wearing a specific coloured T-shirt or having a moment of silence for deranged whales. This was about coercing people to take an injection that could, although exceptionally rare, kill them. At the minimum, notice of liability forms should have been signed by someone with the company (or government), or the company should have demanded their labour lawyers respond to employee concerns relating to this topic. But the government mandate was the government mandate, and management at Canada Post would follow orders and never answer any earnest questions from employees. There were supervisors at Canada Post against this policy, upper-level managers against this policy, and many that supported the policy had doubts over what longer-term consequences may follow. Very few, however, openly voiced their dissent.

The first call to EI I made was brief, and I discovered that it usually took between 1-28 days for a request to be completed, but since EI was getting backed up, Anna told me it could take a little longer. I inquired about the mechanics of the appeals process, and I pencilled in a note to call back on January 6, 2022. The one curious note during the call was when Anna asked if I was off work due to the company's vaccine policy. It was oddly placed in the conversation as if a new training bullet point compelled Anna to ask it. I answered that I did not know, which was true.

The next call went swimmingly and fast. My claim was still in the first round, but an answer was expected shortly. I inquired about the appeals process and was informed that all appeals were forwarded to a separate department. There were particular forms to fill out if my claim went this route. Thank you, Mitch; talk again soon.

The next call on January 11, 2022, went poorly. I was speaking with Chi, who you could tell was having a stressful time with what he no doubt thought was selfish anti-vaxxers bothering him. Chi didn't want to divulge anything and was borderline rude, so I reciprocated his curtness and asked who do I send the lawsuit materials to when I sued for my EI. Soon after, Chi dropped the big no-no and asked why I didn't just take the vaccine. I immediately asked for a supervisor to put in a complaint about Chi. When the supervisor got on the line, I informed him what Chi had asked me and informed him my medical information is private and protected by law. The supervisor was sympathetic and assured me this would not happen again. I then called an EI complaint line, and unlike vaccine hotline questions that are left unrequited, this complaint service returned their calls immediately. I reiterated my gripe and then proceeded to send off some emails to MPs and anyone related to EI, complaining that what the government was doing to hardworking Canadians who should qualify for EI was tantamount to harassment. I made a day out of it. I had the time.

My triggered cantankerous mood was probably overcooked a bit, but the reality was Trudeau had declared war on people like me on August 13, 2021, and the only way to fight this war was to have a militarist' posture. Outside of his vaccine-influenced haughtiness, Chi was probably a nice enough man. Even as I pursued every avenue available to get his behaviour checked and have him reprimanded, I didn't wish him personal harm or ill will. The Geneva Convention of Pandemic Warfare clearly stated that all medical information is still private. To this end, my employer set up an attestation labyrinth for employees to attest to one of many options, and managers would never actually know an employee's vaccination status, only whether they had attested or not. This idea that anyone on the street or working for EI could just ask you if you had a certain medical procedure was batcrap bonkers. I would never comply with this!

The next call went well. Amanda informed me that there were four levels of escalation and that I was on level two. Each of the first two levels took about a week, and the last two had to be handled within days. When I inquired what the difference was, she told me the last two resulted in direct emails to the person charged with making the decisions. I spoke with EI's Barb, from Newfoundland, later in the day. She was a delightful lady that asked a few questions about my business income. Her accent was thickly coated in Newfoundland splendour. By the end of the call, she informed me that my business income, or lack thereof, would not negatively impact my claim.

By January 14, 2022, I was on level four. Kevin confirmed that at this level, it should be a daily update. I called back on January 17 and 18, and on each day, I was told an update was expected any day, but since EI was backed up by thousands of cases, it might take a little longer. I vehemently protested that level four was supposed to be a one-business-day turnaround and implored that my claim be escalated again. Ensuring that another email was sent out would eventually break this wall, or so I thought.

On January 19, 2022, I got a call from Catherine. It was nice to be the one receiving the call and not making it for a change. It made me feel special, even though I knew whoever was calling was a compensated foot soldier in the EI vs. ME mêlée. Cathy and I had a verbose conversation, and she thoroughly examined my situation. Cathy, unlike Chi, never assumed I was unvaccinated or asked any such meddling questions. Instead, she adroitly inquired about my dismissal, my suspension, or my misconduct, and she invited me to share what information the company provided during our final meeting. I responded to each question with a never-ending story, literally. When asked what the company told our group in a final meeting on November 28, 2021, I took almost two minutes to respond before she interrupted me. In those two minutes, I explained that our boss said they would answer any questions, but when we started asking questions, she had no answers. I then explained we asked questions to the employer in October, sent numerous emails, I didn't fully understand the ramifications of each attestation option, the intricacies of third-party privacy company holding our personal information, liability concerns, etc.

Breaking up my garrulousness Cathy astutely asked, *'but you say that they gave you a form letter at the last meeting. What, exactly?'* Crap! During my incessant blathering, I had voluntarily mentioned the company gave us all a form explaining why we were on LWOP, and Cathy had keyed on this potential weakness. I hesitated before speaking, then launched into another endless session, saying the letter was about the attestation program and forcing employees out on LWOP, but in our contract LWOP can only happen if the employee requests it, and we asked numerous questions but none were answered, and...Cathy had heard enough and interrupted me:

"Okay, okay, I see. So, in this case, because in cases like this we must obtain the employer's version before being able to make a decision. But then, when I spoke to the employer yesterday, they said that they refused to provide any explanation in regards to the reason why you were put on a leave of absence. Then in such a case, the decision is made only based on the client..."

Cathy approved my EI claim, on the telephone, because of a, *'lack of information on the employer's part.'* She further said that because there was no misconduct in these circumstances, the client's version of events becomes fact. I was pleasantly surprised.

No one else in the groups I was in had been approved for EI. From my informational sources, no one else across Canada had been approved. I shared my experience online and welcomed any questions. Many on forced LWOP were, justifiably so, livid that EI was backed up, and it could take weeks or longer before the backlog was cleared. My paranoid self knew this was, by design, another Trudeau tactic to get more people to take his shots and accept his tyranny. Many would fold in the coming weeks because the EI funds were not coming. Those under duress that took the shots to pay the bills were freedom fighting casualties in Trudeau's malicious EI war of attrition.

While I like to think that my approval was the result of my persistence or cunning, it was more likely that I was fortunate in my timing. The fluke loophole I exploited to take advantage of Canada Post's lack of knowledge would not take long to close. By the time others in the group reached the end of their hellish EI journey Canada Post had refined their story, and their cases would need to go to appeal.

Cathy informed me the company had 30 days to appeal the decision. Until the money arrived and this 30-day period passed, I was not officially done playing the piano in the enchanted EI-woods just yet.

Chapter 17 - The Government's Last Stand?

While the tentative EI victory took the cement brick off my jugular, this battle took place inside what can now, with all hope, be called the most intense period of political and policy turmoil of the entire pandemic. At very few points in life have I ever considered myself completely flummoxed. With the COVID-19 news cycle changing by the day, and capricious policy decisions arriving hour-to-hour, no one had the mental agility to congregate common sense. To begin with, Trudeau started the year off with the same old hateful song:

January 5, 2021 - *"When people see we're in lockdowns, or serious public health restrictions right now, because of the risk posed to all of us by unvaccinated people - people get angry. I'm extremely frustrated...it's a slap in the face to see people putting themselves, putting their fellow citizens, putting airline workers at risk by being completely irresponsible."*[225]

Months after he barely won a senseless election and after the onset of the game-changing omicron variant, in reaction to the above quote, I had to ask myself, what the hell was this nutbar doing? Then in the span of only a couple of weeks, Quebec Premier François Legault announced a flurry of COVID-19 edicts that suggested he wanted to dethrone Trudeau to become King Nutbar.

December 30, 2021 - A curfew will be in force from 10 p.m. to 5 a.m.[226]

January 3, 2022 - Canadian army rolls in Quebec to hasten COVID-19 vaccination[227]

January 7, 2022 - Quebec will require people to show vaccine passports at liquor, cannabis stores[228]

January 11, 2022 - Quebec to impose health tax on unvaccinated Canadians[229]
"...the premier announced that it would be the first in the nation to

financially penalise the unvaccinated"

January 13, 2022 - Quebec...imposes vaccine passport on large stores[230]

That Legault could prove more treacherous with his actions than anyone in Canada before, including Trudeau and Higgs, was astonishing. Following the wacky curfew scheme, which Quebec tried before and said there was no evidence it worked, there were videos of blackened vans roaming the streets of Montreal shortly before 10 PM warning people over a loudspeaker to go inside that curfew was coming. People walking their dogs and talking to their neighbours wondered what was going on. It was utterly surreal and made absolutely no sense on any scientific level.

What could be deduced is that Quebec was exercising more control, or perhaps further training, of citizens under the guise of fighting the increase in COVID-19 cases. However, the old argument from 2020 that policymakers had to do something, no matter how crazy, because the fearful people demanded it was no longer applicable. Most people in Quebec were already so conditioned to follow mandates (and blame the unvaccinated) that they would have done anything they were told. Legault could have told people the colour pink fights COVID-19 and the next day Quebec would be bathed in pink. It was, during this exceptionally odd interlude from common sense, that simple.

Some might counter that Legault was enacting these policies to intentionally anger unvaccinated people and supply further enticement so that they would get the shots. This likely has an element of truth, as does the circular near psychotic motives Legault expressed back in early 2021:

"We've had no choice but to lock down, reopen, lock down, reopen...When we lock down, it's to protect people's physical health; when we reopen, it's to help their mental health."[231]

It goes without saying that if the above represents was what policymakers believed, we are all doomed.

Despite being politically extremely popular in Quebec, with every new enforcement announcement, a smidgen of rage against Legault built. I thought of and tried to plan driving over the border to protest as Legault stirred Boyce Market-type feelings. Then I recalled the recent news that, *'Canada's public health agency admits it tracked 33 million mobile devices during lockdown.'*[232] Maybe the EI pogey narcs were watching me? Watching and waiting.

For whatever reason, Quebec's nightmare wasn't internalized inside me to the degree events in New Brunswick were. It was as if the border was a barrier to my disdain. Maybe a different type of border could also explain how the vaccinated acquired apathy when it came to the poor unvaccinated bastards they ostracized.

The curfew nuttiness was finally relaxed on January 13, 2022, the same day Legault imposed vaccination passports on big box stores. Big box stores sold food. Another test. Legault squirmed around the issue of banning people from 'food' by basing his new proof of vaccination on store size. Many freedom fighters in New Brunswick and across Canada launched boycotts and made calls of protest to Costco and Wal-Mart. More battle lines were drawn, apparently to implement a corrupt political agenda.

Around the time Legault was etching his 'evil' name into the minds of freedom lovers across Canada, Canadian Health Minister, Jean-Yves Duclos, was taking his new marching orders from Trudeau. The headline from the CBC was something the conspiracy crowd had been warning about for years. It was still nonetheless disturbing when the CBC Twitter note dropped:

"Duclos said that provinces likely will start turning to mandatory vaccination policies to deal with swelling COVID caseloads threatening to overwhelm hospitals."[233]

For those unfamiliar with Duclos, if Trudeau were playing the part of Hitler, Duclos would be his Himmler (or right-hand man). Duclos could, at any moment, blurt out nonsensically hostile proclamations about COVID-19 that contradicted known science. For example, with natural immunity spreading rapidly, very rapidly, the vaccines having been proven useless against COVID-19 and Canada still one of the most vaccinated countries in the world, Duclos stated that the '*the only way that we know to get through COVID-19, this variant and any future variant, is through vaccination.*'[234] This was an absolute lie. Duclos simply didn't care.

As the triple jabbed caught and spread COVID-19 and case counts went well above the testing capacity of the country, it was pretty obvious the vaccines were failing in front of our eyes. Duclos was told to fight for universal vaccination - so he, like a mindless drone, did. Incidentally, for those that may be thinking I never heard of this Duclos guy, please stop exaggerating his importance; when Ontario Premier, Doug Ford, ended Ontario's 'basic income pilot' in 2019, the WEF noted the following:

"There was also an unexpected postscript. In December, the Canadian prime minister, Justin Trudeau, and the social development minister, Jean-Yves Duclos, said in interviews that a guaranteed national minimum income could be an option as they sought ways to support Canadians to adapt to an unsteady, shifting labour market. Duclos predicted it would come."[235]

Who the hell was Duclos in 2019 to predict that a 'guaranteed national minimum income' would be coming to Canada? He was Trudeau's Himmler, that's who.

As the 'mandatory vaccination' jingle was being played for the wind chimes across Canada, other countries were also dancing around this idea. In fact, Austria had been trying to make the shots mandatory since November 2021, and Ecuador, led by President Guillermo Lasso of WEF fame, became one of the first countries to actually make mandatory COVID-19 vaccination a law on

December 23, 2021. Then there was Germany's Chancellor, Olaf Scholz, and German President, Frank-Walter Steinmeier - both with WEF stripes - pledging that mandatory vaccinations were coming to Germany. Lastly, Italy and Greece tried to make COVID-19 vaccination punishable by fines for those over 50 and 60, respectively. Rumour has it that at a UN 'Circle of Leadership' meeting, Italy's Mario Draghi and Greece's Katerina Sakellaropoulou slipped away, and both got secret 'We Love WEF' tattoos.

That certain, almost exclusively, WEF-aligned leaders were trying to adopt forms of mandatory vaccination around the same time Duclos was dropping the idea helps put the weirdly timed January 7, 2022, CPAC stream into perspective. The CPAC event[236] was layered in cringe-worthy political theatrics and had planted questions about Italy and mandatory vaccination teed up for Duclos to take his swings. Like most CPAC streams, barely anyone was watching except for the government-sponsored media waiting for their choreographed headlines.

Some Premiers, like Alberta's Kenny, immediately said his province would not adopt mandatory vaccination, while others, like New Brunswick, started spreading the news. That Higgs was triple dosed and most of his family, also triple dosed, had just had COVID-19 evidently didn't mean anything. After meeting with Trudeau, Higgs either cashed his cheque or cashed out his common sense and told the world:

January 11, 2022 - Province may revisit mandatory COVID-19 vaccines, says Higgs[237]
"...it's something that will get further discussion in New Brunswick and probably across the country."

At this point, over 90% of eligible people in New Brunswick had reportedly had their first dose. Let that sink in. This wasn't about health and safety. It was about everyone taking the shots and people accepting a QR code vaccine pass (or some derivative thereof). That someone with Higg's limited intellect and lack of ambition was reading a piece of paper saying mandatory vaccination should be back on the table was sheer insanity. It was obvious that either Cardy's ideological persistence or Trudeau's monetary tentacles had gotten to Higgs again.

As the debate over provincial mandates filtered through, Duclos made a point of distilling and sharing his beliefs: *'I personally think we will get there at some point - mandatory vaccination.'* Duclos' 'personal' thoughts were not just his opinion - he was our Health Minister and had a great deal of sway as to whether mandatory vaccination of all Canadians would one day happen.

The ensuing verbal skirmishes following Duclos' hand grenades were not as rancorous as one might expect. Sure there was Legault, who was pretty much open to anything save murdering the unvaccinated, and Higgs would follow the script even if people were rushing his office with pitchforks (which was discussed), but the rest of Canada wasn't complying. Along with Kenny from Alberta, Saskatchewan's Mo was also against mandatory vaccination, and BC's Dr. Bonnie Henry, whose motto was 'no mandate is too fucking crazy for me,' said *'I don't foresee making it mandatory for vaccinations for everybody in the province.'*[238] Oddly quiet at this time was BC Premier John Horgan. Horgan might be the only WEF acolyte that took a knee, at least for this brief moment. He had just finished cancer treatments which may explain his silence. Feel better, Horgan, and end all mandates!

As mandatory vaccination was likely to remain atop the agenda for some time, New Brunswick's health god, Shephard, issued a call for volunteers to help with the COVID-19 response.[239] When asked how she would use the volunteers, Shephard responded, *'it will be triaged, and we will utilize everyone to the best of their ability'*. When pressed further, she responded they wanted *'anyone that can administer a vaccine'* (her words, not mine).[13] Omicron was spreading COVID-19 around faster than

---

[13] If volunteers could administer a vaccine, why couldn't they also administer

turkey dinner, New Brunswick had the highest vaccination rates in Canada, and the vaccines take a bit before they prime the immune system for battle (and many studies suggest they weaken the immune system first). The profound silliness of Shephard's statements made you wonder whether New Brunswick was the test province for an upcoming healthcare volunteerism push in Canada. Having volunteers administer care in any form was a slap in the face to unionized healthcare workers sitting at home on LWOP. Shephard was, in my mind, little more than a disgrace.

As it would turn out, zero volunteers worked. Of the 4,000+ people that applied to help, 45 were selected and pitched in, and all 45 people were paid.[240] This, in a nutshell, was Dorothy Shephard. She was given a silver dollar to run to the grocery store to fetch eggs, and she came back with a watermelon and said the driveway needed de-icing. From a policy perspective nothing this person ever did made a lick of sense during the pandemic. I applied to volunteer and sincerely would have helped out if it was a non-unionized position. On my resume, I noted that my medical information is and will always remain private.

The Shephard development, which attracted Canada-wide coverage, reeked of being even more theatrical than the non-medically trained army personnel being summoned into Quebec to help with vaccinations. It was like both of these stories were fabricated and part of a marketing campaign to demonstrate just how serious rising COVID-19 cases were. With the mandatory vaccination feelers coming back cool, getting the fear gauge back to some form of heat was desired.

The next notable event was scheduled to occur on January 15, 2022, and involved mandating truckers. A contentious issue since initially announced in November, some said it would threaten border flow between the U.S. and Canada. Many also pointed out that truckers were the heroes during the pandemic and that most of their time working was spent alone in a cab. The idea that this

---

monoclonal antibodies (which at the time were producing excellent results at limiting hospitalization and death if taken early after infection)?

group needed to take a vaccine didn't seem warranted, at least from a purely logistical and common sense standpoint. It also made no sense with the new reality of omicron now fully formed. Seemingly coming to their senses only days before the January 15, 2022 deadline, the news crossed the wires:

January 12, 2022 - Feds make last-minute reversal on vaccine mandate for truckers.[241]

The Canadian Press article was spreading across the internet like wildfire, with the Globe and Mail picking it up and even Reuters covering the story. This was really happening! A major federal mandate was tossed aside due to a lack of merit. Alcohol could be used to celebrate something meaningful rather than to simply drown out the mandated depression spirits. Hooray! Let's go!

Just as the celebration started the next day, the news crossed the wire. It was like a punch in the guts:

"Today, the Minister of Health, the Honourable Jean-Yves Duclos, the Minister of Transport, the Honourable Omar Alghabra, and the Minister of Public Safety, the Honourable Marco Mendicino, issued the following statement:

On November 19, 2021, we announced that as of January 15, 2022, certain categories of travellers who are currently exempt from entry requirements will only be allowed to enter the country if they are fully vaccinated with one of the vaccines approved for entry into Canada.

These groups include several essential service providers, including truck drivers. Let us be clear: This has not changed. The information shared yesterday was provided in error."[242]

The news about the trucker mandates brought a lot of people, me included, from a feeling of jubilation to sorrow in less than a day. How exactly did a Department of Transport employee call the Canadian Press and say the mandates were over by 'error'? It was one of those things that you knew was a waste of time to lament deeply over, because we were never going to find out the truth, but that didn't stop you from trying.

The working theory I concocted was that Duclos, Omar, and Marco, at the behest of Trudeau, botched the releases on purpose. The goal being to aggravate those that had not fallen into line to take their government-approved vaccines. This open hatred would align with the rhetoric coming out of France just a week earlier when Macron dropped the following:

"The unvaccinated, I really want to piss them off. And so we're going to continue doing so until the end. That's the strategy."[243]

Macron reportedly used the word "*emmerder*", which meant to put in the "*merde*" (shit). It was vulgar and used intentionally. The argument could be made that Macron was taking cues from Trudeau and using divisive and hateful language for political purposes. France's election was only weeks away.

If not at the hand of Trudeau, this tactic of intentionally trying to annoy the unvaccinated was likely orchestrated by Duclos as Omar and Marco seemed too dim-witted to come up with this scheme on their own. I'll be the first to admit that the plan to enrage those keying on this event worked as planned. Saying the trucker mandate was abolished and then hours later saying the mandate was back on was genius-level evil. As if climbing feverously for an award for most despised, Duclos was working up the ladder.

The fella I had arranged my pretend illegal gun purchases from was likewise feeling stressed. He noted after the trucker mandate flip-flop fiasco, and I quote, *'those fuckers better hope I don't get a terminal disease. I'll drive up there and take them all fucking out.'* Five months earlier, I would have thought this guy was nuts. Today I wondered if I might do the same. He was probably, joking, of course, yet it was coming from a serious place of misery that was being provoked and stoked intentionally by our dictators. This person wasn't part of a militia, he didn't want to bring down the government unless it was by a vote, and he wasn't racist. Rather, he was married with kids, and he liked to farm and spend time in the community. He was happy. But he had seen enough.

This feeling that something had to be done to stop the likes of Trudeau, Duclos, and Legault, to quickly name three, was growing like a smouldering cyst behind your eye. Left unchecked, sooner or later, it is all you are going to think about and all you are going to see. Simmering underneath our dictators' rampage of trickery, there was an indescribable suspicion that Trudeau's devotees were behaving recklessly and desperately for a reason. What was the big push for more mandates and the threat of mandatory vaccination really all about? Did Trudeau plot his last big stand against the unvaccinated, and if so, why now?

As despair, uncertainty, and confusion threatened to be all-consuming, in the background, unnoticed at first, was a little GoFundMe fundraiser named 'Freedom Convoy 2022.' I recalled the old movie 'Convoy' starring Kris Kristofferson, my mom's favourite singer. My mother and I had another argument wherein she, perhaps forgetting round one, brought up the vaccines and started to tell me what I should be doing. The periods of black rage may have been far less frequent, but they still happened. We made up quicker than before, but I absolutely knew that I was done catering or feeling sorry for those who stood idly by with myopic apathy as the unvaccinated endured Trudeau's mandated trauma. If you wanted to take the shots, take them (that is your choice), but please do then shut the fuck up about it. The days of playing coy or speaking softly for fear of upsetting someone had long passed. The time to stand up and be proud of common sense was rising. Those chemicals that satiate or reinvigorate after extra-long work shifts were coursing through my heroin-friendly veins as moments of clarity surfaced. Omicron had Trudeau and his thugs rattled. Let's see where this goes...

Chapter 18 - The Undercurrents

"The real voyage of discovery consists not in seeking new landscapes, but in having new eyes." ~ Marcel Proust

The negative news rattling the cages of the unvaccinated as 2022 began caught most of the headlines and coincided with Trudeau trying to turn up the speed on his mandatory vaccination mission. But in the background, the highly infectious omicron variant was, quietly and below the surface, making a mockery of the mandates and altering the manner in which information was being gathered and shared. To play on Dickens, even as Trudeau's were doing their worst, the best of times was calling.

On January 10, 2022, a meeting between Trudeau and Canada's Premiers resulted in no consensus, with only a handful of Premiers voicing the possibility of a national vaccine mandate. This was one of the first indications that the Premiers may have no longer been firmly in Trudeau's pocket, either financially or in (the WEF kindred) spirit. The tacit thought, if you dared think such things, was that maybe provincial leaders wanted to get off of Trudeau's mandate-mania-ship, and they were just waiting for the opportune time politically to jump. If this were the case, Trudeau would require another shake of his pandemic-money tree to avoid a rupture of the political policy harmony that had been steadfast since August 13, 2021.

Before the full force of omicron hit, Alberta - previously one the strictest provinces against unvaccinated healthcare workers - dropped a pleasant Christmas surprise:

December 24, 2021 - With Omicron surging, Alberta Health Services offers COVID testing option to unvaccinated staff[244]
"In light of the risk posed by the Omicron variant, we need to adjust the policy to maximize capacity and avoid losing any staff if we can while still keeping patients safe"

Even as the small Alberta win was drowned out by Trudeau's omicron fear machine, it nonetheless highlighted a couple of crucial questions: why couldn't unvaccinated healthcare workers throughout Canada also test and return to work? Was catching COVID-19 from someone that was fully vaccinated somehow different than catching it from someone that is unvaccinated?

If the pleasant news from Alberta was the Christmas miracle, then the news about to come out of Quebec was the miraculous New Year bombshell. Right before Legault went bonkers with more mandates, curfews, and his unvaccinated tax, Quebec did the unthinkable:

December 28, 2021 - Quebec to allow some healthcare staff infected with COVID-19 to stay on job[245]
Provincial health minister Christian Dubé on Tuesday described the decision as a necessity born of a difficult situation caused by the Omicron variant's unrestrained spread.

This is what Canada had become, a stark raving mad country so hell-bent on punishing the unvaccinated that it would allow COVID-19 *positive* people to work while the unvaccinated were forced to sit at home. Some people believed that Quebec Health Minister Dubé, who doesn't appear to have any WEF affiliations, did not get along with Legault. There can be no doubt that Legault was furious by the word 'unrestrained' that Dubé was slinging:

"Dubé...described the decision as a necessity born of a difficult situation caused by the Omicron variant's unrestrained spread."[246]

Legault's mandates were supposed to ensure hospitals could not be overrun, and now Dubé was suggesting unless the province adopted policies that made the mandates look ill-conceived, the hospitals would be overrun. It seems obvious that Dubé was part of the reason why Legault went berserk to begin

2022. Would-be dictators, drunk on power, do not take kindly when their powers threaten to be undermined.

The news out of Alberta and Quebec helps us understand why Trudeau's clan was putting on a desperate face in January 2022. And although not immediately echoed elsewhere in Canada, left unchecked, failed healthcare mandates could spark a complete revolt against the COVID-19 narrative. What good are mandates in compelling greater vaccination if they get tossed aside when cases start to climb because the immunization campaign failed to produce its promised effects?

As these subplots were churning below the calm waters, some people were starting to ask questions about the statistics. Provincial policymakers were warning that they may have to ration care if omicron kept shattering their models and, almost like a military that had gotten used to the drill, many people were immediately scared and looking to blame the unvaccinated. And then there was Brampton Mayor Patrick Brown calling bullshit:

December 29, 2021 - December Brampton mayor speaks out on Ontario's misleading COVID hospital data[247]

Questions about the statistical sleight of hand that had been going on for some time were left unanswered in emails to PHAC, Dr. Tam, Dr. Russell, Shephard, Higgs, and countless others. And at risk of more calls from the RCMP, I admit to calling and leaving assertive messages to countless statistical purveyors across Canada. By withholding or purposely contorting information to further a pro-vaccination agenda, these individuals were attacking transparency and, in my opinion, behaving like criminals. Now, finally, there was an elected official, Mayor Brown, joining what had previously been an arcane fight with these shysters:

"It's what's known as incidental hospitalizations - people who are included in the Ontario government's daily count of people in hospital with COVID-19, but who aren't actually in hospital for the virus.

Brampton Mayor Patrick Brown is now looking to draw attention to this under-reported issue, which is only getting bigger. "I've been told it's about 50% of cases," Brown said in a phone interview with the Sun, referring specifically to Brampton hospitals.
This means the actual number of people in hospital with COVID-19 throughout Ontario may be half of what the official numbers indicate."

On January 11, 2022, for the first time, Ontario *'started distinguishing between patients admitted to hospital due to COVID-19 and incidental admissions'*, with the smug Dr. Jüni adding, *'This is addressing the concerns of various people...'*[248] These nameless 'various people' that Jüni mentioned were anyone that demands transparency and honesty from their leaders and health-related policymakers. As one of the most fanatical model-based prophets in Canada, Dr. Jüni was, and again this is my opinion, a corrupt hack. Once people were told that Jüni and their government had been lying to them, would they slowly start to wake up?

Even as other provinces started becoming more transparent, change was happening slowly, and the conditioned government-sponsored media really didn't know what was going on. As a quick example, the ominous headline on January 7, 2022, read *'COVID cases are pushing hospital capacity in N.S. to the limit'*,[249] but in the article, the reality eked out:

"Two-thirds of the people in hospital with COVID-19 were not admitted because of the disease [COVID-19], and their cases are not considered severe."

Were COVID-19 cases really responsible for the healthcare capacity stresses in Nova Scotia when two-thirds of COVID-19 cases were not severe? No. They were not.

So accustomed to pushing fear, what many CBC reporters didn't understand, even as they unwittingly reported it to us, is that

COVID-19 was not responsible for all of the healthcare problems in Canada. Rather, and unfortunately, Canada had been dealing with healthcare stresses well before COVID-19 came along. For example, in the decade leading up to COVID-19, there were countless incidences of hospitals being overrun, surgeries being delayed, and doctors and nurses being pushed past the brink of exhaustion because of capacity issues. Here are a few:

January 10, 2013 - Hospitals overwhelmed by flu and norovirus patients[250]

December 29, 2014 - Ontario ERs 'overwhelmed' as flu hits harder than usual[251]

April 27, 2017 - Surge in patients forces Ontario hospitals to put beds in 'unconventional spaces.'[252]
"Patient capacity at about half of Ontario's 145 hospital corporations exceeded 100 percent and reached as high as 130 percent."

January 25, 2018 - Hospital overcrowding crisis caused by more than just flu, says Ontario Health Coalition[253]
Patients are receiving "substandard care" in hallways at hospitals across Ontario due to a crisis in capacity that leads to increased infection rates, more violence, and higher mortality rates.

November 13, 2019 - Ontario residents urged to get flu shot, as hospitals brace for the worst[254]
"We are actively advertising for people to go and get the flu vaccine, if not for themselves to protect others around them."

Prior to the arrival of COVID-19, The Fraser Institute looked at twenty-eight developed countries and concluded that Canada ranked last on the number of hospital beds and last on hospital wait times.[255] This Canadian healthcare crisis had existed for a long time, and jabbing people with vaccines was never a solution so much as a diversion from this fact.

In the case of where I live, New Brunswick, prior to January 18, 2022, the province did not report incidental hospitalization figures. If you showed up to hospital with a broken arm and happened to also test positive for COVID-19, you would be logged as a COVID-19 hospitalization. This made COVID-19 hospitalizations much higher than they should have been and, likewise, probably also artificially inflated ICU and the death 'with covid' statistics.[14] I used the word 'probably' deliberately because I have emailed and called every major New Brunswick policymaker imaginable, and none will answer my questions.

To get an idea of what the mentally tormented contrarians in New Brunswick were dealing with, consider the following chain of events:

January 11, 2022 - *A record high 88 people are now hospitalized because of the virus. "The next few weeks will be intense"..."We are at the start of a very high tidal wave," Dornan said. "It's creeping up now, but in the next two or three weeks, it's going to crash over us, like no one's business. The worst is yet to come."*[256]

Thanks to multiple doctors using their models to warn of an upcoming wave, we were absolutely bombarded by Dr. Russell and Premier Higgs, every day and every hour, with calls for vaccination to stop omicron. New Brunswick was over 90% first dose vaccinated, and it took a couple of weeks for the shots to kick in. Any sensible person would know that the current upswing in cases would be over by the time any protection could be offered from the shots. But with Higgs one of the few puppets still dancing on Trudeau's strings, rubbish ruled the day:

January 13, 2022: *"We're not going to go through 2022 with our province in lockdown," he said, hinting mandatory vaccinations could be coming. "We're going to do what is*

---

[14] ICU and death statistics were massaged in N.B. and across Canada as well. COVID-19 hospitalizations are the focus on this chapter. Some provinces also started to report, sometimes, 'incidental' ICU cases in 2022.

necessary to protect all of New Brunswickers and to compel people to get vaccinated. Life will become increasingly uncomfortable and more difficult for those who are able to be vaccinated but choose not to be. ["257]

Baselessly blaming the unvaccinated for his lockdowns and trying to top Legault as King-crazy with more threats, Higgs was proving there was no ceiling to his corruption and deception. People protested outside of Higgs' home and left curse-laden messages constantly at his office (don't look at me) precisely because he was paid off ornament in Trudeau's trophy case. Then finally, this hallelujah moment:

January 18, 2022 - *"Of the 113 people hospitalized, 15 are in intensive care, a decrease of one. Four of them are on ventilators, also down one. Fifty-nine of the people hospitalized were already admitted for other reasons when they tested positive for COVID-19."* [258]

Did you catch it? Of the 113 people hospitalized with COVID-19, only 54 went to hospital for COVID-19. This meant, according to our corrupt New Brunswick government, during the strongest increase in COVID-19 cases during the entire pandemic, officially reported COVID-19 hospitalizations were declining!

This was the first time New Brunswick released incidental hospitalization numbers, and it should have caused a riot. Only one week earlier, policymakers lied when they said, *'a record high 88 people are now hospitalized because of the virus.'* All 88 of these people were not hospitalized because of the virus! Instead, an indeterminate number of these people went to hospital for a reason other than COVID-19 and just happened to test positive. After two years, New Brunswick policymakers were willfully misleading people by exploiting fraudulent statistics to generate fear-driven models, and these corrupt activities were being used to undermine the very premise of medical choice. Whether you were for or against the COVID-19 vaccines wasn't the point.

Next, the words below were digitally printed by the CBC, and people still had jobs after this. New Brunswick's Bruce MacFarlane, who never responded to multiple requests, was reading like a drunk:

"Although the deaths are all reported as COVID related, the people didn't all necessarily die from the virus, according to a Department of Health spokesperson.

The province has changed the way it reports deaths "due to increasing caseloads" and its "desire to be transparent," Bruce Macfarlane told CBC News.

"Public Health does not have enough time to determine whether cause of death is COVID-19 related prior to announcing the death publicly," he said in an emailed statement.

As a result, when a person with COVID-19 dies, they will be counted as a COVID-19 death "unless there is a clear alternative cause of death, such as a car accident."[259]

Public Health didn't have enough time to determine cause of death, so they just called it a COVID-19 death? Wow. Who is in such a mad rush to know the cause of death that they can't wait until officials determine the cause of death? And even if placating the impatient was the intent of rushing the cause of death, why label it a COVID-19 death instead of say 'unknown'? Vaccine deaths can take weeks, months, or even years (if ever) to be confirmed, but if a person dies during a pandemic, COVID-19 is the cause of death until further notice? Of course, New Brunswick was following the tutelage of the WHO's first rule (Chapter 4) - call everything a COVID-19 death and mark the comorbidities below because this makes life easier for those pushing fear and vaccines. The above article, in the running for most convoluted mess of the pandemic continued, and please do brace yourselves:

"Macfarlane did not say when the new way of reporting deaths began, but on Monday, Public Health changed the wording in its

daily news releases to say, "people who had COVID-19 have died." Until then, Public Health had been reporting that people died "as a result of COVID-19."
Macfarlane did not respond to questions about whose decision it was to group the deaths together or whether they will each eventually be followed up on."

'...*people who had COVID-19 have died*"? Jesus Christ, please help us now. New Brunswick wouldn't tell people when the new method of reporting COVID-19 deaths began? It seemed to be a pretty basic question - when did you start making the daily death numbers up? This wasn't a Babylon Bee or Onion news article (or, in Canada, The Beaverton). This was supposed to be the news! Nearly two years into a global pandemic and News Brunswick was reporting rubbish data from someone that appeared to be using the old my dog ate my homework routine.

Canada's second-largest province by population, Quebec, was supposedly more transparent and consistent with its data delivery. Then Quebec one day decided to say the secretive stuff out loud. Like the New Brunswick debacle, what sits below should have been front-page news on every Canadian paper (no, not the Pfizer documents[260]), but it is likely you have never read it before. Here was the bombshell some knew was happening but could not prove, buried in a single Canada Press article:

"Quebec's interim public health director, Dr. Luc Boileau, has acknowledged that the province has seen a "huge" number of deaths linked to COVID-19. Quebec's high death toll, he said last Thursday, is explained by the fact the province counts a COVID-19 death as any death involving someone who has the disease.

He said a government study from January indicated that around 30 percent of the official COVID-19 deaths in the province's hospitals involved people who tested positive for COVID-19 but whose principle cause of death was not the disease. He said about 40 percent to 50 percent of official COVID-19 deaths in the province involve people who had the disease but who died of other causes."[261]

When I ranted and raved to people that a WHO document from April 2020 could be artificially inflating COVID-19 death numbers, most people thought I was crazy. The above proved, at least in my minds frantic search for validation, that I may not have been crazy. According to Quebec's interim Public Health director, Dr. Luc Boileau, 40-50% of the COVID-19 deaths in Quebec may not have been from COVID-19. If similar statistics were replicated across Canada, it is possible that COVID-19 was never any deadlier than influenza and pneumonia. Was it all just a big lie? The snowball continued to gather speed down the hill:

January 8, 2022 - Saskatchewan changes up hospitalization reporting, includes 'incidental' cases[262]

January 12, 2022 - Two-thirds of HSC's COVID-19 patients incidental, Manitoba says[263]

January 18, 2022 - *The province of Alberta is beginning to differentiate its statistics on patients hospitalized with COVID-19 and those where it is unclear if the virus contributed to their admission.*[264]

February 1, 2022 - Nearly half of all COVID-19 patients in BC hospitals were likely not admitted due to COVID-19.[265]

Every time New Brunswick's Jennifer Russell or BC's Bonnie Henry mentioned COVID-19 hospitalizations to convey how critical it was that everyone gets vaccinated, which was nearly every time they spoke, were they being deceitful? The other option was that our top doctors had no idea about incidental COVID-19 hospitalizations, which is too fantastic a speculation even to consider. How long did policymakers know that the statistics they were using to make the scary models and push vaccination were phony? Also, and most critically, how long would Canadians continue to drink the government's poisonous pablum? Surely the exposing of the rigged data would make more Canadians open their eyes, wouldn't it?

What the undercurrents helped bring to light is that it wasn't COVID-19 or bad flu seasons that were causing the healthcare crisis. It was the inefficiencies in Canadian healthcare and, put simply, the overall lack of healthcare capacity. In 2013 in New Brunswick, *'nearly a third of NB hospital beds tied up with seniors waiting for nursing home spots'*,[266] and in 2019 the Toronto Star noted, *'Nobody wins when hospitals become long-term care homes.'*[267] That many of Canada's hospital beds were being used by the elderly was not a new phenomenon when COVID-19 arrived but an old and growing problem in Canada. In 2018 a Nova Scotia a freedom of information request revealed the following:

"Over the last five years, 718,230 bed days in our hospitals were used for people who were not hospital patients at all, but were waiting for placement in a nursing home."[268]

718,230 divided by 5 equals 143,645, and this number divided by 365 equals 393. This means that in the average year from 2014-2018, there were 393 'not hospital patients' per day for the entire year, taking up a hospital bed in Nova Scotia. Had Nova Scotia hospitals not been inundated with the elderly awaiting longer-term care placement, or the real crisis, the COVID-19 pandemic would have never pushed hospitalization capacity anywhere close to 100%.

The fragile Canadian healthcare system didn't get this way overnight but languished into a sad state over many years, with hospital beds on a per capita basis in precipitous decline. It was in this state of disarray because instead of coming up with long-term solutions, some policymakers were too busy blaming the flu outbreaks, the long-term care crisis, the lack of nurses, or COVID-19 every time capacity limits threatened to be breached. It is understood that the election cycle is shorter than the time it would take to properly fix healthcare in Canada.

Understanding the undercurrents of 2022 is not about denying COVID-19 cases added some strain to already overburdened Canadian hospitals. It is about recognizing that anyone that thought the mandates were a long-term fix to a grossly inadequate healthcare system was either disingenuous or delusional. Investing our time and resources enacting mandates, vax-passes, rigorous hospital screening processes, painting everything in Plexiglass, and adding universal testing to healthcare turned out to be time and money that was completely wasted when omicron arrived.

The brainwashed and paid off didn't like the building undercurrents. So, those that pointed at the statistical corruption and continued coercive mandates in early 2022 were either ignored or aggressively overpowered. It was even suggested, no longer quietly, that those pointing at rigged hospitalization and ICU stats didn't care about others. It will all be over soon, the story continued, if we all just take the vaccines and the boosters and remain locked down for a few more weeks.

Despite being scoffed at by many, the undercurrents did set precedents and started to allow once conspiratorial questions to slip into the mainstream. If Quebec could allow COVID-19 positive healthcare workers to work, why couldn't New Brunswick or Nova Scotia? If Alberta healthcare officials could offer the testing option to healthcare workers, why couldn't BC or Ontario? The public discourse was changing, albeit very slowly, as these types of questions, much like a virus, threatened to become contagious. Although not in this arena quite yet, the contrarian inclined could not help but ask:

What would it take for the indoctrinated majority of Canadians to start understanding that all of the vaccines, mandates, masking, and resources that were being used to monitor, trace, and track people may have had little or nothing to do with COVID-19?

Chapter 19 - The Great Canadian Dictator

January 2022 is what they call a change in momentum in the sports world. It was, with little risk of exaggeration, one of the most memorable months in Canadian history. With Trudeau focused on increasing vaccination rates of the only segment of the population where rates could be significantly increased (i.e., kids), his cronies vying for mandatory vaccination nationwide, and nameless soldiers re-wiring EI rules and devising bills that would limit free speech, the hammers continued to be dropped by the government-sponsored media:

January 12, 2022 - Majority of Canadians polled support healthcare fines for unvaccinated, survey finds[269]

January 19, 2022 - More than one in four Canadians support jail time for the unvaccinated, poll finds[270]

Amidst this craziness, the final push of Trudeau's hatred, there was the sound of a truck starting in Delta, British Columbia. It was quiet at first, but more and more engines would soon join that faint rumble. These trucks represented a predicament that Trudeau's calculus was unable to anticipate. Per *The Joy Luck Club*, these trucks were coming from afar, but they were carrying all the good intentions of freedom-loving Canadians.

There are precious few moments in this life that bring you unadulterated joy. The picture of a big rig driving away from a couple of small kids almost brought tears to my eyes. To many, Trudeau's mandates stood for a form of pure evil that had to be stopped. The trucker driving away from his children, not knowing when he would be home, was a heroic fight against this evil. I don't use the word heroic lightly, as this is what I sincerely believe.

Trudeau's Canada was starting to punish the unvaccinated with a health tax, and we were a hair-trigger away from mandatory vaccination nationwide. These trends also underscored the threat of permanent digital vaccine IDs, government tracking and tracing of all citizens, and, eventually (possibly), a Chinese-style social credit system. Those who didn't want government tyranny and preferred that Canada keep existing medical consent (without coercion) and privacy laws intact needed to take a stand now before it was too late.

While the image of this trucker driving away was magnificent, some of the first videos of the convoy taking shape out West were eye-dropping. People were lining the roads waving flags up in the frigid BC mountains. And in the background, like a litmus test of how successful the Freedom Convoy was becoming, was the GoFundMe page, which after less than seven days of being active, had more than $1 million.[271] Fourteen days after this, it would have attracted more than $10 million.[272]

As a rule, I don't generally give to many charities or causes simply because I have kids and debt, and I work under the assumption that I will have more to give when I pass if I successfully invest any excess funds I have today. I gave a small amount to the convoy after seeing a handful of images and videos. I planned on giving more.

Like millions of Canadians, both unvaccinated and vaccinated, I watched the building convoy with the sense that I was part of it. Some would later argue that this convoy wanted to bring the government down. On the contrary, despite a handful of bad apples, the majority of convoy protestors desperately wanted to bring the government back up to a level where existing laws were followed. One person should not have the power to strangle or give breath to freedom merely by saying the word 'pandemic.' Quite simply, if the mandates were gone, this event would not have happened.

As the convoy strengthened, there were reports that it was the longest convoy in history and that more than 50,000 trucks were on their way to Ottawa. The contrarian in me knew that some of this was hype, but I didn't care. It was great! Give me more!

When I read on a crackpot cavern of the internet that 10,000 trucks were also coming from the U.S. to support the cause, a sense of warmth came over me (it wasn't the whisky).

As the excitement built, there were also many politicians and media calling the convoy a bunch of anti-vaxxers, which was an increasingly unsuitable word to use as omicron spread through people with all medical backgrounds with ease. What was lost in this name-calling was the fact that two of the three convoy founders - Tamara Lich, Chris Barber, and BJ Dichter - were vaccinated. This was an anti-mandate convoy, not an anti-vaxx convoy. If you want to take a vaccine, take a vaccine.

The media, predictably, didn't want anything to do with a serious discussion about why thousands of Canadians were cheering along with their kids on the side of roads across Canada. Instead, they attacked the character and historical activism or political leanings of anyone or thing remotely associated with the convoy. Along with the key three founders, another main character was Pat King, who had a checkered historical record. Early on, the eventual three 'founders,' like a political party vetting candidates, distanced themselves from Pat King and others. While logical, this was also not the real story. To reiterate, the convoy wasn't about this person or that person. It was about ending the mandates! Using the same playbook to attack those in the convoy that they would use to attack anyone that dared call Trudeau a dictator, the MSM conspired to quarantine the convoy into its box.

As the trucks put the hammer down toward Ottawa, the money donated by Canadians to the cause grew above the amount raised by any political party in the fourth quarter of 2021.[273] Accepted the moment as significant, Trudeau stood up, and...gave yet another divisive speech.

"It's important to underline the close to 90% of truckers in this country are vaccinated, like close to 90% of Canadians. Over the past many months and years now, Canadians have stepped up to protect each other, to protect our frontline workers, to protect our

The terms 'small fringe minority' and 'unacceptable views'
alluded to how out of touch with reality Trudeau had become.
There was a window of opportunity for Trudeau to offer a
conciliatory viewpoint or extend some variant of an olive branch to
the truckers who were now two days outside of Ottawa. But
instead, Trudeau chose to use inflammatory language and degrade
the views of millions of Canadians. Some wondered why people
were so angry with the mandates, the lies, and the push for a
Chinese-style governance system. It was because Trudeau was a
belligerent and malicious son of a gun.

There were people at my workplace outraged they had been
coerced by Trudeau to take a vaccine they never wanted, and their
outrage expanded exponentially as Trudeau was now using them to
build his dictatorial case that 90% of the popular was right and the
other 10% were wrong. For me, this was when Trudeau, who had
been skirting around the idea of putting on his full führer costume
before, had officially gone from being a docile despot to a historic
dictator. He no longer cared whatsoever about the citizens of
Canada - he would demolish the social fabric of the nation to push
his vaccines and punish those who stood against him. This man
had an insane lust for his vision of Canada, period.

There was no other way for me to interpret what Trudeau,
the power-hungry mobster, was doing as omicron rendered vaccine

efficacy useless. Everyone, except Trudeau, was slowly acknowledging this. To reiterate, on January 26, 2022, our pandemic dictator arrogantly and ignorantly shared his delusions with the following:

"We know the way through this pandemic is by getting everyone vaccinated."

These were not the words of a sane individual. Full stop.

Mounting some feeble multi-fanged media attack, these exact words were echoed a day earlier by Transport Minister Omar Alghabra and Employment Minister Carla Qualtrough, among others.[275] After Carla reiterated that 90% of truckers had been vaccinated, the reporter asked her how many truckers were unvaccinated. Carla answered, *'I don't have that data; I apologize.'* This was our Employment minister, preaching vaccination for everyone and oblivious to everything else. Other questions Carla would no doubt be unable to answer would be how many people didn't want to take the shots and how many do you think will outright refuse a booster? The talking points Trudeau gave Carla were '90% vaccinated' and 'they stepped up to do their part.' That is all she knew.

The timing of the renewed pro-vaccination campaign was astonishingly out of touch, and it also went against the undeniable trend emerging elsewhere in the world. For example, as of December 31, 2021, South Africa didn't report any significant spikes in deaths, and the omicron strain had peaked within four weeks, leading *'some scientists...to forecast the same pattern elsewhere.'*[276] Then, on January 19, 2022, one week before Trudeau would quintuple down with *'getting everyone vaccinated,'* UK's Boris Johnson announced that England would be ending mask requirements and dropping its so-called 'COVID Pass.'[277] Johnson was one of the first major world leaders to drop the sentiment *'we must learn to live with Covid in the same way we live with flu.'* He would not be the last.

On the surface, that Johnson was declaring some strain of victory against COVID-19 was more than a little shocking. After all, Johnson was flirting with the idea of mandatory vaccination only weeks earlier,[278] and he had attended Davos on three occasions while he was a London Mayor (2012-2014). But alas, Johnson had said the WEF was *'a constellation of egos involved in orgies of adulation,'*[279] and he started banning his cabinet from going to Davos beginning in 2020.[280] Johnson didn't aspire to Trudeau-level dictatorial eminence. He was only in it for the money:

2019: *"You just have to chuck a snowball into a cocktail party at Davos, and you'd hit someone with a sovereign wealth fund who would fund a piece of infrastructure."*[281]

To further highlight how quickly perceptions had changed in the UK, on January 2, 2022, Dr. Hilary called unvaccinated doctors 'selfish'[282] and strongly supported the mandates, but by January 20, 2022, he said the mandates should be scrapped.[283] Not even the idea that Boris Johnson was looking for a distraction from his penchant for partying during COVID-19 lockdowns[284] could explain this groundswell of change. Maybe, just maybe, omicron could supply the much-needed death blow to the mindless vaccination dogma?

Rather than entertain the idea that omicron was spreading natural immunity with such force the pandemic had permanently changed, Trudeau's cabal was mounting an attack. Instead of mentioning the exceptionally positive developments in places like South Africa and England, Trudeau's favourite henchman, Duclos, preferred to focus and mention places like Italy and Austria or where mandatory vaccine policies were being tested. This oversight was not lost on South Africa's top coronavirus experts, and shortly before Trudeau gave his 'great dictator' speech, the BBC asked - *'Why Was South Africa ignored over mild Omicron evidence?'* The content of the article was most interesting:

"It seems like high-income countries are much more able to absorb bad news that comes from countries like South Africa.

When we're providing good news, all of a sudden, there's a whole lot of scepticism. I would call that racism.''[285]

A prickly amount of blackface photos aside, I would be the first to say that Trudeau, Duclos, Omar, Carla, and others in Justin's cult are not 'racist.' I am of the mind that in order to levy such a charge, some material evidence is required. Nevertheless, the question of why South Africa was applauded for its expeditious work in tracing and monitoring the ominous omicron variant early on but almost completely ignored when the data turned positive is absolutely valid. Not only was the South African data telling us omicron had basically a six-week life cycle (for those looking for curve flatness), but a study out of South Africa on January 19, 2022, before Trudeau's official crowning date, suggested that *'MRNA Boosters Don't Block Omicron.'*[286] Why were high-income countries ignoring the science?

You may recall that Cardy deceitfully cited a South African study to spread bogus info that kids were in more danger from the omicron than the delta. Why was this fake negative news out of South Africa picked up instantly by Cardy and countless news organizations across the world while studies and data that suggested omicron was a sweet puppy out of South Africa shunned? Did it have anything to do with people like Cardy and Trudeau corruptly pursuing their agenda at any and all costs?

As the truckers were one day out of Ottawa, Canada's sergeant-at-arms, Pat McDonell, sent letters to MPs warning that if protesters came to their homes to *'not get involved'* and to *'avoid physical altercations, even if provoked.'*[287] Then there was CTV, which claimed, *'Most federal politicians and their staff are already being warned to avoid the parliamentary precinct while the convoy is in town because of the security risk.'*[288] Apparently, someone forgot to tell Trudeau's big brother apparatus that the truckers wanted to end the mandates, not start a war. The media and politicians, perhaps nervous that some form of retribution could be coming their way, were acting oddly paranoid, even for them.

As if to say the most ludicrous and shocking thing they could possibly think of to avoid an honest discussion of when the mandates were going to end, the media dropped:

"...some people claiming to be affiliated with the convoy have discussed online overthrowing the government and going after Prime Minister Justin Trudeau and other MPs. One person said that "the only way that this is going to be solved is with bullets," and it has been suggested that the event on the Hill could turn into Canada's version of the Jan. 6, 2021 insurrection at the U.S. Capitol."[289]

'Some people'? A violent threat of shooting Trudeau (was this reported to police)? And who exactly suggested this could be an insurrection? Suffice to say, if you have the time and energy, you can find threatening words on basically any topic or political person imaginable on the internet. Trudeau had wondered if we should 'tolerate' the unvaccinated, newspapers and doctors on social media openly wished the unvaccinated would die, polls said Canadians wanted to throw the unvaccinated in jail, and mandatory vaccination for all was being discussed as Quebec was about to fine and then ban the unvaccinated from Wal-Mart. Would it really be all that shocking if that somewhere, someone on the internet was wishing ill will against Trudeau? I did it daily, in some form or another, but that didn't mean I wanted to go to Ottawa and...

Commenting on the internet phenomenon that empowers the extremists, a professor said the following:

June 7, 2020 - 60 minutes Australia[290]
"It's that sense of vulnerability that scientist Professor Stephan Lewandowsky sees as giving rise to conspiratorial thinking - fringe ideas of a small percentage of people given power by social media."

Lewandowsky bled the WEF colours, and he may have been the originator of the 'fringe' and 'small' lexicon Trudeau fancied. Nevertheless, he was wrong about social media giving power. Social media was the comparatively safe and preferred outlet for the raging inferno of Trudeau-inspired disgust to be offloaded without actual bloodshed. People that had been forced out of their jobs and couldn't travel to see loved ones were not 'given power' by social media. They were desperately venting and crying on social media.

That the MSM was sensationalizing nameless online posts and misconstruing the fairly basic 'end the mandates' mantra of the Freedom Convoy was, of course, not surprising. Along with the much-beaten drum - Trudeau bought the media! - there was also the fact that many journalists and television personalities had an irrational fear of COVID-19, and they bought into the brand of hate Trudeau was selling. Finally, some might ask that if this station or that news organization never got government money, how could they be biased? The speculation is that some outlets that never got a lot of government affection were biased, based on the belief that their efforts might yield future Trudeau-funded dividends. Many journalists also aspired to work at the CBC, and it was common knowledge that a reporter would never land a coveted CBC position if they spoke critically of Trudeau.

As Canadian media chiefly focused on only one side of the story, the entire conversation was happening elsewhere. In the U.S., this entailed a debate between people like Donald Trump Jr., who endorsed the truckers for fighting 'tyranny,"[291] and the Washington Post (Bezos) that screamed Canada must confront the 'toxic' Freedom Convoy.[292] That the left versus right political gears were grinding hours before the truckers reached their destination was to be anticipated. Co-opting movements is what each of these elements, at the extreme, habitually tries to do. Even so, and as the National Post succinctly put it, one side was currying more favour: the convoy *'has caught the attention of foreign anti-mandate sympathizers who are framing Freedom Convoy 2022 as a popular uprising against the pandemic strictures of Prime Minister Justin Trudeau.'*[293] When asked if the Freedom Convoy was a code-red-global-freedom-phenomenon, the unnamed online sources covered by CTV put on their best Jack Nicholson face and answered - 'Your goddam right it is!'

Before the truckers started rolling into Ottawa on January 28, 2022, expectations were high, and tensions were already hot. Trudeau's speech and attempt to frame the protest as 'small' and 'fringe' were equivalent to throwing gasoline on an inferno. Even those who thought Trudeau was a diabolical genius executing some globalist master scheme didn't think he planned properly for this. Saying a segment of society holds 'unacceptable views' brought a few brainwashed and righteously vaccinated out of their slumber and onto team Trucker. Views are views; let's all try to get along.

Trudeau had tried desperately to keep his August 13, 2021 lie big and simple, but the spread of omicron and the threat of endemic status were choking his narrative. Trudeau had completely ignored natural immunity, and Dr. Tam did too. By doing so, they would also have to ignore a January 19, 2021 study from the CDC, which said natural immunity (delta) was stronger than two doses of vaccine.[294] Even when NACI recommended people delay getting vaccinated if they had a recent infection, Trudeau ignored the advice.[295] Our dictator wanted to force vaccines on all Canadians, and the pursuit of this goal was no longer aligned with any pragmatic understanding of COVID-19.

The truckers were coming for their great reset, and many said they would not leave until all the mandates were dropped. Something, as the saying goes, had to give. Enter Ottawa Police Chief Sloly, who, like a referee in a boxing match saying he wanted a clean fight, had this to say before the truckers arrived:

"Let me be very clear: we are prepared to investigate, arrest if necessary, charge and prosecute anyone who acts violently or breaks the law in the demonstrations, or in association with the demonstrations."[296]

With the Great Dictator in one corner and the Truckers in the other - Ding, Ding!

Chapter 20 - The Truckers Cometh

'Canadian truckers rule' ~ Elon Musk[297]

When the trucks finally arrived in Ottawa, it was a glorious sight. Like soldiers marching into battle, many truckers planned to fight, meaning stay in Ottawa until victory was had and the mandates were dropped. Already accustomed to being away from home and sleeping in their cabs for extended periods, with enough fuel, the truckers could conceivably stay in Ottawa forever. Some truckers also brought their families, the kids, and pets. Freedom was for everyone.

Leading up to this moment, Canada by no means had a monopoly on protesting COVID-19 restrictions. Elsewhere in the world, protests against lockdowns, restrictions, masks, and mandates had been taking place for almost two years. Even in China, there were early reports of people forming groups to protest restrictions and business closures. These people were quickly arrested for *'picking quarrels and provoking trouble'* - a criminal offence in China.

The basic correlation was that more COVID-19 cases or hospitalizations meant more restrictions, and more restrictions resulted in more protests. Shortly before the Canadian Freedom Convoy, other European countries, including Austria, Germany, Italy, Belgium, and France, were holding massive demonstrations, primarily in response to the discussion of mandatory vaccination. South Africa, where the omicron mutation was first discovered, had already seen its protest curve flatten.

While a wide variety of actors and protest methods were deployed across the globe, in late January the tiny and typically reserved country of Canada had tapped into an original and creative way to protest the COVID-19 mandates - a convoy! And for this brief moment, or the next 23 days to be precise, all eyes were glued on Ottawa. The movement was all the rage and resonated in so many countries that copycat convoys popped up in

France, Belgium, The Netherlands, the U.S., Australia, New Zealand, and others. The Canadian-instigated Freedom Convoy was a worldwide sensation.

Ottawa police estimates put the total amount of people flooding Parliament Hill on January 29, 2022, between 5,000 and 18,000.[298] Much like the models that gave ridiculously wide ranges for COVID-19 deaths and cases and still ended up being wrong, allow me to say with great confidence well north of 25,000 Canadians braved the frigid air to try and go to the hill that day. There were trucks backed up Wellington Street as far as the eye could see, bridges were swarmed with people trying to make their way downtown, all streets in the downtown core were closed, and the cold and weary packed Rideau mall in an attempt to get warm and not wear a mask in a mall (which was the equivalent of a high crime).[299] In these early moments, the police were either pro-protest or neutral on the subject. While you may not like the topical matter of a protest, the act, and the right to peacefully assemble, are protected under Canadian law. Even when the owners of the Rideau Centre voluntarily closed the mall, and some media tried to blame it on the unruly protesters, police interjected and said, *There is no threat to public safety.* That the mall was closed and businesses in the downtown core were asked to close was suspicious and, potentially, politically motivated. Playing the role of Switzerland, the police were, in the opening days, delighted by the peace. After four days, Police Chief Sloly noted the following:

"No riots, no injuries, no deaths. That is a measure of success for any jurisdiction in Canada, and quite frankly anywhere in the world."[300]

Early in the protest, there were a handful of not-so-pleasant occurrences, including a Nazi flag briefly waving on a high balcony, a person dancing on the Unknown Soldiers' grave, a U.S. confederate flag, and some freedom materials placed on Terry Fox's statue. Defending a Nazi flag or the unfortunate dancing incident is not something anyone should be doing, and no one did. As for the Terry Fox statue - which protestors quickly cleaned up -

another Terry Fox statue had previously been dressed up with Pride regalia, and the media and politicians adored it. I don't really have an enlightened opinion on statue wardrobe etiquette, but do some people believe that Terry Fox was for Pride and not Freedom?

Amidst the distractions, the media conveniently forgot to mention the protesters were exceptionally, and quite shockingly, peaceful. There was no significant damage to property, no brawls, and no statues torn to the ground and decapitated. And the desecration of the Unknown Soldier was an accident, the lady was very remorseful, and later she would not be charged. Things could have gone bad on the first weekend in Ottawa, but they didn't. I was surprised that grandpa from the bridge opening was not in Ottawa looking to stir some violence up for the cameras. If the best the shadowy government could do to make the protests look horrifying was a single Nazi flag, it was stunningly pathetic.

Relentless in trying to force a false narrative, the CBC interviewed Canadian Anti-Hate Network Chair Bernie Farber, who made a remarkable claim:

"...worst display of Nazis and racist propaganda that I have ever seen in this country."[301]

A single Nazi flag that every protester conceivable denounced is the worst display of Nazis and racist propaganda ever seen in Canada. Really?

As the Truckers were landing in Ottawa, a blockade was forming at the Coutts border in Alberta, one of the busiest borders for trade between the U.S. in Canada. Where the protests in Ottawa would likely be tolerated as emergency lanes were left open and the public seemed, initially, somewhat supportive, the blockade at the Coutts border was potentially a more serious matter. There were also protests taking place across Canada, with huge crowds in Calgary, Toronto, and Vancouver, where Brian Peckford - the last living signer of the Canadian Charter of Rights and Freedoms -

gave an impassioned speech on January 29, 2022.

Peckford: *"We have to send a very clear and unmistakable message to every leader in Canada - all fourteen governments - that we will not stand to see our freedoms taken away...and just because you remove the mandates, it's not all over, it's just beginning! Because we want those rights and freedoms re-established in our Charter of Rights and Freedoms because they are sacred and permanent for all of Canada."*[302]

The adrenalin coursing through the veins of people across Canada was not reserved only for the speakers and protesters. Rather, as the convoy arrived in Ottawa, Saskatchewan's Scott Moe sent a letter to the truckers[303] saying the end to the mandates was coming, and Ontario's Doug Ford stated it was time *'to live with covid.'*[304] There were also politicians, primarily Progressive Conservative party members and Maxime Bernier, who spoke with protesters, and soon-to-be interim Conservative Leader, Candice Bergen, had dinner with some protesters. Suddenly, openly talking about ending the mandates was no longer forbidden. It was even becoming popular! Nearly everyone, it seemed, was having a gay old time.

The one person not having an enjoyable time was our dictator, Justin Trudeau. As all this positive enthusiasm and love was building, Trudeau was covertly trucked to an undisclosed location. Our dictator was afraid to be anywhere near Canadians that had driven from every direction across the country to peacefully protest in their capital. Not only could Trudeau no longer perpetuate barefaced lies to defend his segregationist mandates, but he also lacked the ability to speak on the protests. The cowardice of our dictator, at this moment, will never be forgotten.

As days of nonviolent protesting were about to turn into a week, the MSM avoided almost any positive coverage and instead asked all the tough questions that Canadians wanted to know:

"There is concerns that Russian actors could be continuing to fuel things as this protest grows, but perhaps they were even instigating it from the outset?"[305]

My first response to the Russia angle was outstanding - Russians love freedom too! But when CBC government personality, Nil Koksal, didn't offer a punchline to this outlandish comment, I sat mystified. Amidst drawing up plans to invade Ukraine, Russia gave some truckers in BC gas money to drive to Ottawa? The protests in Canada had been happening since the first restrictions were announced in 2020. Was Putin also giving all these protesters Tim Horton's cards to stand out in front of local city halls across the country? If any of this made-up garbage was true, where was my Russian compensation for protesting, and why wasn't anyone I knew driving to Ottawa with a fistful of rubles?

CBC had the nerve to double down on the Russian theme by giving airtime to 'New Brunswick cyber security expert' David Shipley. Shipley was adamant that the Russians were behind the protests, or maybe China was too, and he provided zero evidence to support any of his speculations.[306] Shipley's conclusion was the Canadian government needed to regulate the internet. The entire interview was little more than an infomercial spreading conspiracies and laying the foundations for Trudeau's upcoming internet censorship quest.

The funding from Russia chicanery must have played in a focus group because following Koksal's and Shipley's baseless comments, others would start guessing that that money being funnelled to truckers was coming from primarily foreign actors or right-wing extremist groups, or Elon Musk, or possibly even terrorists. This, of course, was all for show. I gave money, and I knew plenty of people that gave money to the Freedom Convoy. The more the media pushed on something, the more you knew they were doing it for a reason.

On Monday, January 29, 2022, Trudeau announced that he had caught COVID-19. Thankfully, Trudeau had three doses of newly defined 'vaccines' in him, and this, and this alone, would successfully beat back the disease. In hiding and now COVID-19 positive to ensure more hiding, Trudeau's hypocrisy would be put on full display by India's Palki Sharma.[307] Ms. Sharma had been saving up her words for years and did not hold back:

"There's a new trend on social media tonight hashtag where is Justin Trudeau. It's not a rhetorical question. It's not funded by Canada's opposition, either. It's a genuine query of ordinary Canadians, where is their Prime Minister? Unfortunately, nobody knows. Trudeau says he has contracted the Wuhan virus. But no one knows where he's isolated. Normally, he would be in his office on Mondays. Today he wasn't. He and his family were moved to an undisclosed location. In other words, he fled. Do you know why? Because the white knight of democracy could not handle a protest."

Delivered with perfect comedic timing, Ms. Sharma was just getting started:

"Around the time...farmers were protesting in India, that Trudeau [from 2020] was full of ideas how to reach out how to handle the protests how to broker peace. He was passionate and proactive in offering advice. Let me quote what he said about India. "The situation he said is concerning. We are all very worried about family and friends. Let me remind you Canada will always be there to defend the rights of peaceful protesters. We believe in the process of dialogue. We've reached out through multiple means to the Indian authorities to highlight our concerns." If only we could get this message to Trudeau's secret cubbyhole..."

Like the unvaccinated taking some guilty pleasure every time a triple vaccinated person was shocked when they caught the virus they supposedly took their shots to guard against, karma was rearing its handsome head. Many Canadians may have been blinded by Trudeau's empty charms, but much of the world, including those with decent memories in India, were not. Sharma continued her evisceration:

"The protests are certainly daunting. But there hasn't been violence. So far, the protests have been peaceful. So why hasn't Prime Minister Trudeau reached out to the protesters where is the process of dialogue?... his response is two-faced. When the protests happened in India, it's the government's fault. The cops are tyrants the ministers are unresponsive. But when the protests happened in Canada, the narrative changes...Trudeau calls these truckers a small fringe minority holding onto unacceptable views - his words...I'm not saying Trudeau should surrender to these anti-vaxxers. I'm saying he should stick by his own words. He should reach out to them... This whole controversy is a lesson for all self-righteous leaders out there - stop meddling in the affairs of other countries, and if you do, if you do, make sure you hold yourself to the same standard if not, you're just a hypocrite, wavy hair or not."

For executing one of the best takedowns of Trudeau during the entire pandemic, Ms. Sharma is forgiven for using the derogatory and misplaced term 'anti-vaxxers.'

After the first weekend of protests, Trudeau was a weakened man thrown onto a deserted island searching for a new food source. For whatever reason, Trudeau had gambled either on the protesters withering away on their own or that the crowds would turn violent, and this would hasten an aggressive police or military response. As neither of these events happened, and weekend number two neared, it quickly became clear that Trudeau had no backup plan. Our great dictator, who encouraged other nations to have a dialogue with protesters, refused to speak with Canadian protesters on his doorstep, and beyond parking violations, there was insufficient cause to start arresting thousands of truckers and protesters. The tension, as per the maxim, was beginning to build.

On Friday before the second weekend, Police Chief Sloly announced a 'surge and contain' strategy. This strategy, to be perfectly frank, failed beyond anything imaginable. The police surge ended up being more police watching protesters do whatever they wanted. The protesters let the music blare and, peacefully, danced the weekend nights away. It looked like a fantastic party. The police watched. Some police shook protesters' hands. Peace was the theme. End the mandates!

Some people may have the misconception that someone in my position -disgruntled and on forced LWOP - is politically resolute on bringing Trudeau down or exacting revenge all the day long. Sometimes grievances are cast aside as pointless whimsy triumphs in unexpected ways to enhance this life. With this in mind, when Ottawa Mayor Jim Watson had a conniption on live television about the protesters having bouncy castles, I smiled and thought, it doesn't get any better than this. It was ridiculous, obviously, that instead of listening to protesters' demands and trying to bring Trudeau to the negotiating table, Watson was attacking bouncy castles. Ridiculous but also splendid.

"It's disturbing when you see the protest turning into what looks like some kind of a fun carnival, where they've got bouncy castles and hot tubs and saunas..."[308]

During the truckers' stay in Ottawa, there were many whimsical moments like the bouncy castle one, including the pig roasts, the trucked-in saunas, cops giving protesters hi-fives, cops helping the protesters unfetch their tent structure from a fence, and the professionally built sound stages and structures. If the truckers' and protesters' goal was to aggravate the Mayor and make the coward Trudeau stew in befuddled silence, per Bush's big lie - mission accomplished!

There were also, contrary to the MSM coverage, heart-warming stories, including the homeless being fed and having a place to socialize, local shops (that stayed open) seeing business boom, and crime in Ottawa crashing. As the fact that crime was down since the truckers arrived became widely known, Ottawa police's Steve Bell aimed to fix the narrative: *there is currently an underreporting of some crimes of the unlawful demonstrators.*[309] Wouldn't the reports of underreported crimes constitute said crimes actually being reported? For that matter, why were demonstrators exercising their legal rights to peacefully protest, most of which were not illegally parked, now considered 'unlawful'?

As the second weekend ended, police pledged that more troops were coming, words like 'unlawful' and 'occupation' were repeated ad nauseam, and police started to go after truckers' fuel supplies. Then, on Monday morning, an Ottawa court injunction banned the honking of horns. Hours after the horn ban was made into a ten-day law, an older man was aggressively arrested for honking his horn nowhere close to the protesters. The 4'10 man was 78 years old and meant no harm, saying, *'I just gave the trucker a thumbs-up and a honk.*'[310] Placing a freedom hat on a Terry Fox statue was reported like a murder on the CBC, but forcibly arresting a great-grandfather for honking his horn (and not a single trucker for honking theirs) didn't make the cut into the nightly news. Even if the man was a little testy, which he was, it was because he didn't even know a new law existed. The arrest was an instant reminder of how seemingly well-intentioned actions can produce harmful effects, especially when placing new powers into the hands of some overzealous police that were not fond of protesters and horn honkers.

The energized and chaotic words and actions of policymakers and the police showed that everyone was starting to feel the heat. The first weekend was peaceful, and government/media attempts to paint the protest as violent or racist-driven failed miserably. The second weekend was a party more than a protest, and this infuriated those more versed in traditional anti-protest war measures. As the third weekend beckoned, with only small signals of protester fatigue, the already anti-protester narrative escalated abruptly to the protesters are unlawful and dangerous. It didn't matter that the protesters weren't doing anything specifically that unlawful or that dangerous; just being in Ottawa, or 'occupying' Ottawa, was close to being decreed illegal.

With the new no-honking injunction in place and funds from the GoFundMe campaign already frozen, the government managed to freeze more than $8.2 million (USD) from the Freedom Convoy's new GiveSendGo campaign, or the funding system set up to counteract the freezing of GoFundMe funds.[311] With fuel confiscations becoming more widespread and monetary streams potentially running dry, rumours that the protest may only last a few more days abound. The Freedom Convoy talked a tough game, as they should, but at this point, it was starting to become clear that an end to the federal mandates would not happen anytime soon with Trudeau in charge. This led to speculation that Freedom Convoy representatives were looking for an exit strategy that might satisfy both sides. Getting truckers on the road again before being arrested or having their trucks impounded and sold (which was threatened at the time) was the favoured path. But with Trudeau not saying anything and walking out of the House of Commons when being questioned on the protests on February 9 and February 10, 2022, a breakthrough deal, unlike breakthrough COVID-19 cases, was highly improbably

"...representatives of the Ontario government declined a third invitation to participate in trilateral talks to deal with ongoing vaccine mandate protests."[312]

As the third weekend neared, hundreds of citizens staged what the National Post coined a *'gas can subterfuge to frustrate police.'*[313] As a mob of people marched toward downtown, some were carrying gas cans filled with water, and some were full of fuel and, by design, there were too many people for the cops to search unless they wanted to risk a riot. There were families with kids pushing strollers with a gas can buckled inside them instead of babies. These actions were memorable and highly effective and were the average person's way of not complying with authoritarianism. Unfortunately, this would also be one of the last moments of unexpected joyful glee as the tide was about to turn.

The street BBQs and hot tub beer drinking managed to keep going for the third weekend even though everyone knew, like how a massive high school party pisses off the neighbours, that the cops would be clearing house soon. The protesters were not scared of the flyers and rhetoric that said the 'illegal occupation' must end, and those who stayed bravely surrendered to the idea of being arrested. These dead-enders were to be applauded for standing up to tyranny and exercising their lawfully protected rights to peaceful assembly and protest. The government doesn't get to decide when and how Canadians protest; the people do!

After the third weekend, on Monday February 14, 2022, Trudeau invoked the Emergency Act for the first time in Canadian history. The coward that refused to meet or listen to a single protester was now showing Canadians his iron fist. The Emergency Act that our dictator opted not to use during the pandemic was unleashed because peaceful protesters wouldn't go home when Trudeau demanded it. Try as you might, you cannot find a single shred of evidence that Trudeau opened any channels of meaningful dialogue with the protesters, even as almost all provinces adopted timelines for abandoning the archaic and fruitless mandates.

His legacy already firmly cemented in the dictator column, Trudeau's flippant invoking of the Emergency Act was now dragging him into the realm of worst Prime Minister in Canadian history. There was no manner by which to tweak or pervert the facts to even remotely suggest that Trudeau dealt with the Freedom Convoy well, and there was more than enough evidence to suggest he handled the protest as poorly as anyone could have ever imagined.

Chapter 21 - Farewell Truckers

After three weekends of glorious protesting (and dancing), policymakers were divided. Some politicians wanted Trudeau to negotiate or talk with the truckers, while others wanted to steamroll the truckers out of town. And still other leaders were so indecisive, so frustrated, that one moment they would blame the ineffective police that seemed to be in cahoots with the protesters while the next praise the police for getting ready to kick some ass. The onlooker watching this Olympic-level dithering could not help but marvel how people like Mayor Watson and soon-to-be former Police Chief Sloly ever achieved their leadership positions.

Then there was Diane Deans, a member of the Ottawa City Council and Chair of the Ottawa Police Services Board. Ms. Deans was, to be kind, a person in a world all her own. Soon after the peaceful protests started, Deans was already starting to become unhinged, saying that *'...Heavy trucks that can be used as weapons.* '[314] While Watson's bouncy castle statements were hilarious, Deans' televised meltdown on the subject was the stuff of legend:

"I was just aghast this weekend that there was a bouncy castle and there's a hot tub...I wanted to go up there and poke that hot tub myself...and unplug that damn bouncy castle because it's just a symbol of what has gone for 19-days in the capital."[315]

A real reporter may have asked Deans what she thought about those who had been under constant attack by their Prime Minister for 187 days. But this was the CBC, and to talk about why the protesters were in Ottawa and whether their demands were legitimate was unthinkable, especially when those dirty and likely unvaccinated trucker kids were playing on bouncy castles. The most exquisite meltdown from Deans arrived shortly after the bouncy castle remarks and was the pinnacle of greatness. I am not picking on Ms. Deans when I say that her words were the most salacious sequence of propaganda I have ever heard in my life. Judge for yourself:

"I think there's been plenty of counts of how our residents have been subjected to racism and sexism and misogyny and just the most boorish and ugly, hateful behaviour that one could ever expect, and you know, it has increased... it's not a target on the City of Ottawa. It's much bigger than that. It's really an insurrection. It's a, it's an attack on our democracy. It's an attack on our federal government. It has a lot of international elements to it. The money is flowing from the US, it's right out of the Trump playbook...This is not something this country has ever seen before. I understand Mark Carney referred to it as sedition today. I think that's exactly what it is. This is treason. This is way bigger. This is a group of well-polished professional people that are trying to overthrow the government. The government of democratically elected government of this country...."[316]

With the possible exception of Baghdad Bob, the above is some of the most blatant delusions ever expressed on television. As stated, Deans was in a world all her own.

With Trudeau's Emergency Act invoked and people like Watson and Deans taking their rhetoric up 100 notches, the sledge-hammers were about to start dropping. A day after the Emergency Act was invoked, Police Chief Sloly was let go, Steve Bell was named interim Police Chief, and Deans' Police Service Board stated, *'The Board is already working to put in place a new command structure and will be appointing a new Chief soon.'*[317] The logistics of what happened next cannot be corroborated given that he said/she said dynamic developed. What is known is that Bell, who had only been in his acting position for a day, was ousted, and Deans' Police Service Board hired former Waterloo Regional Police Chief Matthew Torigian to take over as Ottawa Police Chief. This chaotic series of events upset Watson, councillors, and anyone that thought an uncontested new Chief picked by Deans' group was not legitimate. A full-fledged orgy of backstabbing, media whoring, and name-calling ensued. The drama was more intoxicating than the protests themselves.

In the span of a few days, Deans was pushed out of her role by Watson, Torigian was given his walking papers a day after he signed his contract, three Police Service Board members resigned in protest of Watson's move, and Steve Bell was back in as interim Police Chief. As I believe Watson and Deans are cut from the same cloths of nuttiness (as elected leaders, not necessarily as people), please understand I am not taking sides in these action-packed escapades. Watson was a buffoon flip-flopping with the tides, but absolutely nothing from Deans, who announced in December 2021 she was running for Mayor,[318] ever made much sense.

"What's more, Deans said, bringing in a seasoned outsider to lead the police service through the crisis meant that interim Chief Steve Bell would not be "out in front" of the response to the occupation - something that could diminish his chances of becoming Ottawa's next permanent Police Chief."

So, to be clear, Deans ousted Bell from interim Chief the day after she approved him as interim Chief because her split personality told her this might improve his chances of being the next permanent Police Chief? And, for good measure, Deans did this because if Bell had been 'out in front' of the occupation response as interim Chief, he would have probably looked bad (I am sure this made Torigian feel wonderful). At the risk of a severe headache, a common side effect of mRNA vaccines,[319] let us stop here.[15]

With a new Police Chief in charge and the reinforcements streaming in around the city, interim Chief Bell said on February 16, 2022, *'some of the techniques we are lawfully able and prepared to use are not what we are used to seeing in Ottawa.'*[320] These tactics and a fascinating 96-hour period started on Thursday,

---

[15] For those that like soap-opera-like drama, 1-day Police Chief wonder, Torigian, was alleged to have been involved in a sexual harassment/discrimination lawsuit that some Ottawa Police Service Board members disapproved of, another Ottawa Police Service Board member attended the protests on a couple of occasions, and Sloly's contract was supposedly paid out in full by a Deans' decree.

February 17, 2022. Per Sloly's referee impersonation made 21-days earlier, ding, ding!

Right out of the gate, the police tried a decapitation attempt and arrested two of the three founders of the convoy, Tamara Lich and Chris Barber. Also picked up, without any resistance, was notable loudmouth Pat King. Hopes that these arrests might convince many protesters to go home were quickly dashed as the charges didn't scare protesters into submission. If the leaders of the protest were being charged with 'counselling to commit mischief,' something that kids seemed to like to do, those peacefully protesting were unlikely to be locked away.

On February 18, 2022, the police and RCMP started to aggressively deploy unusual tactics and reclaim territory. In the Netherlands, weeks earlier, dogs were used to attack anti-lockdown protesters as police crushed the crowd with batons.[321] Apparently, Canada couldn't find any dogs and had to use horses. The police version of events on this topic was as follows:

"The protesters continued their assaultive behaviour with the police line, to prevent an escalation or further injury, mounted officers were sent in to create critical space between the police line and protesters. This is done to create a safe distance."[322]

Oddly, the 'assaultive' actions of the protesters didn't seem to result in any actual assault charges, and by assaultive 'behaviour,' what the police meant was that people were standing still and peacefully protesting. The resulting carnage from horses, which were essentially used as bulldozers, was that two people got trampled underneath the horses. The video was shocking.[323] Most of the people in the crowd didn't own trucks or honk their horns. They were simply standing still to show solidarity against Trudeau's medical tyranny. On this sad day in Canadian history, the 'assaultive behaviour' fabrication was compounded by even more police lies:

"As this was happening, a bicycle was thrown at the feet of one of

The Ottawa police never did say who was arrested for trying to harm a horse, and the flying bicycle, with magical properties, was never seen again. Unfortunately, the 'small fringe minority' of Ottawa police that were perpetrating untruths were personifying the cowardice of their leader, Justin Trudeau. Trudeau ignored the protests completely to keep his mandate-supported agenda in place. The Ottawa police needed to get the protesters gone quickly and, sometimes, ignored the tenet of honesty. Fibbing or exaggerating how docile police were in rounding up the violent hooligans was part of someone's job. As for the flying bicycle, it turned out to be the mobility scooter of a lady crushed underneath the 1,200-pound horses.

Having watched hundreds of hours of footage and following newsworthy development very closely, the only notable incidences of violence were police or security forces, many without any identifying insignia, harming protesters. There is not a single video to my knowledge of any protester taking a wild swing at a cop. In Australia, one man took down five cops in a video of protesters rampaging through police lines. In Ottawa, not a single cop was clothes-lined. This, above anything else, is what protesters should be most proud of.

Police also arrested many others but, in most cases, simply let them go. It was surreal watching social media reports trickle in of these supposedly aggressive, unhinged, and hateful protesters being heroically rounded up, and then driven off to a field on the outskirts of town and released. The attempt by Trudeau and the Ottawa Police to make standing still and protesting freedom illegal was not so illegal as to warrant many actual arrests.

On day three of the crackdown, Daniel Bulford was arrested. Mr. Bulford was intimately involved in the Freedom Convoy planning and also happened to be *'a former RCMP officer who was on the prime minister's security detail.'*[325] Mr. Bulford saw on the news the police were looking for him, so he turned himself in. He was charged with 'mischief' and held in a cell for approximately ten hours before being let go with no charges.[326] Arresting people that didn't fit the police narrative, Trudeau's narrative, would have meant bad publicity. So the corrupt media focused on the big game catches of Tamara Lich and Pat King and, to a lesser extent, people like Chris Barber and Tyson Billings. These would be the villains in Trudeau's story that didn't have any villains, so much as downhearted truckers and protesters.

By February 20, 2022, the police had achieved their goal, and the protest was dispersed. Along the way, the Ottawa police may have played their propaganda game too emphatically for some tastes. The police said they didn't point guns at any protesters. Video evidence proved they did. The police said they didn't fire tear gas at protesters. Video evidence proved they did. The police said the protesters might have had weapons and guns. In time this would be proven false. I could go on, but you get the idea.

As for the subject of guns, a topic used to bolster the otherwise unfounded insurrection clams, some history is helpful. On February 2, 2022 Reuters' reported that, *'Police in Ottawa see signs that guns have been brought into a truckers' protest'*,[327] on February 19, 2022, Bell said *'we have several criminal investigations ongoing that relate to the seizure of weapons,* and on March 19, 2022, the Toronto Star reported that *'police sources indicated that loaded shotguns were found in trucks at the Ottawa protest.* '[328] It took until March 24, 2022, before Bell finally confessed that zero weapons charges had been filed.[329] While I don't claim to be an aficionado of historical insurrections, for some reason, I think that weapons are required for such a label to be applicable? For the entire duration of the peaceful protest, we were told illegal and dangerous protesters wanted to topple the government. Was this all just another big lie?

Another glaring lie was that since all the tow truck companies in Ottawa sided with the protesters or did not want their business logo to be seen towing the trucks, no tow trucks could be hired, and this is one the reasons why the Emergency Act was needed. First, removing the protesters and drivers of the trucks could have been done well before any real need to tow the trucks.

Second, in February 2022, you could have gotten on the phone and found a few greedy tow truck companies in Canada that hated the unvaccinated and would have gladly driven to Ottawa to tow the trucks for the right price. Truckers came to Ottawa to protest from all over Canada, but our government wants us to believe that no tow truck company anywhere in Canada would come tow trucks in Ottawa? If this were true, it meant all of Canada was for the protests! Third, the U.S. was offering to tow trucks at the Ambassador Bridge blockade.[330] These tow trucks could have, and absolutely would have, driven to Ottawa should the need and payment for their services been requested. Finally, on February 7, 2022, then-Police Chief Sloly stated, *'we have towed vehicles, and we have towed trucks.'*[331] Did the tow truck(s) used up until February 7, 2022, suddenly stop working?

To be fair, there were 'lies' happening at both extremes. For example, the online freedom community said that police had killed many protesters and that indigenous reinforcements were coming to face off against cops after the horses trampled the disabled, indigenous woman. These lies were unnecessary and spread by those looking to provoke. But are these fraudulent memes from faceless fanatics the same thing as the Ottawa police and Toronto Star willfully spreading what they knew was false or unverified information? For that matter, like the old couple ready to fight at the bridge opening, the mysterious pebble thrower at the Trudeau rally, or the sole Nazis flag waver (probably), who is to say that some covert government faction was not responsible for instigating the reprehensible acts and misinformation that was being attributed to the freedom protesters?

People often see the pig roasts or truckers drinking beer in a hot tub and assume it was a party. Perhaps it was. But perhaps also, the Freedom Convoy was a necessary form of psychological therapy to deflect some of the pain and suffering that Trudeau's six-month campaign of division and hate had caused. With almost all nations dropping or at least rethinking mandates after omicron, why not Canada? Trudeau could have given any timeline he wanted to end the mandates and the truckers would have likely left Ottawa without the need for arrests. Instead, our dictator walked out of the House of Commons (again) when questioned about the Emergency Act on February 15, 2022, and (once again) on February 16, 2022, after he accused a *'Jewish Member of Parliament for Supporting Nazis.'*[332] The actions of Trudeau were almost too unbelievable to be true. Maybe cracking heads and punishing the protesters was his plan all along?

With Trudeau having completed his journey from one-time substitute drama teacher to playing the role of obstinate dictator, the Freedom Convoy travelled beyond vaccine mandates and became the fight for freedom and Canadian rights. I still remember the image of the kids watching their father drive off to battle in Ottawa. I also remember the kids drawing pictures of flags and truckers at a Nova Scotia daycare, and the kids lined up holding hands on the Ambassador Bridge to help ensure traffic remained stopped. People that despised the protesters were shocked that kids, in their minds, were being used as pawns to further the pro-freedom agenda. Yet some of these people months earlier had no problem forcing kids to take a vaccine to play sports or attend a school function, and many also thought kids should be able to take vaccines without parental consent. The incoherent logic was kids can't possibly be old enough to fight for freedom and bodily autonomy, but they damn well know they want to take an experimental vaccine that is safe and effective and brought to them by Pfizer.

As the protest wound down, it was clear much work still had to be done to change the hearts of minds of many Canadians. There were also some people that simply needed to be ignored as a sane society persisted. Consider these comments from Global New's Mercedes Stephenson:

"There was some people alleging police brutality. I didn't see that. I did see people absolutely getting hit by batons and some rough arrests. Those were people who did not move back as the police line advanced. Sometimes they were on their knees, begging with officers, some veterans saying please don't do this. But if you did not move when they told you to move, that was the fate that you suffered..."[333]

Immediately after saying she did not see any police brutality Ms. Stephenson perfectly describes that she saw police brutality. People on their knees begging couldn't be arrested without incident? How many people in Canada were as loopy as Ms. Stephenson, and could this damage be repaired, or was it permanent? If the latter, communism is probably closer than we think.

Amidst the protests' end, or pause depending on how you look at it, a Johns Hopkins study was released called *'A Literature Review and Meta-Analysis of the Effects of Lockdowns on COVID-19 Mortality'*. Some of the conclusions from the paper were not what the Trudeau camp wanted to hear:

"We find little to no evidence that mandated lockdowns in Europe and the United States had a noticeable effect on COVID-19 mortality rates. "[334]

A year earlier, such thoughts might get you banned from social media, and six months earlier, making such claims would definitely get you branded an 'anti-vaxxer.' The Chinese censor agents hit delete, delete, but it was too late. Shortly after the Johns Hopkins study, and as if to cackle at the fading force of the pandemic, Iceland became the first country to recommend people run out and catch COVID-19, so the odds of herd immunity might increase.

"Widespread societal resistance to COVID-19 is the main route out of the epidemic. To achieve this, as many people as possible need to be infected with the virus as the vaccines are not enough... "[335]

Iceland was previously one of the strongest proponents of 'zero-covid.' Not anymore. Added to the Iceland news were Ireland, Denmark, Sweden, and many other countries that had vowed to end all mandates. A convoy of countries realized the mandates were not working, so get rid of them.

As the truckers were scattered, the final tally, according to Bell, was 230 arrests and 118 criminal charges. With authorities having all the means necessary to mop up the border protests and blockades prior to the Emergency Act, Trudeau was left to contemplate how to spin invoking the Emergency Act to thwart one of the most non-violent protests in history. Yes, the Ottawa protest was loud, and it lasted much longer than it should have, but of the 118 criminal charges, none were for weapons, sedition, treason, attempted murder, etc.

As other papers, doctors, and politicians began to question the value of lockdowns and mandates more critically, there was a renewed hope that tyranny could be slain, even if the Freedom Convoy was not the vehicle for the final kill. In the background, Trudeau soaked up his losses, fumed, and schemed. Like a barracuda being released into a bathtub, all Justin could do was panic and squirm.

~ Contextual Interlude Activated (sub variant BS.05) ~

Whether or not the Freedom Convoy was successful is a matter of great debate. Until the last protester was banished from Ottawa, I was unequivocally of the mind that the protests were the greatest thing since sliced bread (you may have smelled an oven-baked whiff of my bias in the preceding two chapters). Scientists call how I and others were absorbing and disseminating news that may not have been entirely accurate *'prosocial lies,'* and they believe these types of lies can enhance *'benevolence-based trust.'*[336] It wasn't wrong to say Trudeau's Gestapo goons were pulverizing old men for honking their horns, and killer horses might have murdered some people; it was, at least for a moment during wartime, virtuous.

This said, scientists also note from the same study that *'although prosocial lies increase benevolence-based trust, they harm integrity-based trust.'* With integrity a pursuit of mine, and the days of contorting truthfulness for some moralistic higher protest purpose having passed, let's try to objectively delve into the post-Freedom Convoy success/failure theme.

Initially, the Freedom Convoy was phenomenally successful because some mandates were dropped, and the size and peaceful execution of the protests helped change the public discourse. Quite frankly, as soon as trucks started rolling toward Ottawa, there was no longer any debate about whether Canada should adopt a mandatory vaccine strategy or tax the unvaccinated. Moreover, by the time the trucks started reaching Ottawa, any chance of Trudeau regaining control of his COVID-19 narrative had vanished (much like Trudeau himself). Importantly, this happened even as hospitalizations and deaths from those with COVID-19 continued to increase in Canada.

The protests also ushered in and expedited a period of necessary change. In the days following January 29, 2022, Progressive Conservative leader, Erin O'Toole, stepped down, Premier after Premier across Canada acquired the courage to openly talk against mandates, and Legault - yes, even Legault - had started rolling back some of his crazy as he called for *'social peace.* '[337] It was, thanks to the truckers, becoming a political minefield to attack the unvaccinated. You could say the first truck horn that honked in Ottawa was the death knell for the outrageous and hateful bombs that had previously been dropping on the unvaccinated. Given that Trudeau had been mercilessly attacking the unvaccinated since August 13, 2022, this helps explain his loss for words.

But these initial successes do not necessarily tell us if the Freedom Convoy will be perceived as a long-term benefit to the cause of freedom. Recall the protests were responsible for or at least provided the excuse for the government to enact far-reaching new powers, including the expansion of anti-money laundering rules. Should these intentions persist, it is conceivable that new governmental powers or the intrusion into our daily lives could become more onerous following the Freedom Convoy than the vaccine mandates themselves. Also, consider that in the span of only a couple of weeks, Nova Scotia ordered people to stop standing close to highways,[338] Calgary had an injunction to curtail excessive horn honking and protesting,[339] pre-crime RCMP forces disabled excavators sitting innocently in a field,[340] and Trudeau was illegally using drones to spy on protesters (don't worry, Trudeau found a loophole).[341] Demonizing or fighting to limit the right of Canadians to protest is, in a word, deplorable. Did the Freedom Convoy inadvertently legitimize even more government overreach in this area?

You could also make the case that when the truckers didn't leave at an opportune time, this led to dictator Trudeau invoking the Emergency Act for the first time, thus setting up another potentially treacherous precedent in Canada. I don't blame the truckers and protesters for their dead-end ways, as many of these dedicated freedom fighters held true to their promise of not leaving until the mandates were gone. Nevertheless, in hindsight, voluntarily leaving around the third weekend may have turned out to be a genius move and would not at all have stymied the progress, both in perceptions and the falling mandates, that had been achieved since January 29, 2022. By not leaving or supplying some form of a bookend to the protest, the conversation has now switched to Tamara Lich and others being political prisoners. How this tangent will play out is uncertain. Lich and Barber are scheduled for trial in September 2023.[342]

In short, the problem with declaring the convoy a definitive success or failure after a week or two, or even after a year or two, is that Canada is currently being run by an unpredictable lunatic. I am fully aware this may sound excessive, but when you, metaphorically, try to fight a dictator to the death and said dictator is showing zero movement, it is highly likely they are not in their cubby hole chewing bubble gum. Trudeau was standing so close to complete political failure, and he lived to reign another day. Given time and presented with the opportunity, there is the possibility, however remote it might seem, that our narcissistic commander could be emboldened by the protest and do something even crazier than any of us thought possible.

So, was the Freedom Convoy a success? Yes, and no. Or, more succinctly, using a Chinese proverb, we'll see...

Chapter 22 - Can You Help a WEF Brother Out?

"Love is a secret society, a community for two." ~ Melvin Burgess, Bloodsong

After unnecessarily invoking the Emergency Act on February 14, 2022, Trudeau was being bombarded by negative sentiments and criticism, leading many people, myself included, to think that the dictator wouldn't last much longer. What no one knew is precisely how or when Trudeau would or even could be ousted. The House vote to approve the Emergency Act was to take place on February 21, 2022. Some speculated, and a lot prayed, that behind-the-scenes wheeling was happening to get a vote of no confidence to trigger an election. Could this be the end of Trudeau?

The problem with speculating about Trudeau's demise was that despite his simpleton-like persona and overly incessant need to apologize for everything (except his mandates), he had a level of cunning few lay credit to. Quite frankly, you do not get to become a dictator of one of the supposedly freest countries in the world without knowing how to stir the pot and make the stew. In the span of a few days, Trudeau cutely, without saying it, turned the Emergency Act vote into a confidence vote on the premise that NDP party leader, Jagmeet Singh, would side with him. Despite the fact that he was already Prime Minister, if this worked, it would almost be like a coup d'état for Trudeau.

The NDP's financial woes had been a much talked about topic for some time, with many noting in 2021 that the NDP keeps Trudeau's minority government propped up.[343] It would be difficult for Jagmeet to concur with the calls of no confidence with his party's coffers not exactly flush and election ready.

By way of a quick backdrop, Jagmeet graduated from the WEFs Young Global Leaders Academy in 2018, he was as pig-headed on mandates and climate change as Trudeau, and he was furious when his brother-in-law, Jodhveer Singh Dhaliwal, donated $13,000 to the Freedom Convoy. Although Jagmeet's freedom-loving brother-in-law was one of the top donors to the convoy and he never came out against the protests, the CBC and other media outlets cited nameless sources saying Dhaliwal rescinded his donation and *'didn't fully comprehend what the money would be used for.'*[344] Apparently, Jagmeet convinced his brother-in-law that the Freedom Convoy was evil and, doing his best Diane Deans impersonation, this is the story Jagmeet was sticking to. Here is a couple of takes from Jagmeet on the Freedom Convoy.

January 27, 2022 - *"I am concerned by extremist elements that are spreading misinformation and attempting to turn the convoy into a Canadian version of the terrorist attacks on the U.S. Capitol."*[345]

January 29, 2022 - *"...today Conservative MPs have endorsed a convoy led by those that claim the superiority of the white bloodline and equate Islam to a disease."*[346]

Saying that everyone is racist was, of course, Jagmeet's shtick. In 2020 Jagmeet falsely levelled the 'racist' charge and was kicked out of Parliament,[347] and after a couple of days of amazingly peaceful protests in Ottawa, he did what he does best:

January 30, 2022 - *"The display of racism and anti-Semitism we witnessed by the flying of Confederate flags and Nazi swastikas is vile, violent, and hateful. MPs who attended and failed to confront it should look into a mirror and ask themselves what kind of Canada they're building for our children."*[348]

The Nazi flag was briefly dangled by a nameless person on a balcony and, from what I saw, was denounced by everyone. No sensible individual would try to besmirch the massive protests happening across the entire country based upon a flag. Jagmeet did. Jagmeet was a predictable manipulator who, when cornered by something he didn't care for, instinctually hurled preposterous character assassination grenades. Jagmeet voted in favour of the Emergency Act. In his rambling statement, Jagmeet covered climate change and the need to vaccinate kids without actually mentioning anything tangible about why the Emergency Act was necessary. Here are three quotes that tell you all you need to know about Jagmeet:

"What has become very clear in this crisis is that there needs to be a serious examination of policing in Canada. Occupiers get hugs from police, while Indigenous and racialized people are met with the barrel of a gun. There are several accounts of current and former law enforcement and military members involved in these occupations."[349]

There were people of all races, colours, and creeds protesting mandates across Canada. That Jagmeet was pushing complete rubbish is appalling. Next:

"This is not a protest. It is not peaceful. The organisers of this illegal occupation have been clear from the beginning. They came here to overthrow a democratically elected government."

Ending the mandates was the only real demand in the mission statement from the three founders of the Freedom Convoy.

"The use of the Emergencies Act is a clear admission of failure for the government, we should have never gotten here. But the crisis situation in Ottawa requires additional action to prevent something serious from happening. We take the use of the Emergencies Act very seriously."

So, Jagmeet voted for the Emergency Act *'to prevent something serious from happening.'* Exactly what was supposed to happen, he apparently didn't have time to delve into. Remember, get vaccinated to save the world.

After the Emergency Act vote in the House, it was on to the Senate for debate and, eventually, another vote. The Senate usually rubberstamps everything, so when the debate turned feisty on February 22, 2022, some started to speculate that the Senate might actually vote against the Emergency Act.[350] Sensing a Senate loss would prove rather embarrassing and undermine his unscrupulous meddling, Trudeau revoked the Emergency Act on February 23, 2022. As if preparing for his upcoming world democracy speech tour, our dictator said:

Jagmeet had egg on his face. He had just reluctantly gone along with the Prime Minister's Emergency Act scheme to save his political skin, and now, less than two full days after the House vote passed, the emergency was supposedly over. Lies would have to be piled on top of lies to explain not only the justification of the Act but the curious timing in revoking the Act. Saying the unprecedented state of Emergency in Canada was over because of the worrisome prospect of an unfavourable Senate vote was likely too wacky a theory for even Trudeau.

The sense of listlessness Trudeau was coping with following revoking the Emergency Act was quite daunting. The provinces had lifted or were planning to pull most mandates, and much of the world had already accepted COVID-19 as a virus to live with. With the three week protests messily mopped up and the Emergency Act haphazardly invoked and revoked, it was understandable that Trudeau would not be mentioning the federal vaccine mandates anytime soon. I use the word 'understandable' because had Trudeau given any hint that his discriminatory mandates would be relinquished, he would have been mercilessly crucified for not at least discussing the mandates with the protesters. Like it or not, Trudeau was married to his mandates, at least until more distance from the protest had transpired.

Then, on February 24, 2022, Russia invaded Ukraine. It was as if the political gods had somehow bestowed Trudeau with the ultimate distraction-worthy event. Trudeau set up the cameras, tested to see if he didn't have COVID-19 again, removed his cloth mask, and started dancing in front of the lights:

"Make no mistake. Russia's attack on Ukraine is also an attack on democracy, international law, human rights, and freedom. Russia's

actions stand in direct opposition to the democratic principles that generations of Canadians have fought to protect democracies. And Democratic leaders everywhere must come together to defend these principles and stand firmly against authoritarianism. Russia must immediately cease all hostile actions against Ukraine. All military and proxy forces from the country Ukraine's sovereignty and territorial integrity must be respected. And Ukrainian people, like all people, must be free to determine their own future."[352]

The irony for many Canadians not being free to work and travel unless they took a government-mandated medical procedure was extraordinary. Russia had listened to its people (at least on the vaccine matter) and scrapped its mandate plans in January, and despite his WEF habits, Putin had only been briefly locked down the country twice in 2020.[353] By contrast, Trudeau arrested peaceful anti-mandate protesters and froze bank accounts literally days before lambasting Russia and speaking of 'democratic values.' With narcissism exuding from every pore on Trudeau's face, he continued:

"I want to be clear, our quarrel is not with the people of Russia. It is with President Putin and Russian leadership that has enabled and supported this further invasion of Ukraine..."

The words 'our quarrel' signaled that Canada was now a passive participant in the conflict. Days earlier, Trudeau drafted Jagmeet to do his bidding, and now it was on to the President of Ukraine, Volodymyr Zelenskyy, to present the mother of all distractions. Trudeau had never once spoken to a protester in Ottawa. He spoke with Zelenskyy on February 24, 2022, and many times in the following weeks. Trudeau had gone literally weeks without answering any specific questions about his vaccine mandates and policies. Trudeau's first Ukraine streaming show lasted an hour. To the wounded and perhaps also sometimes self-absorbed unvaccinated Canadians, everything Trudeau was doing was orchestrated to distract from his social control and mandate experiments and/or to further his agenda.

This is not to suggest the Ukraine conflict didn't deserve Canada's attention. Perhaps it did (or perhaps, per Professor Mearshiemer[354] and The Pope,[355] the conflict was provoked?). The curious observation was that the Ukraine-Russian situation wasn't receiving just some of Trudeau's attention but all of his attention. The zeal with which Trudeau immersed himself in everything Ukraine was more of a rebranding effort than a call to arms to fight one of the world's most potent nuclear powers. Trudeau myopically seemed to sincerely believe his pro-democracy cheerleading and token amounts of capital sent to Ukraine (compared to the U.S.) would somehow resonate and restore Canada's standing in the world.

Over the coming days and weeks, Trudeau would announce sanctions against Russia, weapons for Ukraine, and plans to bring Ukrainian refugees to Canada. Unvaccinated Canadians couldn't get on a plane or train in Canada, but unvaccinated Ukrainians were permitted to fly into Canada unscathed. Canadians that didn't take the vaccines were selfish and should be removed from society, but the people of Ukraine, one of the least vaccinated countries on earth, were delightful? This tangent is not intended to insult the Ukrainian people, which in many cases had gone through hell and watched loved ones die, but to highlight Trudeau's unrelenting hypocrisy. There were plenty of unvaccinated Canadians that would gladly denounce Putin if it meant they could be treated as well as unvaccinated people from Ukraine.

Despite Trudeau's attempts at distraction, the key issue causing many Canadians grief - the mandates! - had not been solved and was absolutely not going away. Like Pfizer's well-orchestrated efforts to subconsciously insert the word 'Pfizer' comfortingly into my mother's mind, Trudeau seemed to be using the power of repetition to try and establish an association between himself and the word 'democracy.' During this time, I, and many others, could not watch this maniac lie anymore without becoming infuriated. Perhaps this was partly the point as Trudeau endeavoured to cement his shaky political base and reimagine divide and conquer.

A January 31, 2022, Angus Reid Poll said that the majority of Canadians wanted COVID-19 restrictions to end,[356] and nothing had happened since then to even remotely suggest that the number of people wanting the mandates to remain in place had grown. Trudeau could babble on about democracy all he wanted as the mandate issue had long ago reached the cyst behind the eyes of most Canadians. The heartbreaking situation in Ukraine would not change this.

Then, in an unexpected move, Trudeau called up his old WEF buddy Jagmeet and convinced him that if band-aided together, two failed political parties could equal one gigantic failed political empire. Jagmeet de-soured from being played like a violin on the Emergency Act and acquiesced, and Trudeau's unofficial Liberal/NDP majority was born. With momentum at their backs following the protests, the Progressive Conservatives decried the move as an outrageous power grab and this played well in the polls. Unfortunately, the options to stop it were not apparent. Trudeau wanted to rise from weak minority leader to King, and so long as he shared the crown with Jagmeet, he had found a suitable path to coronation.

The 'confidence-and-supply agreement (CSA)' between Liberals and NDP was hashed out on March 22, 2022.[357] While not necessarily binding in a strict contractual sense, if they could continue massaging each other's interests, the deal did give Trudeau and Jagmeet safe passage until October 2025. Jagmeet initially got some money thrown at his dental plan by Trudeau and Trudeau got his budget passed thanks to Jagmeet. The memes depicting this love affair were comical, gross, over-the-top, and copious. Many said Jagmeet was holding on for his full pension in 2025, and others speculated that the J-twins both saw the writing on the wall - that their political careers were nearing an end - and opted to go out with one hell of a bang. Whatever the case, Jagmeet bestowed upon Trudeau the means to remain a dictator for a little while longer.

Despite Jagmeet noting that CSA could end anytime if Trudeau acted in bad faith, these WEF brothers had been in lockstep since the big lie was told. In fact, Jagmeet often displayed a zest for one-upmanship when following Trudeau's train to kooky town. It was as if Jagmeet was clapping like a seal for Schwab to throw him the fish.

August 29, 2021 - Jagmeet: *"...we absolutely believe that there needs to be mandatory vaccines and there would be consequences for those who are not able to, or not willing to do that."*[358]

That these mandate buddies had banded together was disquieting, and it shattered the theory that Trudeau might soon embrace common sense, end the mandates, and adopt realistic COVID-19 policies. As Jagmeet and Trudeau bonded, the often spurious connections many drew between the WEF and Canada suddenly seemed not so spurious. And while people like to disregard the connection because the WEF doesn't have an army or it's just a place for wealthy and powerful people to stroke egos and chug caviar, consider the words of former Prime Minster and WEF glorifier Stephen Harper:

"Take a moment to offer my personal congratulations to you [Klaus Schwab]. On this, the 40th annual gathering of your creation, the World Economic Forum you chose, as its motto, committed to improving the state of the world. I would observe that few who have set such a lofty goal have more reason to be pleased with their accomplishments to have conceived of the need for such an institution as this required insight. To have established it took commitment, but to have that nurtured, it is a podium from which business and political leaders could nudge public policy by addressing their peers from around the world. That is a formidable achievement, and Professor this gathering."[359]

The key word from the above heartfelt speech is *nudge*. Whatever you may think of the WEF, it is clear that political boundaries are no barrier to WEF groupthink, as all political parties had been 'penetrated' by the WEF in Canada. Also clear was that the ideological similarities between lovebirds Jagmeet and

Justin, beliefs that were gained in part due to WEF influence, had nudged these venerated WEF scholars together. Disagree with this dynamic duo, and you were a racist Nazis.

Chapter 23 - Twinkle, Twinkle, Little Chinese Star (Part I)

"There is a level of admiration I actually have for China because their basic dictatorship is allowing them to actually turn their economy around on a dime and say we need to go green, we need to start, you know, investing in solar" ~ Justin Trudeau

When trying to examine Trudeau's state of mind, remember that his first instinct when asked which nation's administration he most admired in 2013 was to blurt out China. Trudeau has never apologized or revised his 'admiration' for China's 'basic dictatorship.' At the time, the CBC punched out the headline *'Justin Trudeau's 'foolish' China remarks spark anger.'*[360] It is difficult to find a CBC headline as cutting as this one in 2013, even as Trudeau went from merely admiring a dictator to becoming one.

Speaking of dictators, the President of the People's Republic of China, Xi Jinping, has been running the show since 2013, and he is, colloquialism armed, widely considered to be a real son of a gun (that gun being Chinese Communist veteran Xi Zhongxun). Soon after Xi was in charge, China started building islands in the disputed South China Sea. The international uproar and condemnation were widespread and continuous. And although China continually asserted that they would not 'pursue militarization' of the islands, in March 2022, a U.S. admiral contended all three islands had been 'fully militarized'.[361] It is this type of patience, planning, and execution that, in part, has led many to conclude that China will be the world's next superpower.

The world's current superpower, the U.S., helped enable China's meteoric economic rise. For example, the U.S. backed China's entrance into the WTO in 2001, and U.S. companies eagerly set up shop in China to take advantage of cheaper labour and profit from the country's fast-growing marketplace. But where economically, China and U.S. were partnered, there has never been an agreement regarding human rights abuses in China or the aggressive posture China has toward Hong Kong, Taiwan, and others. Moreover, the U.S. has long brandished a cold war-type vibe against China, and the feelings given in return have been mutual. You could say the China / U.S. romance is an accident waiting to happen and that it hasn't happened yet, beyond a Trump-inspired mild trade war, is incredible.

When COVID-19 struck, China locked down Wuhan's more than 11 million people for 76-days.[362] This tactic, which China had rehearsed with SARS[363] and H1N1,[364] was shockingly severe by design, although if the only measure of success was to stop COVID-19 case counts from rising, it was highly effective. When Wuhan reopened, people needed QR 'health codes' on their smartphones to work and travel. If your health code scanned green, you could move around with some freedom, and if your health code scanned red, you were limited access and mobility. While health codes and China's social credit system are controversial topics, the fact that many heaped praises on China following the Wuhan accomplishments was not. Consider the New York Times:

"The success has positioned China well, economically and diplomatically, to push back against the United States and others worried about its seemingly inexorable rise. It has also emboldened Mr. Xi, who has offered China's experience as a model for others to follow.

While officials in Wuhan initially dithered and obfuscated for fear of political reprisals, the authorities now leap into action at any sign of new infections, if at times with excessive zeal."[365]

As the New York Times and others swooned over *'How China Beat the Virus,'* they also unintentionally shared the fascinating priorities China had compared to most other nations. For example, when COVID-19 hit the U.S., New York City built a field hospital in Central Park while China's Xi 'commandeered farmland' and got to work building massive quarantine camps.[366] China's planning and execution, from the very beginning, wasn't to save those that happened to catch the virus and wanted healthcare, but to banish, by force if necessary, those infected.

A popular assumption is that China's actions would have crossed lines when it comes to the rights and freedoms that Canadians enjoy. After all, we didn't build quarantine camps in Canada, and we never locked people down for an unbelievable 76-days straight. But before condemning all of China's aggressive policies as somehow unCanadian, please remember that Canada did construct pleasant *'Voluntary Isolation Centres,'* and Canada did hold the record for the longest lockdown in the world (Toronto restaurants at 382 days), and multiple small business lockdowns were *'the longest in North America.'*[367]

While there was no declaration of 'herd immunity' made in China, as Israel did in May 2021, there was a building consensus after victory in Wuhan that China had the right stuff to knock out any outbreak. The WHO was curiously trusting and sent a group to China in February 2020 to glean the methods responsible for the country's successful actions. For anyone who cares for freedom, the statements made by the WHO in their 40-page report were jolting:

"China's uncompromising and rigorous use of non-pharmaceutical measures to contain transmission of the COVID-19 virus in multiple settings provides vital lessons for the global response."[368]

That the WHO cheered everything China was saying and doing while completely ignoring any human rights concerns was more than a little suspicious. Devastating lockdowns that lasted months and complete population surveillance were *'vital lessons for the global response?'* As the U.S., Germany, Australia, and many other countries questioned the WHO judgement, tasked with cooling suspicions was UN Secretary-General António Guterres:

"Once we have finally turned the page on this epidemic, there must be a time to look back fully to understand how such a disease emerged and spread its devastation so quickly across the globe and how all those involved reacted to the crisis. But now is not that time."[369]

Did anyone genuinely believe the pandemic should be allowed to run its course before any investigation into the origins of COVID-19 even started? China and the WHO/UN did. The word coming out of the WHO was profoundly troubling and a large reason for President Trump pulling funding from the WHO.[370] Despite his critics, Trump had made an excellent pro-freedom and democracy decision. After all, the WHO was standing *against* an independent investigation into the origins of COVID-19 and openly *promoting* China's COVID-19 lockdowns as fabulous. Also, from the same February WHO report:

"...the rapid adaptation and tailoring of China's strategy demonstrated that containment can be adapted and successfully operationalized in a wide range of settings."

Along with the signals that the WHO was in China's corner, there were reports that doctors and scientists were 'disappearing' in China, that lab evidence was destroyed, and that China was *'bleaching...wildlife market stalls.'*[371] These reports led to countless and sometimes ominous questions over what might be happening behind the curtain. Maybe China didn't join the COVAX vaccine program to end vaccine nationalism, and maybe Xi's minions were not on a global goodwill tour giving free seminars to countries that wanted to learn how best to oppress, censor, and punish their people. Instead, maybe China was leveraging its early COVID-19 success purely for its self-interests.

Supporting this contrarian take in 2020 was a former Australian diplomat to China that went so far as to explain how China had 'weaponized COVID-19' while on 60 minutes:

"Question: They [China] are the good guys in all of this. The way they managed the pandemic has been highly successful, while the rest of the world has failed.

Answer: This is highly politicized, of course, it is a deliberate effort to take advantage of Western weakness. And it's a time when democracies can be said, I'm afraid, reasonably to have made not the best of this. It also shows how the West has failed to cooperate, whereas China has over a massive area and, with some of its partners, achieved what looks like a much more standardized approach where you can move very rapidly and achieve very quick results in terms of test and trace. So that is undeniably a point. But this is not a medical campaign to say, Listen, you must do as we do. It is a political campaign to say you are weak. Your democracy doesn't serve the right purposes. Look at America - utter horror and chaos. Look at the United Kingdom look at some parts of Europe as well. How on earth can you say that your system is better than ours when it is clearly incapable of doing anything other than making things worse? This is a very powerful political weapon, and it's being used very aggressively."[372]

This strategy of painting the West as 'weak' was partly in retaliation to what China deemed interference by those that questioned their relationship with the WHO. China also had an axe to grind with anyone suggesting that China dragged its heels when COVID-19 was first discovered or that COVID-19 may have come from a Chinese lab. In the case of Australia, which called for an independent review of what happened in Wuhan, China responded by launching a trade war,[373] and for America - which was always thought to be meddling - China launched projectiles like this one through State media in 2021:

"...why does the western mainstream media collectively silence the deaths of frequent vaccinators of Pfizer?"[374]

The Chinese, in some ways, were akin to Donald Trump in that while exerting influence over potential adversaries, they didn't let a single sleight against them slide. President Xi may not have been up all hours of the night, Tweeting threats against his aggressors, but his regime was surely keeping a hit list. Even when the first case of omicron was detected in the country on January 18, 2022, China suggested the virulent strain may have come from Canadian mail.[375] This was likely Xi's unique way of letting fellow dictator Trudeau know that he hadn't forgotten about the arrest of Huawei executive Meng Wanzhou.

In addition to leveraging its '*much more standardized approach*' to COVID-19 (by subverting the WHO), China was also adding to preparations to provoke a great reset in U.S. dollar (USD) hegemony. Warning that U.S. currency dominance was a threat to global financial stability for some time, China, Russia, and a handful of others had been positioning for the day when USD was no longer the world's reserve currency (for Russia, this involved gold purchases, and for China, it meant opening up markets and allowing its currency, the Renminbi (RMB), to float more freely versus other fiat currencies[16]). But getting off the dollar would likely mean that China would need to reduce its $1+ trillion U.S. debt hoard, and RMB would have to become a much bigger reserve asset in global central banks, neither of which was showing much sign of happening pre-pandemic. COVID-19 presented an opportunity to accelerate the timeline for the demise of the USD.

With much of the world mired in COVID-19 cases, China began testing its digital RMB currency in April 2020 and was not shy of its intentions:

"A sovereign digital currency provides a functional alternative to the dollar settlement system..."[376]

This wasn't exactly an axe-to-tree situation or where China's digital currency experiment would cut down USD supremacy. Still, it was another Chinese-made island that might one day end up being militarized. If China embraced a successful and efficient digital currency, this could lend to economic and policy advantages domestically. International trading partners might also take to digital RMB if it was competitive and convenient compared to dealing in USD, particularly countries that may prefer to play outside the realm of U.S. financial sanctions or the SWIFT payment system. Long story short, more countries

---

[16] 'Fiat currencies' refers to all currencies since the end of the Bretton Woods Agreement in 1971. Fiat money is government produced and not backed by gold or silver.

holding more RMB, digital or otherwise, meant more confidence in China. Remember, all China wanted was to be loved.

What the pandemic did was accelerate the trajectory of China's goals of economic and political dominance. In 2020 China surpassed the U.S. in foreign direct investment[377] and was the only major economy in the world to report positive GDP. China ended 2020 at almost 15% of the global economy and was quickly closing on the U.S., which accounted for approximately 22%. In January 2021, Bloomberg noted:

"Based on projections from the International Monetary Fund, China will now overtake the U.S. by 2028, two years earlier than previously predicted, according to Nomura Holdings Inc."[378]

Had the trends of 2020 and 2021 continued, China would overtake the U.S. economically even before 2028. As such, you could say that COVID-19 was a curse for America and the West and a blessing for China, at least economically.

Like New Brunswick's Higgs treating COVID-19 as a proverbial cash cow, China was milking COVID-19 for every drop of prestige and clout it could. On January 25, 2021, China's Xi gave a speech about 'change' and 'new perspectives' at Davos (yes, even Xi dabbled in WEF sorcery).[379] Days earlier, Xi graciously offered another speech suggesting China's time was now.

"The world is undergoing profound changes unseen in a century, but time and the situation are in our favor. This is where our determination and confidence are coming from."[380]

Then in April 2021, a year after its first trials, China launched the world's first digital currency. As the Wall Street Journal noted, this was *'money that isn't linked to the dollar-dominated global financial system.'*[381] By the end of 2021, China's digital currency was being used by 261 million people in China, and some Huawei smartphones had pre-installed digital wallets that could access China's Digital Currency Electronic Payment (DCEP) system. DCEP had crypto-like qualities and could be used without access to the internet (i.e., tap two phones together like exchanging bills). However, DCEP was not decentralized, and only one central bank, the People's Bank of China, controlled the game.

Still coping with wave after wave of COVID-19, much of the world was oblivious as China had fully launched something that had the potential to undermine USD dominance. A nameless banker in the Financial Times described China's digital currency aspirations as follows:

"They are thinking about things that the rest of the world is nowhere near thinking about yet."[382]

The above statement could just as easily describe China's COVID-19 aspirations. When the pandemic started and countries grappled to find tests and hone their tracing skills, China tested '*11 million residents in just 25 days*' so that they could flush out and isolate 335 cases of COVID-19.[383] Being so far ahead on the COVID-19 curve flattening game meant that China was baking Beef Wellington while other countries struggled to try and turn the stove on.

The contrast between China and the rest of the world in other areas was also stunning. As Klaus was calling for a Great Reset and Trudeau was thinking about becoming a great dictator, China had already adopted QR health codes to control movements and protester bank accounts. And by the time Trudeau announced his big lie on August 13, 2021, China had already broached the subject of setting up and operating a global vaccine passport system. This idea would have been the most inconceivable conspiracy that you could dream up in 2019. A year into covid-hell, and it was being discussed.

While I am sure, it wasn't intentional, on the vaccine passport issue China was able to somehow tap into the whimsical bouncy castle melody expressed by Watson and Deans. Consider what the cruel dictatorship that is China proclaimed it could do for the world in March 2021:

"Chinese experts noted on Tuesday that China can help by sharing its experience with and provide technical support to the WHO to organize the issue, as China is the most experienced country in using a health code system in the world while the WHO is the most proper organizer for the matter to ensure independence, fairness, and data security.

Technology would not be a problem, Chinese experts said, noting that if the international community unites to promote the work, a platform can be established within 2-3 months and, optimistically, can be used for the Tokyo Olympic Games scheduled between July 23 and August 8.

"In terms of technology, I believe that Chinese companies can build an international platform in just one week...

Cooperation between WHO and China would be a powerful combination to promote the matter fast with a mature technology while guaranteeing public trust, Chinese experts noted."[384]

To me, the above words and the entire situation were bizarrely comical. People in Canada were upset because Trudeau was tracking cell phone movements during the pandemic (for the greater good). Now the entire planet was comfortable with China constructing a system to monitor their international travel movements? That this idea was mentioned non-satirically was proof that China's ambitions had not only been accelerated by its COVID-19 expertise but teleported to a different dimension. Seemingly sane and intelligent people professed admiration for China's governance style! China was the 'good guys' (we were told). Furthermore, scared and downtrodden people, some of which may or may not have had a pocket full of digital RMB, wanted to travel safely and loved the idea that China had the means to make this happen. Why not let China set up a global vaccine passport?

Just as the WHO coincidentally took advantage of widespread fear to produce its new COVID-19 death coding document at the ideal time, China wanted to set up a global passport system just as many countries were bumbling to implement basic vaccine passes. It was as if China was playing chess while petty baby-tyrants like Trudeau dabbled in checkers. Xi had planned and executed the two-pronged plan of controlling the COVID-19 narrative and creating a long-term alternative to U.S. dollar dominance. This attack was succeeding beyond the wildest expectations.

"The present-day world is undergoing a great transformation of the kind not seen for a century," Mr. Xi told officials at another meeting in January [2021], "but time and momentum are on our side."[385]

China was so successful so quickly that more ominous contrarian questions unintentionally popped into the brain. Maybe all the lockdowns China conducted with SARS and H1N1 were training sessions to further the great long-term communist vision? Maybe China knew beforehand that its governance style and past experience meant that it was best suited to become the key global superpower during a pandemic? And finally, brace yourself; maybe China intentionally unleashed a deadly virus onto the world, knowing they were ready and everyone else was not?

On this last point, which some might say is in bad taste, I said early on I didn't believe COVID-19 was a bioweapon. I still don't. But this is not to say there is evidence to disprove that COVID-19 did not unintentionally or intentionally come from a lab. Was the proximity between the lab messing around with bat coronaviruses and the Wuhan wet market that may have been responsible for patient zero just a mindboggling coincidence? Some powerful players helped fund a paper in July 2021 saying COVID-19 likely came from a Chinese wet market,[386] and many of these same authors were supported by the NIH (and others) to draft another paper in July 2022 telling us the same thing.[387] The only limitation of these studies, which deny the lab leak theory, was that they both were beholden to Chinese-provided data to manufacture their findings. Those that trust any data out of China should not be trusted.

President Xi, a man of planning and execution, upon acquiring power, embraced Chinese history and culture and quoted Confucius: '*he who rules by virtue is like the Pole Star, it maintains its place, and the multitude of stars pay homage.*'[388] Despite the conspiratorial-like questions and human rights concerns, the consensus before omicron arrived seemed to be that China was indeed leading by virtue. Accordingly, world leaders were presented with two roads - constant peril or Chinese-style salvation. Almost all chose the latter.

Chapter 24 - Twinkle, Twinkle, Little Chinese Star (Part II)

As omicron arrived, China would be challenged, potentially in ways, Xi's regime had not yet imagined. The world watched and wondered if China's 'zero-covid' dance could stay alive. Get the popcorn.

Foreshadowing what was coming to China was New Zealand, whose zero-covid model had amazing success at beating back case numbers early on in the pandemic but ultimately failed when the delta variant arrived:

"We're transitioning from our current strategy into a new way of doing things. With Delta, the return to zero is incredibly difficult, and our restrictions alone are not enough to achieve that quickly. In fact, for this outbreak, it's clear that long periods of heavy restrictions has not got us to zero cases."[389]

Prime Minister Jacinda Ardern's admission that her oftentimes fanatical push for higher vaccination rates wasn't working was, to a tiny degree, gratifying. Ardern was, after all, a pandemic dictator that endorsed a two-class system of vaccinated and unvaccinated[390] and also openly threatened, *'there is not going to be an endpoint to this vaccination program.'*[391] It was this insane lust for control that, in 2021, made Ardern's New Zealand, Australia, and China a formidable axis of evil COVID-19 restrictions.

Even as Ardern's advisors tinkered with models, the best estimates with delta they imagined were 20, 30, or 50 cases per day. When omicron finally hit the country in February 2022, the seven-day rolling average for COVID-19 cases in New Zealand skyrocketed above 20,000 cases! Zero-covid, already thought too rigid a standard to uphold with the delta, was inconceivable with omicron. The vaccines and lockdowns had failed, and Ardern knew it. Ever the agitator, the overzealously proud WEF hit-woman would painfully drag her high heels, getting rid of many mandates. Nevertheless, New Zealand was slowly learning to live with COVID-19.

The loss of New Zealand as a zero-covid ally probably caught the attention of China, and if it didn't, South Korea absolutely would. In March 2022, with newly elected Conservative Yoon Seok-youl in charge, South Korea was also adopting a live with COVID-19 strategy. You may recall that South Korea had initial success at quickly containing COVID-19, and for 22 months, the country had exceptionally low case counts, often in the hundreds per day. The seven-day rolling average for COVID-19 cases in mid-March 2022 in South Korea was more than 400,000 (that's per day, folks), and on May 17, 2022, there were a record 628,000 cases of COVID-19 and 429 deaths. Despite producing ludicrously wide forecasts, the models were shattered because they didn't think this many daily cases were possible. Suddenly the memory of how wonderful Korea was compared to the U.S. in 2020 was forgotten. COVID-19 would not be caged any longer.

Interestingly, while much of Canada and other parts of the world may have been over-reporting deaths, South Korea may have sometimes been under-reporting deaths. The observer could not help but ask why.

"KDCA official Lee Sang-won said some 70,000 cases and 200 deaths were missing in tallies over the past couple of days, apologising for errors in its compiling procedures."[392]

As China watched what was happening in New Zealand and South Korea, it braced itself for a war versus the invisible enemy. China's COVID-19 modus operandi had been heralded as god-like for almost two years, but now, with the notable exception of Canada, China was one of the only restriction radicals left as 'live with covid' became ubiquitous. Those who pursued mandatory vaccination or fined the elderly, like Italy and Greece, were planning to drop restrictions and mandates. Austria suspended mandatory vaccination days before it started,[393] and Germany's mandatory vaccine vote failed. The dichotomy was stunning; the world was opening up and growing more confident about this path as China was locking down as President Xi grew more adamant.

"At a meeting chaired by Xi on Thursday [May 5, 2022], the ruling Communist Party's supreme Politburo Standing Committee vowed to "unswervingly adhere to the general policy of 'dynamic zero-Covid,' and resolutely fight against any words and acts that distort, doubt or deny our country's epidemic prevention policies."

This is the first time Xi, who, according to state media, made an "important speech" at the meeting, has made public remarks about China's battle against Covid since public furor erupted over the harsh lockdown in Shanghai."[394]

It was as if the arrival of omicron was regarded by many as a test of Xi's rule itself. The Xinhua government news added that the seven-member committee said:

"Our prevention and control strategy is determined by the party's nature and mission, our policies can stand the test of history, our measures are scientific and effective...We have won the battle to defend Wuhan, and we will certainly be able to win the battle to defend Shanghai."[395]

China defending its 'dynamic zero-covid policy' so strongly even prompted the WHO to miraculously obtain the fortitude to question China's stance against omicron. In 2021, the WHO was asking Western Countries to accept China's vaccine as an equal,[396] and now it was suggesting to China that it had to adjust its zero-covid ambitions.[397] This surprise suggested that while the WHO may have been corrupt, it was corruptible in either direction, probably dependent upon the prevailing monetary winds.

The logic that China was fixated on was that the blowback from opening up and allowing omicron to creep through society would be so great it could have lasting repercussions. Instead, stay the course. But like superman having kryptonite, China had omicron.

With delta, a regular day in China meant 34,000 Shanghai Disney visitors were locked down until they could all be tested because of one positive case,[398] but in April 2022, with omicron, it meant 25 million people in Shanghai had to be locked down. Along with these rolling lockdowns, which were more than double the size seen in Wuhan, quarantine centres popped up all over Shanghai, and COVID-19 positive people, or those suspected as being positive, were taken away in droves. This rush to quarantine people was so frantic that, in many instances, people's pets could not be looked after and were simply murdered. The Wikipedia section 'Pet Killing,' with links to Chinese sources, notes that *'live fish were recorded getting killed by ground impact,'* and people were told to *'give up on their cat'* as they were dragged away. Dogs were also put to death (with one owner compensated as authorities *'didn't think very carefully'*.)[399] I saw a horrific video of a bag full of live cats waiting to be taken care of in China. I couldn't bookmark or even finish the video. This was how China treated animals and, it has been said, how they also treated the Uyghurs people (see Uyghur's genocide).

Just as China had leveraged its COVID-19 success to maximum advantage against the West for almost two years, the West quickly returned the favour. The momentum shift was startling, and it dealt a severe blow to the Chinese pandemic model and to the communist governance style. There were videos on the internet that showed walls being built around apartment buildings to keep people locked inside, people violently resisting China's quarantine police, and citizens in Shanghai scream-protesting uncontrollably from their apartments at night.[400] With omicron and the three-level lockdown system moving from Shanghai to China's capital Beijing, another 20+ million city, there would be no shortage of stories and footage to further highlight China's brutal tyranny. Those applauding China since March 2020 quietly slinked to the back of the room.

This horror show notwithstanding, was it more disturbing to allow omicron to rip through some of the most densely populated places in the world, where the elderly had a low vaccine uptake, or to make lockdowns, testing, and quarantine camps a long-term feature of society? The sad reality was that neither option was being considered. Rather, China, like much of the world, was dealing with COVID-19 while looking through a political lens. Trying to provide the conditions to produce the best outcomes for citizens, or their pets, wasn't the point. Maintaining power was.

As China tenaciously clung to zero-covid and cranked its censorship apparatus up to 11, the perceptions of China being *the good guy in all of this'* were gone baby gone. Instead, given the ideological viciousness on display, more aspersions and foreboding questions were hurled in China's direction. Did China lie about the extent and severity of COVID-19 so it could acquire and hoard masks and personal protective equipment from other countries?[401] Was China continuing to stifle WHO investigators that contended in June 2022 that *'Key pieces of data...are not yet available for a complete understanding of how the COVID-19 pandemic began?'*[402]

Whatever the true motivations of China were, with omicron proving not easily contained, the bloom had fallen off of China's zero-covid-rose, and Xi and company started behaving erratically. When the WHO said China's COVID-19 strategy was unsustainable, China censored the WHO.[403] When 20 academics, led by Tong Zhiwei, a prominent Shanghai law professor and Communist party member, urged authorities to stop *'excessive pandemic prevention,'* they were also censored. Zhiewei sounded like a Canadian protester when he bravely said:

"Pandemic prevention needs to be balanced with ensuring people's rights and freedoms."[404]

Winning the hearts and minds of the world would be impossible when one of China's key allies, the WHO, and their people were openly questioning the communist party's actions and motives.

As quickly as we entertained China becoming the world's leading economic force and using digital RMB as we have our faces scanned everyplace by Chinese tech, the idea had fallen off a cliff. On July 7, 2022, Mainland China officially declared its first vaccine mandate.[405] This was a tacit admission that omicron would not be controlled. In July 2022, China was also using robots to manually test people for COVID-19. Scan your QR code and open your nostrils if you want to do anything[406] - coming to a street corner near you? Months earlier, serious people professed a love for the methods of communist control of pathogens. Now the ineffective and traumatizing lockdowns just looked pathetic, dangerous, and sad. The lockdown situation had become so depressing that in July 2022, Bloomberg reported that more than 10,000 rich people worth $48 billion wanted to leave China, adding, *'but will Xi let them?'*[407] As for the instruments developed to keep people safe from COVID-19, they now had a much broader 1984-style function, and please do not mention this out loud, or you will be punished:

"Earlier this week, dozens of people traveled to Zhengzhou to participate in a protest. But upon arriving in Zhengzhou and scanning QR codes at train stations, buildings, or hotels, they said their health codes turned red.

In recent weeks, people have been taking to the streets in Zhengzhou and Henan, calling for authorities and banks to return their money."[408]

Freezing the bank accounts of those that disagree with you, brought to you by dictators Xi and Trudeau.

In short, with its twinkle no longer quite as bright, China's far from virtuous model of societal tracking and ruthless control would have to wait until another day to completely infect the world.

Yet even as the omicron was proving a formidable foe and exposing China's imperfections, the communist vision and planning for global economic dominance may not have been a shooting star. In May 2022, China's ownership of U.S. Treasury Securities dipped below $1 trillion for the first time since 2003,[409] and in June 2022, a UBS Annual Reserve Manager Survey said that more Central Banks wanted to hold RMB:

"Central banks are increasingly keen to hold China's yuan as a reserve currency, as the country's growing economic and political power threatens to erode the U.S. dollar's global dominance."[410]

Was omicron simply delaying the inevitable? Stay tuned.

Chapter 25 - Liberals Go Off the Deep End
(Some exaggerated speculations, for effect, are made in this
chapter)

*"How many guns need to be seized? How much vitriol do we have
to see of 'Honk' - which is an acronym for 'heil Hitler' - do we
need to see on social media?"* ~ Canadian Liberal MP Ya'ara Saks[411]

The above words from Ms. Saks were said in Parliament, in
front of other people, and with the cameras on. Some in the
medical field suggested that the loud horns from the trucks had
caused citizens 'chronic annoyance and distress' or PTSD. After the
protests, there were even worn down journalists that the CBC hired
'trauma therapists' to help them cope.[412] Was it possible that Saks'
was negatively impacted by the truck horns on some deeply
psychological level and that she started seeing Hitler yelling
'honk!' in her sleep? The only other explanation I could think of
was that Trudeau asked Saks to say something chilling about social
media because he wanted momentum for Canada to adopt China-
style censorship (i.e., ban everything that you don't like). Even
then, her statement was light years out to lunch.

After the truckers were disbanded, the foolishness from
Watson and Deans didn't take long to spread to Liberals and the
pro-liberal media. Part of this was due to the genuine unsettling
sense that the protests were permitted to go on for so long. The
feeling here was that with many people's nerves frazzled after a
few days of non-stop honking, why the hell did it take so long for
authorities to do much of anything? As much as I loved the
peaceful protests, part of me agrees with specific points this crowd
makes, especially given that the trucks were illegally parked.
Another reason for the frantic and almost delusional behaviour as
Ottawa turned truckerless was that omicron had wholly changed
the idea of when COVID-19 might become endemic. The
justifications for vaccine mandates were disappearing. Trying to
reconstruct walls of division against the unvaccinated seemed
impossible, but some thought they were up to this task. Finally, as
more information came out about the Emergency Act being
invoked for spurious reasons, it is likely that the peculiar

distractions in the news were intentional. Quick - look at the baby giraffe!

Right off the jump, before the protests had ended, the headlines started to cross the wires in a weird fashion. CBC noted:

"BC lifts most COVID-19 restrictions as long as masks and vaccine cards are used."[413]

Read the headline and let it sink in. This was either done to intentionally piss people off, which it did, or not so subtly to tell the peasantry the mandates were not going anywhere. Shortly after this odd headline, and as the peaceful protesters were being rounded up by police, Bill Gates, while attending the Munich Security Conference on February 18, 2022, had this to say:

"Question: Where would you assess where we are today in beating COVID-19
Gates: Sadly, the virus itself, particularly the variant called omicron, is a type of vaccine; that is, it creates both B-cell and T-cell immunity, and it's done a better job getting out to the world population than we have with vaccines...That means the chance of severe disease, which is mainly associated with being elderly and having obesity or diabetes, those risks are now dramatically reduced because of that infection, exposure."[414]

Bill the vaccinator Gates echoed what we already knew, or that natural infection imbued powerful protection against COVID-19. Sitting next to Bill Gates, as he explained that he was 'sad' people were getting immunity for free, was Canadian Minister of Foreign Affairs, Mélanie Joly. Wake up, Mélanie! Tell your boss to end the mandates!

The next bout of nuttiness following Gates (a nut in his own right) happened a week after the protests ended when Deputy Prime Minister, Chrystia Freeland, attended a rally to support Ukraine. During the rally, Freeland was photographed holding a flag/scarf associated with Ukrainian OUN, *'a ultranationalist, antisemitic and fascist organization.'* Oops. The statement concocted by Freeland and released by her press secretary was marvellous:

"...there were thousands of people at the event in Toronto, that many were trying to get a photo or give the Liberal cabinet minister tokens, such as ribbons, and that she tried to be friendly with everyone. She added that someone "pushed a scarf (that read "Slava Ukraini") in front of some politicians" including Freeland. "[415]

The massive protest in Ottawa lasted more than three weeks and was constantly ridiculed because, on the first day, one person (possibly a government plant) held up a Nazi flag. Freeland physically holds a neo-Nazi flag, and she gets a complete pass? As if this bizarre hypocrisy wasn't farcical enough, Freeland posted a pic of herself holding the flag on Twitter and then later removed it. Double oops. Finally, remember the Russian-sponsored trucker protest? Apparently, the Russians were also picking on poor sweet Freeland:

"A classic KGB disinformation smear is accusing Ukrainians and Ukrainian-Canadians of being far-right extremists or fascists or Nazis,' Freeland's press secretary said...Freeland's office is saying the whole thing reeks of Russian sponsored disinformation. "[416]

Following Freeland, the Liberal comedy show continued with Trudeau celebrating his anniversary by holding hands with his wife on an indoor swing set, fully masked for protection, of course.[417] This was one of the most ridiculous virtue signalling pictures in history and begged the question: was Trudeau playing mind games, or had he simply lost his mind? In 2018 Andrew Sheer repeatedly asked Trudeau about his secretive $7,500 swing set expense.[418] Was this the swing set?

Oddly enough, Trudeau was able to swiftly trump his family's funky masking predilections by, allegedly, swearing at someone in the House of Commons and then answering media queries with, *'What is the nature of your thoughts, gentlemen, when you say you move your lips in a particular way.'*[419] Smug and flippant may have worked for Trudeau's dad, to who the quote was attributed, but the wrath over mandates was not going away. From playing hide-and-seek during the protest to failing to answer any direct questions about restrictions, Trudeau was wandering aimlessly on thin ice and knew it.

The pattern of skating mindlessly around making shit up continued with the Liberal party calling for mask mandates to be re-enacted in Ontario shortly after masking restrictions were lifted. These statements were so out of touch after omicron peaked in January, and most people were ready to live with COVID-19, that it boggled the mind. With the Ontario Liberal party not doing well against Doug Ford in the polls, this was the first real 'let's get the Trudeau wedge band back together again':

"Speaking of schools, they are now ground zero for COVID spread...Finally, it's also time Ontarians stopped being forced to guess if they're sick or contagious. Ontario Liberals demand that Ford Conservatives make PCR tests accessible to all Ontarians."[420]

PCR tests for everyone? LOL (first and last time using internet lingo)! People of sound mind realized no amount of testing or even harsh lockdowns (i.e., China) could keep omicron in check. Moreover, cases in Ontario were way down from January, contact tracing wasn't being done anymore, and hospitals were not under significant stress. Why, in God's name, were Liberals proposing PCR tests for everyone?

The goal seemed to be that the Liberals wanted to weaponize fear again, in which case they would need to raise the psychotic bar much higher. Enter University of Saskatchewan professor of community health and epidemiology Nazem Muhajarine - a man who was one of the strongest proponents for mandating the 3rd dose of vaccine. With the bulk of mandates at the provincial level already setting out to sea, Muhajarine sailed this gem in April 2022:

Completely idiotic and erroneous fearmongering at its best. But one whacko doctor would not be enough. It was time to call the big gun. Dr. David Fisman was the most pro-liberal die for vaccine mandates and climate change scientist in Canada, and his mathematical chicanery concluded the unvaccinated were dangerous. The Fisman study was a Hail Mary attempt to reacquire control through fear and division that Trudeau desperately wanted back. It was entitled *'Impact of population mixing between vaccinated and unvaccinated subpopulations on infectious disease dynamics: implications for SARS-CoV-2 transmission.'*[422] This paper was bought and paid for by the Federal government.

"This research was supported by a grant from the Canadian Institutes of Health Research."[17]

The conclusion from Fisman and company that the unvaccinated posed a danger to the vaccinated was August 2021 level lies. Like a finely oiled government machine, the media picked up the study with ridiculous speed.[423] Ever anxious to spread the narrative, The Toronto Star contended, *'Remaining unvaccinated increases risk to vaccinated...'*[424] Not as intense as the death wishes it previously espoused, it was nonetheless still fake news. No other serious or unserious study in the world suggested the nonsense Fisman was peddling.

The Fisman paper was torn to shreds by people much smarter than me, including Dr. Byram W. Bridle with *'Fiction Disguised as Science to Promote Hatred.'*[425] As Bridle and countless others pointed out, the assumption for *'baseline immunity in unvaccinated people'* was set at 20% by Fisman. No expert on the planet - as in none - believed only 20% of 'unvaccinated' Canadians had natural immunity. Fascinatingly, as you increased this number to a level around 80%, which was below

---

[17] Fisman did not respond when asked for the monetary value of the grant.

many estimates at the time, the model flipped and said the vaccinated were more dangerous to the unvaccinated.

The idea here isn't to bash Fisman or show that he is a corrupt hack making crap up to scare people. He was, and I am confident Fisman already knows this. Rather, it is to show that as their nonsensical mandates were falling apart, Trudeau's cult did what any animal about to die in nature did - they fought. But would they have the tenacity to fight like a cornered badger?

Fisman's gibberish had to be echoed by as many senior people as possible, including Duclos, who, on May 4, 2022, said, *'We can't have relaxation of Public Health measures - more freedom - without vaccination.'*[426] Linking freedom to a failed vaccine was, in any circumstance, wrong and evil. But in the face of omicron generating mortality rates comparable to the flu, it was also just a bald-faced lie. Next was Mona, the mother of the mandates, reiterating something 100% false - *'The only way to end the pandemic is to make sure that everyone, everywhere, can be vaccinated.'*[427] Reading from a Trudeau French-kissed cue card, what Mona didn't realize is that she was making a fool of herself. Everyone, everywhere already, could be vaccinated - many didn't want to be! As per Moderna's CEO on May 24, 2022: *'It's sad to say, I'm in the process of throwing 30 million doses in the garbage because nobody wants them. We have a big demand problem...we tried to contact every country, and nobody wants to take them.'*[428] Bill Gates and a big pharma CEO were sad. Mark it down.

Finally, Parliamentary Secretary to the Minister of Health Adam van Koeverden continued to disseminate false information during his speech in Parliament:

"Thanks to my colleague for giving me the opportunity to highlight a recent study [Fisman's study]. Unfortunately, the unvaccinated continue to disproportionally risk the safety of those vaccinated against COVID-19."[429]

As the Liberals went full Fisman, it quickly became apparent they had to because it was the only study they could use. I would venture to say that not a single politician or MSM outlet touting the Fisman study knew that the natural immunity of the unvaccinated input was 20%, and that this produced fraudulent conclusions. They simply didn't care. The narrative they wanted to indoctrinate was decided on before purchasing the Fisman study.

As Fisman was spreading propaganda more respected and less biased doctors, like Epidemiology Lead of Influenza & Emerging Respiratory Pathogens at BCCDC Dr. Danuta Skowronsk, were informing us that almost half of Canadians had already caught COVID-19.[430] Moreover, weeks later, the 'COVID-19 Immunity Task Force' would tell us that more than 17 million Canadians had caught the omicron variant within five months.[431] Remember, Fisman's lies depended upon a 20% COVID-19 infection rate in the unvaccinated.

When the 'COVID-19 Immunity Task Force' told us that 17.5 million Canadians caught COVID-19 for the five months ending May 15, 2022, they also informed us that the COVID-19 case fatality rate fell below 0.1%. The government says 10,489 Canadians died from COVID-19 during the period when 17.5 million Canadians caught COVID-19.[432] This equals an all-case mortality rate of approximately 0.061% in Canada. 0.061% was almost half of the 115 deaths per 100,000 cases that Johns Hopkins was reporting for Canada.[433] Further confirmation COVID-19 was more fluffy teddy bear than pissed-off grizzly.

Someone around this time blurted out that there hadn't been a preposterous headline from one of the government doctors in a while. Muhajarine knowing the Liberals were desperate and able to secretly move funds, asked for double his usual research fee. Lack of preposterous headline problem solved - *Fourth vaccine doses could be key to ending pandemic: Sask. epidemiologist'*.[434] Israel had already started the fourth dose of the vaccines in January 2022. All the Fauci ignored research showed an antibody boost but no real protection from transmission. Muhajarine cashed his cheque.

With the Fisman garbage getting debunked and not as many Canadians playing the fool again, there was yet another miraculous Hail Mary attempt to keep the momentum that wasn't going, um, going. At this point, out of sheer morbid curiosity, why the hell not? Show us what you got!

"Liberals would add COVID-19 shots to schools' immunization lists, Duca says" [435]

Wow. I didn't see that level of crazy coming. Duca added that along with mandating vaccines in trials for kids, Ford was *'weak on science and weak on vaccines,'* and he catered to *'fringe elements.'* The use of the word 'fringe' had to have been intentional. It was tasteless and not effective. Shortly before Duca dropped his mandatory vaccination proposal, the CDC released a shiny new study saying, *'As of February 2022, approximately 75% of children and adolescents had serologic evidence of previous infection with SARS-CoV-2.'* [436] Assuming Canada was similar to that of the U.S., which it was, and more kids caught COVID-19 in March and April, which they did, Duca was saying he wanted to force an old, leaky 'vaccine' on kids despite 80+% of them already having natural immunity. With the first major Canadian election since the protests had ended, it was clear in my mind that Duca was done. The promulgation of hate and division cannot be election winners every time. I surmised that Trudeau and/or the Liberal party were losing their minds if this was the platform they deemed essential at this moment.

Even if Trudeau did think he could gain some traction, part of him had to know that it wouldn't be enough. Unlike on August 13, 2021, when Trudeau could easily mask his tyrannical template, the world, and Canadians, now knew what he was about. As Trudeau tried to regain traction, Joe Rogan was calling him a *'creepy fucking dictator,'* [437] and as he attempted to repaint the unvaccinated as selfish clips of Bill Maher were being watched that compared Trudeau's words to that of Hitler.[438] It was so obvious Trudeau had pushed way too far into his mandate-craze that even Conservative MP Rachael Thomas in the House said that *'many Canadians'* believed Trudeau fit the definition of a dictator.[439] A Canadian politician other than Maxime Bernier suggesting Trudeau was a dictator was big news in 2022. The MSM quickly and mercilessly attacked Ms. Thomas for daring to disparage their champion.

What the Liberals were doing wasn't any more militant than their deceptive deeds in late 2021. Still, with so many having caught COVID-19, whether vaccinated or not, the hate-laced rhetoric and *'the pandemic isn't over'* mantras were not compelling enough to spread fear. A brand new vaccine plant opened in South Africa in March 2022 and was at threat of closing by May 2022 because it had not received a single order,[440] and countries were pouring spoiled vaccines out because no one wanted them. Except to the hard-core anxiety-laden pro-Trudeau/Jagmeet mob in Canada, it was obvious the vaccine train had derailed, and there was no putting it back on the tracks.

Epitomizing our dictator's lack of focus and direction, on May 8, 2022, Trudeau tried to raise a Canadian flag while vacationing with Mélanie in Ukraine. Fumbling and bumbling, he could not. The video of this event, that for some reason wasn't destroyed, lasted more than two minutes.[441] The flag incident came after Trudeau and his gang had just finished watching a U2 performance in the war zone that was Ukraine. Unlike how Trudeau always wore a mask when on a swing set with his wife, Trudeau didn't wear a mask during the entire trip. Canadians had one of the highest vaccination rates in the world, and Trudeau almost always wore a mask around his unclean fellow citizens. Ukraine had some of the lowest vaccination rates in the world, and Trudeau felt safe to ditch the mask. One word helps us understand this contradiction. Science.

As more pressure regarding the 'political science' mandates was arriving daily, and as the gaze of Canadians started to affix upon the justifications for the Emergency Act, Trudeau needed another diversion - eureka - bang-bang handguns!

Trudeau: *"It will be illegal to buy, sell, transfer, or import handguns anywhere in Canada."*[442]

Definitely out of left field, Trudeau's handgun law defrayed some of the headline hell from burning him for a spat. But it didn't seem to be holding. What would this madman do next, legalize fentanyl? Yep. That's what he was going to do.

"The exemption will allow adults in the province to carry up to 2.5 grams of opioids - including heroin, morphine, and fentanyl - crack and powder cocaine, methamphetamine and MDMA, also known as Ecstasy."[443]

Trudeau should have looked at the polls, examined the improving COVID-19 metrics, considered why people were calling him a dictator, and let the mandate issue go. Except this is not how dictators think. Xi doesn't suddenly stop lockdowns and follow the rest of the world; he just does lockdowns harder. And so did Trudeau.

Like a pig carcass thrown into helicopter blades, the stench of uncooked sausage filled the air, but it still couldn't camouflage the tribulations Trudeau was battling in his vain effort to resurrect his vaccine-based control paradigm. When I was 13, I deployed asinine confidence and jumped on a forklift, and this unfurled unexpected benefits. Trudeau was proof that the opposite can happen as well. As an asinine, hypocritical dictator, Trudeau looked like a man pontificating about his lost puppy. His big red communist puppy. People had walked too far away from the COVID-19 fearmobile, the seasonal tides were turning, and the Liberal ship was sinking fast.

Chapter 26 - The Walls Come Crumblin' Down

As Trudeau pushed to keep federal mandates in place and considered launching a third dose campaign, Dr. Chagla spoke on May 15, 2022, about dropping the travel mandates altogether. Chagla was speaking softly and impressively when the CBC reporter cut him off:

"Forgive me for interrupting because you know that people are watching at home and they're getting upset because the argument and the pushback to you will be better safe than sorry. Most of us went and got our two doses. Some of us got our third dose. Why do we have to go through these steps for the greater good and others don't, and they'll get to enjoy the same travel opportunities and access that those who feel that they acted quite responsibly did as well."[444]

Many assume the CBC is just a bunch of paid-off government shills. They may be overlooking that people like CBC's Natasha Fatah believed Trudeau's message of hate and segregation. Moreover, these brainwashed people assumed that since they took the vaccine for the greater good, those that did not should be punished. If you are thinking of starting a cult, hit Natasha up. She seems like the type.

Along with people like Natasha still biting mad in Canada, there was BC Premier John Horgan, who had long been Trudeau's rock. Not only did Horgan not rush to vacate COVID-19 related restrictions like many other Premiers, but when the protests continued, he said the protesters should 'get a hobby.' Horgan was blunt and, akin to Legault, vehemently wanted to hold onto special emergency powers and COVID-19 restrictions. However, Horgan shocked everyone when he didn't join Trudeau's anti-unvaccinated Fisman frenzy, and, insofar as Trudeau' was concerned, he was starting to speak blasphemy:

Horgan: *"The prime minister repeatedly said when we get past the pandemic will be the best time to have those conversations [about health transfers]. Well, we're here today, the pandemic is waning, it's becoming endemic, and it's time now to have that conversation.* "[445]

Horgan's words could have been intended to provide a little push so Trudeau recognized that if he wanted to keep buying his support, he would have to continue paying. Nevertheless, the odds of Horgan saying the E word - endemic - paid 15-1. That Trudeau was plotting mandatory vaccination while Horgan mentioned 'endemic' was one of the strongest signals yet that we were not going back to fantasy covid-island.

On May 10, 2022, another honest acknowledgement came from a source that should have been pushing more vaccinations harder than anyone. This was the type of news I trusted, and the kind of news Trudeau's cult mustered the audacity to ignore:

Pfizer CEO - *"working on an annual vaccine, or a vaccine that will last at least a year, is the holy grail right now...We don't have a vaccine that will do the job right now, something that will hold a year."* [446]

The open acknowledgement by Pfizer that their vaccine couldn't last even one year (something we already knew) may have just been a marketing ploy for boosters, but it was also further evidence that Canada's two-dose mandate was preposterous. For most of 2021, the vaccine manufacturers and the countries distributing their products claimed they had no idea that vaccine efficacy waned so rapidly, but they were certain the vaccines were safe. The basic question from any semi-critical thinker was obvious: if they didn't know the vaccines would wane so rapidly, how did they know there were no harmful long-term side effects?

As May 2022 drew to a close, Trudeau cancelled attending a fundraiser in person because, according to a Liberal MP, protesters outside were uttering racial slurs. Hours of video of the protests found the protesters using strong language but no racial slurs. Around the same time, a shocked Jagmeet was being yelled at and pestered by protesters when leaving a store, and one irate man was also giving him the middle finger. Jagmeet did the tour and played the news, saying he was shocked by such hate and racism. Days later, Jagmeet would be swarmed in Brampton, Ontario, because people wanted answers. Jagmeet ignored everyone, as he always did Rebel News, and was forced to quickly flee in a gas-guzzling SUV. Even though people had screamed at him, there was no comment from Jagmeet about this protest. The crowd was primarily Sikh.[447]

The charade and games played by politicians can sometimes be laughable, but Trudeau and Jagmeet were taking it to a whole new level. Canadians were no longer protesting only the mandates. They had already had enough of the Trudeau-Jagmeet love affair.

With cases down, hospitalizations down, deaths down, and more than enough evidence to suggest policymakers had been lying to them for some time, the public's fear began, slowly at first, to change. The only province with strict mask mandates in May 2022 was Quebec, and on a per capita basis, Quebec also had the highest amount of active COVID-19 cases. If the mask mandates worked, why didn't they work?

Duca entered an Ontario election saying he would force kids to take a COVID-19 vaccine. On June 2, 2022, Duca suffered a historic election loss, including in his hometown, and the Liberal party failed to achieve party status in Canada's most populated province of Ontario. Duca stepped down immediately following an election that took all of 20 minutes to be decided on television. NDP mandate backer Andrea Horwath also suffered a horrific loss and immediately stepped down as party leader. This was a repudiation of Trudeau and Jagmeet, and I believe those that deny this fact have unacceptable views.

Incidentally, it wasn't that people liked Doug Ford - who handled COVID-19 like most paid-off Premiers - it was that they despised the alternatives. I knew teachers in Ontario that voted for

Ford even though he had put them through covid-hell, and they knew that with their contracts upcoming, he would probably viciously harass them again. This threat didn't matter; they would not be voting for mandatory vaccination of kids with a vaccine that didn't work. As for the NDP, they lost some unions to the Progressive Conservatives. That traditionally didn't happen, at least not until Jagmeet jumped into bed with the enemy.

After the election spotlight faded, Trudeau and company should have woken up and devised a plan to get off the mandates. Nope. Instead, they watched as chaos engulfed Canadian airports due to useless and time-consuming COVID-19 protocols. They also watched, with their feet immersed in cement, as the investigation into the Emergency Act continued. Had the 'special committee' conducted a serious and unbiased investigation, there is no doubt that people would have been arrested and charged with treason (or, at the minimum, mischief). But this was Trudeau's and Jagmeet's Canada, where anything goes.

First, there was Minister of Public Safety Marco Mendicino, who had repeatedly told Canadians that the Emergency Act was invoked because the authorities requested it. Courtesy of 'The Andrew Lawton Show,' here are some of Marco's statements as and after the Emergency Act was invoked:

- *"We invoked the act because it was the advice of nonpartisan professional law enforcement."*
- *"That's the reason why we had emergencies act, and we did so on the basis of non-partisan professional advice from law enforcement."*
- *"We were following the advice of various levels of the of law enforcement, including the RCMP."*
- *"After calling upon the police forces, we invoked the emergency measures act."*
- *"We wanted to be sure at bottom, that we were giving law enforcement all of the tools and the resources that they needed..."*
- *"It was only after police told us that they needed this special power."*
- *"The Ontario Association, the Canadian Association, law*

enforcement was very strong. I don't want to speak for every last serving member of law, but there was a very strong consensus that we needed to invoke the act. "[448]

During questioning, RCMP Commissioner Brenda Lucki, former Ottawa Chief of police Peter Sloly, and current Chief Steve Bell denied having asked for the Emergency Act to be invoked. There was no testimony from anyone even remotely suggesting any authorities had asked for the Emergency Act. Macro was caught lying. No wiggle room. Despite openly lying about the justification to take away civil liberties, tear up the Charter, and throttle peaceful protesters, Marco wasn't arrested, and frenzied calls for his resignation were ignored.

Next, Deputy Prime Minister Chrystia Freeland was grilled about her role in declaring the Emergency Act. In one of the most evasive interviews in history, Freeland refused to answer if she had ever used the words like 'terrorism funding' or 'money laundering,' and when asked for specifics, she said, to quote, she had *'heard about efforts to block roads,'* there was a *'constant danger of new blockades,'* and *'there was one blockade after another.'* This was our Deputy Prime Minister, which some think could be our next Prime Minister, providing zero reason(s) to justify the Emergency Act. Finally, when asked if the Ambassador Bridge blockade was already taken down when she and her comrades were discussing matters the night before invoking the Emergency Act on February 13, 2022, she answered 'yes'. The blockades were coming down without the need for the Emergency Act. Facts were facts.

Also, a fact, according to Freeland, was that there were 280 bank accounts frozen at a value of around $8 million, and no charges were laid in relation to the freezing of these assets. The deputy director of FINTRAC, an agency in Freeland's department, had previously testified the following:

"It was (donors') own money. It wasn't cash that funded terrorism or was in any way money laundering. There were people around

the world who were fed up with COVID and were upset and saw the demonstrations. I believe they just wanted to support the cause. "[449]

To be clear on this point, Freeland stated in her testimony that there were zero arrests related to the financial assets that were seized using the Emergency Act, and our top watchdog in this sphere of expertise testified that funding was from individual donors. Are we supposed to believe that our government using special powers to seize bank assets when they feel like it, akin to, say, China, are normal and accepted investigation methods?

Interestingly, Freeland also refused to answer, despite being asked multiple times, if the U.S. had offered to tow Canadian trucks during the Ambassador Bridge protests. Powerful politicians saying they couldn't find a tow truck was a key justification for the Emergency Act. Freeland knew this question was better left unanswered.

It was clear, at least in my mind, that Freeland and company used the Emergency Act to expand government powers, take down potential political rivals, and avoid talking with peaceful protesters exercising their Charter rights. You can argue otherwise if you choose, that is your right, but per Freeland and the RCMP, there were zero arrests under the Emergency Act! If I, as a government, say I desperately need special powers to circumvent the court process, and then I never make an arrest using these new powers wouldn't you wonder what the hell I was doing? It was clear that Freeland thought she was above reproach, and she knew most of Canadians never watched CPAC.

As Freeland wasted time quoting news articles as she failed to directly answer basic questions from MP Brock,[450] it was as if all her WEF and Bilderberg training had prepared her for this moment. Just meander on, speak in slow, serious tones, act offended now and then, and try not to say anything. What else could poor Chrystia do in this situation? Anyone paying attention knew the invoking of the Emergency Act was a farce. In her only bona fide words of substance, Freeland testified:

"...our economic reputation with the United States as a reliable trading partner and as a reliable investment destination was being damaged...This is so dangerous to Canada, colleagues. I was deeply, deeply concerned that these illegal blockades and this illegal occupation would provoke a whole new wave of protectionism and deeply erode our trading relationship with the United States. That was a real economic threat."[451]

It is difficult to comment on the above mix-nut trail of lunacy. Should Freeland's deep concerns and unsubstantiated anxieties about protectionism be the standard for declaring what is tantamount to martial law in Canada?

Along with finding out Freeland can play dodgeball, the investigation into the Emergency Act also unveiled that the Freedom Convoy was initially planned with and approved by the relevant parties and that no authority believed the manifesto from Freedom Convoy warranted any charges or arrests. At what point, and why, did this accepted as legal protest become an illegal occupation exactly? A question no one dares even try to answer.

Suffice to say, the investigation into the Emergency Act was a sore spot for Trudeau and company, so much so that shortly after the Freeland debacle, the Liberals decided to share *'cabinet documents'* to try and bolster their case.[452] Not much is likely to amount from the investigation, even though I think most already know what is close to the truth. To recap: there were zero arrests made under the Emergency Act, zero arrests from all of the financial seizures, and Freeland admitted the blockades were being mopped up with existing powers. I sometimes blather on and allow bias to get the better of me. Nonetheless, these three facts do not seem refuted.

Then, on June 10, 2022, Omar consulted the thousands of experts he never once named, punched the data into a model he never produced, and came up with the following:

"Today, the Government of Canada is also announcing that Mandatory randomized testing will be temporarily suspended at all airports between Saturday, June 11 and Thursday, June 30, 2022. Unvaccinated travellers will still be tested on-site. As of July 1, all testing, including for unvaccinated travellers, will be performed off-site."[453]

You couldn't help but wonder if Omar had done some legal BC meth before saying no testing was required from June 11 to July 1, but then testing had to return. Was COVID-19 going on holiday?

After Omar was MP Lloyd Longfield, who, the poor fella, caught the covid. He said on Twitter, *'Having 4 vaccine doses has kept symptoms mild so far!'*[454] You couldn't help but wonder at what point the math became ludicrous. Was it *'having 17 vaccine doses has kept symptoms mild so far'*?

Even as the downpour - make that hurricane - of negative news bombarded Trudeau and the Liberal party, they persisted, in early June 2022, in insisting their vaccine mandates were needed. It was sheer stupidity and so untenable that reports of a 'massive majority' in the Liberal caucus wanted Trudeau to end the mandates.[455] It didn't even matter if stories of the majority of Liberals being against the mandates were true. Sometimes it is perceptions that create reality. The mandates had to go.

Calling people racist and saying the anti-vaxxers were spreading misinformation were, like old party favours, no longer in style. Some unions had rebooted more cases against the mandates because the policy should not have been renewed. On April 6, 2022, the polls broadly suggested Canadians didn't want mandates, and former Newfoundland Premier, The Honourable A. Brian Peckford had his court date against the government set for September 19, 2022.[456] The walls were not just closing in, they were crumbling. And while Trudeau, the dictator, had tried to engineer some unoriginal schemes to make fear great for him again, he had failed to do so, even if he was the last to know.

On June 9, 2022, while giving yet another pro-democracy speech in the U.S., with Mélanie by his side, Trudeau was asked point blank:

"It appears that you wear a mask inconsistently depending on situations...do you still believe in mask mandates...?"[457]

More than a gotcha moment, this was a *'we know you are a slimeball'* question from a media person not in Trudeau's pocket. The smug dictator nodded, briefly thought about pulling a Natasha and cutting the unscripted question off, and then took his medicine like a good boy. Trudeau looked tired. I hoped he was OK.

Chapter 27 - June 14, 2022

"I've had covid a couple times. Super mild symptoms... I'm not going to let Canada tell me what I do and don't do with my body. For a little bit of money, it's just not worth it." ~ J.T. Realmuto on missing Blue Jays series[458]

Kate Faith is a 29-year-old Canadian who lives in New Zealand that wrote to every Liberal MP in 2022 to inquire why the vaccine mandates were still in effect. She had a memorable encounter with an MP on Instagram. Rather than paraphrase, here is most of the chat in full:

"- Katie: So why are they in place? Corruption and MPs who won't do what's right.
- Liberal MP: Well, you sound a lot smarter than the epidemiologists I speak with. Sorry I responded.
- Katie: What do they say? Does the jab stop transmission? We all know it doesn't. Is there any reason a 29-year-old who has already had covid should not be allowed on a flight?
- Liberal MP: Not here to inform you, Kate, later
- Katie: You are a disgrace of a Canadian.
- Liberal MP: Fuck you."[459]

The colourful language at the end was from Liberal MP Adam van Koeverden. Trudeau and the Toronto Star approved of his message. Katie was shocked and spoke for those that had been under siege in Canada for almost a year:

"I'd like him to apologize to Canadians for saying 'f— off' and for making anyone feel belittled or ostracized due to medical choices."[460]

Adam van Koeverden did apologize on social media and in the House for swearing.[461] His deep heartfelt contrition aside, keep in mind that Koeverden was the same MP that previously quoted the hack Fisman study. Those who advocated for vaccines and mandates but didn't have the time or inclination to defend their position were intellectually disgraceful and, you could argue, criminals. Koeverden had long ago added his name to those that will never be forgotten by freedom-obsessed Canadians. Science is replete with studies on why it is unhealthy to hold a grudge, even against people like Koeverden. So be it.

On June 11, 2022, Mona Fortier announced to the world that although very thoroughly vaccinated, she was feeling a little unwell due to catching the covid. Mona oversaw TBS, which was in charge of the federal vaccine policy, keeping myself and others out of work. She was supposed to produce an update on her policy 'at a minimum' every six months. That sixth-month window ended on April 6, 2022, and we were now past eight months. Mona's phone messaging system had been full since April 6, 2022, she did not return multiple messages left with one of her two receptionists, and she (and TBS) never responded to emails. She instead travelled around Canada taking pictures, eating and drinking, and laughing, even as her vaccine policy wrought psychological and financial harm to Canadians.

As Mona nursed her illness, mayhem was breaking out daily at Canada's busiest airport in Toronto (the airport is actually located in Mississauga, where I was born, but I digress). Toronto Pearson International had always been a poop-hole airport, but legacy COVID-19 policies made it much worse. There were reports of stranded passengers, cancelled flights, labour shortages, and long line-ups. Former NHL superstar, Ryan Whitney, made a video detailing his nightmare.[462] He said it was *the worst airport on earth.* Politicians took notice of the viral video, as did industries and companies demanding the vaccine mandates and restrictions be dropped. This was Trudeau's airport - locked in protocols, mandates, and policies every other major airport in the world had already abandoned. It was scandalous and unnecessary.

As the airport nightmares grew, reports started to emerge that more Liberals, quietly, of course, wanted Trudeau's mandates gone. The tension seemed to be building. Adding drama to the mix was Dr. Tam, Canada's top doctor that had previously been dead wrong about vaccines being able to end COVID-19. Even Tam was openly saying in early February 2022 that we needed *a 'more sustainable'* approach to COVID-19 and that *'we do need to get back to some normalcy'* because *'this virus is not going to disappear.'*[463] These words were exactly what many smart and informed scientists had started saying in July 2021. Better late than never, Tam.

Some might ask why Tam didn't speak against the mandates if she felt this way in February 2022. Despite her long history with the WHO, let's give Tam the benefit of the doubt and recognize that she was, in her way, speaking out. The problem was no one was listening:

"According to sources, Tam has recommended lifting the vaccine mandate and changing travel restrictions more than once. In March, bureaucrats informed the airline industry that the travel restrictions currently causing delays would be lifted by May 1."[464]

It doesn't take Bobby Fischer level genius to figure out Tam was abiding by Trudeau's orders. Trudeau didn't want the mandates gone, so they were not gone - it was this simple. Like a good little foot soldier, Tam shelved her *'live with covid'* thoughts and reluctantly kept playing in Trudeau's 'keep on vaccinating!' campaign. Starting a war against a dictator wasn't exactly in Tam's basket of tricks.

Not only did Tam never (to my knowledge) openly talk about the science and benefits of natural immunity, but she also ignored any hint that the shots might eventually harm the immune system. Remember, these shots were still in Phase 3 clinical trials, and Tam should have been more open about the long-term risks we may not yet be aware of. At the very least, Tam should have made some attempt to stratify the risks COVID-19 posed to different segments of society. She did not. Instead, when it came to vaccination (Tam's wheelhouse when she was with the WHO), someone near the end of their natural life and extremely sick was lumped together with the young and healthy. It was like Tam was a triage nurse walking into an emergency room and yelling, *'Tylenol for everyone, now get out!'*

Then, like an annoying cuckoo clock, Trudeau had something hypocrisy-laden to say: *'Everyone should be able to live a life free of discrimination and to be able to make their own choices for their own body.'*[465] Shortly after his pointless speech in the U.S., Trudeau and Mélanie skipped onto a plane back to Canada. After arriving home on June 13, 2022, Trudeau told the world he had caught COVID-19 again and that since he was vaccinated a bunch, he was handling it fine. The online rumour mill churned frantically - *'Trudeau should drop the mandates quickly because he knowingly broke the law and entered Canada while positive for COVID-19.'* Chuckle. And for good measure: *'when the going gets tough, Trudeau catches COVID-19.'*

As the chuckles from rumours were about to subside, a new tale emerged, started by various legacy news informants, that the government would allow unvaccinated people to travel. Then, inexplicably, on June 14, 2022, Mona's TBS announced the *'Suspension of the vaccine mandates for domestic travellers, transportation workers, and federal employees.'*[466]

My first instinct when hearing the news wasn't how great it was that I may be going back to work but that now, pardon the language, we must all focus and take these bastards to court and fight like rabid animals to ensure this never happens again. Back in January, when the trucker mandate was cancelled (for one day), there was a feeling of joy and relief. On June 14, 2022, there were no such feelings. The overriding question was, what took so long to rescind a policy that was an abysmal failure?

Having not watched many recent conferences due to the possibility of ruining the day with anger, I tuned into the CPAC event on this historic day. Before it started, the CPAC announcer asked the sea of journalists to keep their comments brief to give everyone an opportunity. This was the most people attending one of these events in more than two years. I wondered why journalists and the media previously didn't care why Canada was one of the last countries on earth being strangled by a pandemic dictator. It didn't matter - let's go!

First up was Omar, who had days earlier posted a graphic of a mask on Twitter to justify why Canada was the last major country on earth still enforcing strict travel mandates. Omar said in the Tweet, *'We are keeping Canadians safe when they travel by air and rail, by making masks mandatory for everyone on board.'* [467] Below this statement was a picture of an N95 mask, on which Omar's pro-masking study was based. Little did Omar know his department does not and never had mandated N95 masks. If you ever want to see Omar flustered, ask him if he knows the difference between cloth and N95 masks.

Regardless, Omar was Omar; he had stumbled through numerous interviews in recent months mentioning the word 'science' to justify the mandates without ever actually mentioning any scientific particulars. Like Mona, he never returned phone calls and didn't respond to emails. His words were often infuriatingly dubious. But today was a new day. Go for it, Omar:

"...it's clear that the COVID situation is not the same now as it was last fall when we implemented the vaccine mandate...The suspension of the vaccine mandate was informed by key indicators including the epidemiological situation and modeling, vaccine science, and high levels of vaccination against COVID-19 in Canada."

Nothing too earth-shattering and only semi-painful to watch. Next up was Mona. The bullshit started right off the bat (which COVID-19 probably did not come from) as Mona said, *'The policy has done what it was meant to do.'* This was a blatant lie. Before the mandates, we had zero cases of COVID-19 at my workplace of more than 400 people. Shortly after the mandates, fully vaccinated people were spreading COVID-19 to other fully vaccinated people readily and easily. Similar trends, with varying differences in numbers, of course, were happening Canada-wide.

The mandates were supposed to limit the spread of COVID-19 in the workplace and, per Trudeau's words, 'end covid.' If Mona believed that the vaccine policy did what it was 'meant to do,' then I truly feel sorry for her. Get help, Mona.

Usually, at this point, the rage would build to a level where I needed a walk away (or, in December 2021, have a sip). Serenity now. Mona continued that all options were on the table going forward, including *'reintroduction of vaccine mandates if necessary.'* As a wise militarist might counter, you keep the element of surprise in your pocket Mona. Threatening us with mandates would only keep those impacted in a heightened state of awareness. Finally, Duclos took the mic:

"Our government's response has always been informed by evolving science, research, prudence, and expert Public Health advise..."

No, Duclos, it hasn't. This is a lie. Duclos continued:

"The Omicron has shown us that two doses are no longer enough because immunity acquired through two doses varies and wanes over time."

The early Israel data told us vaccine efficacy quickly waned even before the delta. Pfizer told us vaccine efficacy waned spectacularly with delta. There was little, if any, transmission limiting efficacy from the shots with omicron. Trudeau's Himmler Duclos was the most difficult to watch as he proudly stated untruths, put a positive spin on the mandates, and informed us the government must rely on a new definition of fully vaccinated. Just a month earlier, you may recall that Duclos contended, *'We can't have relaxation of Public Health measures - more freedom - without vaccination.'* Put simply, Duclos was a sick man that proved he would do or say anything to force more of these shots into people's arms.

As Duclos closed out his remarks, it went to a Q and A. The first reporter asked the following:

"Is there specific data that leads to this decision...what's different about today and June 20, 2022, that could not have been done a month ago?"

They must have allowed someone in that wasn't wearing an 'I love Dictator Trudeau' pledge pin because such an elegantly simple question was never asked during these CPAC meetings before. Directed at Omar, his response, with all the stuttering and baloney, was classic Omar. Having never answered a single fact-based mandate question with a single fact, Omar sounded off after hitting his maximum ramble button. This man made up shit all the time, he repeatedly lied, and, most of all, he did it because Trudeau's mandates were simply indefensible:

"Um. Um. I mean, I'll ask Mr. Duclos as well, ah, ah, to guide his own comments, but I'll tell you this decision today took a lot of discussions and consultations, so the decision today is not based on something that we woke up yesterday or this morning and decided to do, we take we've done our homework. This is what Canadians expect us to do. They've seen us focus on their health and safety and that every time we put in place a measure or lifted a measure, it's done guided by science with the aim of protecting the health and safety of Canadians. So what got us today was a period of discussions of consultations of looking at the big picture, preparing ourselves for a potential wave in the fall, but the current situation today so we have to look at all the options and all the data that we have, and after a thoughtful, deliberate, prudent discussions, we've reached this decision. So it's, it's what Canadians expect us to do. We will always err on the side of public health and safety."

OK, Omar, but why weren't the mandates dropped a month ago or four months ago? Omar, the incompetent, didn't have a clue.

Duclos went next and spoke about how great Canada has done vaccinating people. He provided a smidgen more information about the alleged thought process used to make the decision:

"Two doses are not enough now to protect against infection and transmission. And that is why we are transitioning now to an up-to-date vaccination definition of what it means to be adequately protected against COVID-19. Fully protected with two doses doesn't work anymore. Dr. Tam said that last Friday..."

While these types of comments may seem ordinary, the reality was people had been screaming since August 13, 2021, that these vaccines waned terrifically fast after a few months of getting two doses. Almost a year later, Duclos confessed that policymakers had been ignoring the science. When, precisely, did you know Mr. Duclos that two doses were not enough and why the hell didn't you mandate the third dose then or stop the mandates immediately?

"Two doses are not enough now to protect against infection and transmission."

Rereading it makes the blood boil even more. To reiterate, when did you know this Duclos!? Because a wide variety of reliable sources knew this was the case a long time ago! Here are a few:

November 29, 2021 - Moderna chief predicts existing vaccines will struggle with Omicron[468]
I think it's going to be a material drop. I just don't know how much because we need to wait for the data. But all the scientists I've talked to ... are like, 'This is not going to be good.'

December 13, 2021 - Omicron evades Moderna vaccine too, study suggests, but boosters help...[469]

December 13, 2021 - Dr. Peter Jüni: *"This variant here is so absolutely infectious now... This will reach every single person. Statistically speaking, there will be very few lucky ones."*[470]

December 15, 2021 - Neither vaccination with two doses of AstraZeneca nor Pfizer were able to stimulate an antibody response strong enough to neutralize Omicron[471]

December 21, 2021 - Most of the World's Vaccines Likely Won't Prevent Infection From Omicron[472]

December 23, 2021 [Study release date]: No Omicron immunity without booster, study finds[473]

January 6, 2022 - Moderna CEO: *"We have been saying that we believe first this virus is not going away. We're going to have to live with it. I will be surprised when we get that data in the coming weeks that it's holding nicely over time — I would expect that it's not going to hold great."*[474]

January 10, 2022 - Pfizer CEO says two Covid vaccine doses aren't 'enough for omicron.'[475]

January 12, 2022 - Fauci (he is the science): *"Omicron, with its extraordinary, unprecedented degree of efficiency of transmissibility, will ultimately find just about everybody."*[476]

January 29, 2022 - Dr. Kieran Moore: *"In the face of Omicron, I absolutely think ... we have to learn to live with this virus."*[477]

January 29, 2022 - Saskatchewan Premier Scott Moe: *"An unvaccinated trucker does not pose any greater risk of transmission than a vaccinated trucker."*[478]

February 13, 2022 - Doug Ford: *"We also know that it doesn't matter if you have one shot or ten shots, you can still catch COVID-19."*[479]

April 21, 2022 - *"Primary immunization with two doses of ChAdOx1 nCoV-19 or BNT162b2 vaccine provided limited protection against symptomatic disease caused by the omicron variant."*[480]

Like a dying general going down with a fight, Duclos adopted a revisionist and bogus interpretation of history to explain why the government did not remove ineffective restrictions months ago. He should have been taken to task by the media, dragged away by the RCMP, and brought up on charges for making threats of bringing back mandates while providing no evidence they did anything but harm Canadians.

Omar, Mona, and Duclos were not heroes giving us back our freedoms; these were the villains that helped steal freedom from us and held onto much longer than the pandemic suggested they should. They should have been apologizing and begging for forgiveness as they were dragged away in cuffs for following Trudeau's demands, but instead, they were patting themselves on the back. The religiously inclined might have thought, *'Father, forgive them, for they do not know what they are doing.'* The informed pragmatist had a different take - *these bastards knew exactly what they were doing, and they should burn.* For the record, I land someplace in the middle: perhaps they didn't deserve jail or hell, even though they most certainly should have been abruptly tossed from their jobs. Why should a gang of thugs that caused so much needless pain and suffering with vindictive policies and politics be permitted to remain in leadership positions?

Omar, Mona, Carla, Duclos, Legault, Mélanie, and even Trudeau were all human beings. They were sometimes going to make mistakes, and it's not like I or anyone else levitates above these policymakers simply because we were right that the mandates would do a Hindenburg. This said, honest mistakes are not exactly the same thing as willfully inflicting harm on Canadians and then lying about your intentions. When the dust settled on June 14, 2022, some mandates remained, including:

"Truckers looking to cross the Canada-U.S. border will still need to be fully vaccinated against COVID-19, despite the federal government lifting other health measures for travellers Tuesday."[481]

Unvaccinated Canadians could soon drive and fly to the U.S., and if so inclined, they could even take a boat, walk, or bicycle to visit our neighbours to the south. But what they couldn't do was drive a tractor-trailer across the border. This wasn't a mistake. It was intentional. This was Trudeau and his 'just following orders' subordinates, in a nutshell: vindictiveness and irrationality to the end. Like a cloud covering the light of freedom and never leaving. Truckers were, rightly so, not impressed.

"If you're going to drop mandates, you drop it for everybody. It shouldn't be pick-and-choose. We stood up for what we thought was right and what was fair, and now everyone else can do their thing, but we can't."[482]

I sincerely hope the court system can rectify this pattern of government overreach and Charter breaking spitefulness. The government previously discriminated against one segment of society supposedly for the greater good. Now, they had narrowed this discrimination to one subset of society that happened to drive trucks. Two doses are no longer enough, according to Tam and Duclos, but if you are a trucker, it is plenty to keep the mandates going?

The reason why President Xi didn't adapt to omicron like New Zealand, Australia, or South Korea isn't that he lacked the acumen to read the COVID-19 tea leaves. It was because, in his mind, he had to, at any and all costs, save face. A part of Trudeau must have long ago accepted that he was being viewed by many as a pandemic dictator, and this realization surely modernized his intellectual armoury. In Trudeau's mind leaving reminders that he still had some clout was his way of saving face. Incidentally, Trudeau's basic fear, just like Xi, was that losing the component of control deemed most vital could severely weaken his broader agenda. Maintaining some mandates and the ArriveCan app may seem trifling, but to Trudeau, these actions delivered a form of psychological satiation.

Ultimately, the lesson is that no leader under any circumstances should ever be permitted to treat one segment of society as disposable. The antithesis of a free society is Trudeau's mandates and restrictions that eventually he, and he alone, wanted never to relinquish. Had Trudeau acknowledged that the mandates were failing in late December 2021 and quickly changed course, he may have one day outgrown his failed authoritarianism experiments. The Canadian people can be forgiving should the act of contrition be genuine. People reacted so strongly in January 2022 and will continue to respond strongly until Trudeau takes his last breath because his words and policies were repeatedly and purposely unsubstantiated and malicious. Many politicians say Trudeau's mandates are vindictive. Well, here is a newsflash: many that cherish medical freedom will never forget and will remain actively agitated against Trudeau. This wasn't a leader; it was a spoiled child intentionally bullying Canadian citizens. Always remember!

September 1, 2021 - Trudeau: *"The folks out there tonight shouting, the anti-vaxxers, they're wrong. They are wrong about how we get through this pandemic. And more than just being wrong, because everyone is entitled to their opinion, they are putting at risk their own kids, and they are putting at risk our kids as well...Everyone needs to get vaccinated, and those people are putting us all at risk."*[483]

Sean Hartman was a healthy 17-year kid that wanted to play hockey, so he took the vaccine. Shortly after taking his first shot, Sean died suddenly at his home on Monday September 27, 2021.[18] That Trudeau, the top leader in Canada, was preaching kids should ask their parents if they could get vaccinated and dividing Canadians when he should have been protecting Sean Hartman's rights is unforgivable. That Duclos, Omar, Mona, and many others

---

[18] Despite Sean Hartman's 'slightly enlarged heart' his death was ruled 'unascertained' by Chief Medical Officer of Health with the Simcoe Muskoka District Health Unit, Dr. Charles Gardner. Sean's Dad sought another opinion and a second pathologist, who wanted to remain nameless for fear of losing his job, concluded Sean had died from the COVID-19 vaccine.

blindly parroted Trudeau's diktats was, likewise, unforgivable. To reiterate: the mandates failed, and Trudeau was 100% wrong to enact them and enforce them upon society.

As Duclos meandered on and pledged to terrorize Canadians again in the fall, it was clear he was deflecting. This was no longer Duclos The Terrible; it was Duclos The Pitiful. Threats that the definition of 'fully vaccinated' would be changed, that the mandates could return, and that Canadians must be ready for the fall were a mild tap on a drum. The days of the big, bold, timpani booms were long gone. Then Duclos, in a moment of unwitting clarity that would serve to deprecate his boss, let one honest viewpoint slip through the stream:

"Our rate of boosters is too low. It's lower than all other G7 countries, and that is not good."

Teach a person about vaccines (that work), and you will end up with a vaccinated person. Force Phase 3 trial vaccines on people and many will resist and fight to the death. The reason why our uptake of boosters was lower than any other G7 nation was because of one person and one person only - our dictator, Justin Trudeau.

June 14, 2022, was a victory, but it wasn't a victorious day that book-ended the pandemic in any meaningful way. It was a day when many policymakers admitted their guilt.

Honk, Honk!

Chapter 28 - The Government Is Not Your Doctor

"You can trust us as a source of that [COVID-19] information. You can also trust the Director General of Health and the Ministry of Health...Otherwise, dismiss anything else. We will continue to be your single source of truth...Unless you hear it from us, it is not the truth." ~ New Zealand Prime Minister Jacinda Ardern[484]

In late 2021 the NTD News network reported that *'Taiwan's health authorities say that...deaths after vaccination reached 865 while deaths from the virus are at 845.'* Proof for this claim came directly from a Taiwan CDC report which covered deaths *'suspected after vaccination'* between March 22 and October 11, 2021.[485] That more people could be dying from the vaccines than from COVID-19 in Taiwan, which is officially the Republic of China, quickly went viral.

It turns out NTD, which stands for New Tang Dynasty, doesn't exactly admire communist China, and the report may have taken some journalistic liberties. On December 17, 2021, the Taiwanese CDC responded with a vastly different interpretation of the facts:

"These adverse events occur after vaccination in time sequence but do not necessarily have a causal relationship with vaccination. It needs enough time to determine whether they may be caused by vaccination based on empirical evidence after investigation or data analysis."[486]

Much like Amina passing five days after her H1N1 vaccination, 17-year-old Sean Hartman passing shortly after he took his first COVID-19 shot, and the FDA flat out denying any Janssen-induced case of GBS was directly caused by the vaccine, Taiwan knew that a 'causal relationship' between the vaccines and injuries was next to impossible to prove. While NTD surely slanted its reporting of 'suspected' vaccine deaths for shock value, Taiwan rocket launched in the opposite direction:

"...according to Vaccine Injury Compensation Program, there has been no 'death directly caused by vaccination' case found in the evaluated cases so far."

Does anyone believe that despite 865 *'suspected deaths after vaccination'* that Taiwan had zero deaths from the vaccines by the end of 2021? Anyone? Even more audacious than the rigged Taiwan statistics was China, which after administering more than 2 billion doses of vaccine, the most by any country in the world, had reported zero vaccine deaths.[487] Deaths were rare, absolutely, but were vaccine deaths in China zero after 2+ billion doses?

A Chinese mother whose daughter died shortly after being vaccinated pleaded for a probe into her daughter's death. Beijing authorities would not oblige and detained the mother to possibly, educate her on the intricacies of the term 'causal relationship' in private.[488] People in China were being detained for protesting vaccine injuries. Peaceful protesters were being jailed in Canada for mischief. As the authoritarian world turns.

Incidentally, I have used the word 'induced' on multiple occasions because, in my mind, if a young, healthy person takes a vaccine and is injured soon thereafter with a medical episode that typically doesn't happen to young, healthy people, I call this a vaccine injury or death. But that's just me.

When it comes to concealing, delaying, or simply lying about vaccine injuries and deaths, it doesn't matter whether a country is a democracy or a dictatorship. The inherent bias was to under or not report deaths from COVID-19 vaccines. In Chapter 10, the feeling that media coverage of vaccine injuries seemed to vanish as Trudeau prepared his dictatorial mandates was thoroughly discussed. In July 2022, former CBC reporter turned whistleblower Marianne Klowak stepped up to provide further evidence that the CBC had abandoned its journalistic integrity in June 2021. In her stunning and informative interview on Trish Woods' Podcast, Ms. Klowak stated, *'at breakneck speed, we were cancelling one whole side of the [COVID-19] debate.'*[489] Ms.

Klowak discussed how her articles relating to the new COVID-19 vaccines were either redirected toward pro-vaccine sources like Pfizer or Toronto Health Unit or how her vaccine injury stories were flat-out rejected. Ms. Klowak helped remind us that those contrarians watching the world turn authoritarian in 2021 were not going crazy. The suppression of vaccine injuries and the cancelling of healthy debate from doctors about COVID-19 really happened. We didn't imagine it.

Ms. Klowak's depiction of a CBC gone corrupt was previously echoed by Tara Henley, who left the CBC in January 2022 because she couldn't take it anymore. Henley had this to say as she departed:

"To work at the CBC in the current climate is to embrace cognitive dissonance and to abandon journalistic integrity. It is to allow sweeping societal changes like lockdowns, vaccine mandates, and school closures to roll out - with little debate. To see billionaires amass extraordinary wealth and bureaucrats amass enormous power - with little scrutiny."[490]

Congratulations to Ms. Henley and Ms. Klowak for escaping and sharing their ordeals after working at Trudeau's propaganda network. Every Canadian would benefit from being made aware of these stories of courage and censorship. Allow us to never forget that, per Section 2(b) of the Canadian Charter of Rights and Freedoms, everyone has *'the freedom of thought, belief, opinion and expression, including freedom of the press and other media of communication.'*[491]

It was only once the mandates finally started to fall, and someone finally convinced Jughead Trudeau that his dream of universal vaccination was impractical, that stories of those injured by the vaccines in Canada finally started to be heard. In the case of Ross Wightman, he was hospitalized with Guillain-Barré Syndrome shortly after taking AstraZeneca's vaccine in 2021. He was one of at least ten individuals in BC that had GBS after the vaccine, and he was one of the first in Canada to get compensation from the government's VISP:

"...it has been determined by our Medical Review Board that there is a probable causal association between the injury(ies) sustained and the vaccination."[492]

You can bet your last digital RMB the word 'probable' was added in by lawyers. The money Mr. Wightman will be receiving will be less than he could have earned working, and he says the lump sum payment was *'not something that I'm overly excited about.'* I sincerely hope Mr. Wightman explores his legal options and that either the VISP or courts can make Mr. Wightman whole.

One of the doctors consulted by the VISP to decide Mr. Wightman's fate was Dr. Kumanan Wilson, who is *'also the CEO of CANImmunize, the tech company behind the digital vaccine tracking platform of the same name.'*[493] Some might argue that since Dr. Wilson runs a company that *'collects vaccination records'* and *'encourages vaccine uptake,'*[494] maybe he should have been disqualified from ruling on vaccine injuries given a possible conflict of interest.[19] Still focused primarily on one side of the story, the CBC gave Wilson lengthy coverage:

"We did tell people you need to get vaccinated, and in many cases, mandates were brought in. We needed to hold up our end of the bargain, and that was making sure that these individuals were treated fairly if something untoward were to happen. I'm a very strong believer in the safety of vaccines. They go through rigorous phase three trials, but rare events can happen, and in those circumstances, those individuals need to be supported."[495]

Dr. Wilson did not respond when asked when Pfizer and Moderna's Phase 3 studies were completed. Perhaps he didn't know the trials that he felt compelled to mention were still ongoing, which would make him incompetent. Or maybe he did know the trials are not done, which means he is a dishonest con

---

[19] Mr. Wilson's CANImmunize company is funded by the Bill & Melinda Gates Foundation and the WHO.

artist. In either case, I see him as immoral, but that's just me.

Pfizer: *"The end of the study is defined as the date of last visit of the last participant in the study."*

Moderna: *"Participants will have one final visit to the study site approximately two years from the date of their second injection."*[20]

The government and people like Wilson say they are of the mind that paying out those harmed by the vaccines is the right thing to do. However, despite having $75 million at their disposal, only 8-people had been compensated for vaccine injuries in the VISP's first year of operations.[21] I am aghast that it takes so long for vaccine injuries to be compensated, and the conspiratorial spirit in me believes this is by design. The VISP also missed its own deadline to update its activities by June 1, 2022. Instead of being transparent and on time, perhaps the VISP gang was too busy square dancing with Mona, who also missed her deadline.

Another person injured by the vaccines was Julian Scholefield, who took the Pfizer vaccine in July 2021, and within a couple of weeks, he was paralyzed from his waist down with a myelitic form of acute disseminated encephalomyelitis. A year later, still paralyzed and unable to work, the CBC finally picked up the trail. Below are Mr. Scholefield's sentiments, which appeared at the bottom of the CBC article:

"I'm paralyzed now, not because of a reckless accident, but because I followed the guidelines of our government, and so that validation and recognition is definitely something that would mean a lot to me."

---

[20] The 'end of study definitions' from Pfizer and Moderna clearly state the studies are not over until the last patient visit takes place.

[21] In an email PHAC responded that VISP has $75 million for the first 5-years, the program will be independently administered by RCGT Consulting, and that four staff members from PHAC work on the VISP.

*So far, recognition of his injury, beyond his team of doctors, has
been hard to come by.*

*Scholefield said provincial and federal government officials have
not responded to emails and letters he has written explaining
his case.*

*"To be ignored and feel like you are swept under the rug is really
hard, especially after going through something like this," he said. "*[496]

Even while reporting these newsworthy facts - which
should have been done in July 2021! - the CBC quoted Dr. Brian
Conway in their article first. Conway previously speculated young
people would receive great benefits from the vaccines against
'long covid' and that BC should enact more authoritarian mandates
like Quebec. This was the doctor the CBC called on to offset Julian
Scholefield's vaccine injury. Conway noted the requisite words
'very rare' and the total shots of vaccine administered were shown
as were total COVID-19 deaths. Missing was the total vaccine
injuries number, which was supposedly the subject of the article.
As of July 22, 2022, there had been 49.921 vaccine injuries logged
in Canada's AEFI system, and more than 10,000 have been
deemed serious.[497] I know of four cases close to me that were
vaccine injuries but where no AEFI report was filed. So make that
at least 49,925 vaccine injuries in Canada.

Even as CBC started providing some coverage of the
vaccine injured, the question these and similar reports evoked was
how do we know that vaccine injuries are 'very rare' when Canada
does such a terrible job documenting and confirming vaccine
injuries?

Until June 1, 2022, there were 733 claims filed with VISP,
and a total of eight people in Canada had received some form of
compensation.[498] The BC Centre for Disease Control says that ten
cases of one specific disease, GBS, have been confirmed from the
COVID-19 vaccines in BC alone, and there have only been eight
people compensated for all vaccine injuries in Canada? In Canada,

a 'with covid' death can be ascertained almost instantly and, in many cases, even before the death certificate has even started to be filled out. An injury from a COVID-19 vaccine can take years to be adjudicated, if at all. The next update from Canada's vaccine injury program is expected by June 1, 2023. The betting line pays even money that they will be late.

The outrageous suppression of debate in the media, the grotesque assault on medical freedom, and the crooked machinations to keep vaccine injuries and deaths concealed. Welcome to Canada. We may never really arrive at an accurate number of those that got injured or died from the COVID-19 vaccines because it is in the interests of powerful people to keep this knowledge obscured from public scrutiny. What we did know in mid-2022 was that the leading cause of death in Alberta in 2021 was 'unknown causes', even though this death category didn't even exist before 2019. That Canada has a technologically advanced healthcare system and the leading cause of death in Alberta is 'unknown' is disconcerting, to say the least. Not to fear, a media celebrity doctor is here to explain:

Dr. Daniel Gregson: "*We do expect that there will be deaths that aren't directly related to COVID, but indirectly related to COVID to occur after the diagnosis in patients after the first month of infection...One would expect that some of those patients are going to survive the COVID and then die at home from other complications.*"[499]

Gregson never did explain how he knows that 'unknown' deaths are the result of COVID-19. But please do remember anything deemed bad medically since 2020 is the absolute fault of COVID-19, and the vaccines are nature's perfect elixir.

Sensing a disturbance in the force, another article dutifully found someone to tell us that *'Vaccines not causing unexplained deaths in Alberta.'*[500] No one had a clue about what caused these deaths (hence the word 'unknown') but what was firmly established, according to Alberta Health spokesperson Lisa Glover, is that they were absolutely not caused by the safe and effective vaccines and anyone that thinks this is just being silly. The article ended with *'we continue to encourage Albertans to get every dose which they are eligible for.'* An article about 'unknown deaths' in Alberta ends with a vaccination advertisement. The propaganda was almost too much to bear.

Not to be outdone by Alberta, New Brunswick's Shephard once again caught the attention of shocked Canadians when she announced that New Brunswick's unknown deaths in the latter half of 2021 were nearly 24% higher than expected (excess mortality).[501] This was the highest rate, by far, in Canada. An infectious disease/researcher at the University of Toronto, Tara Moriarty, flippantly speculated that it was probably COVID-19 deaths that were missed because, well, people were catching COVID-19 around this time:

"The overlap is almost perfect in time. So that's a really important clue that a lot of it is likely COVID related. The level of excess mortality in New Brunswick during that period is enormous. And if it's not COVID killing people, what the hell is it?"[502]

The 'overlap' was aligned with the vaccination campaign as well. But, once again, it is silly to think the vaccines had anything to do with all these unknown deaths, and you were smart as a whip if you speculated COVID-19 was responsible. Little did Ms. Moriarty realize that in New Brunswick, everything that possibly could be branded a COVID-19 death was recorded as a COVID-19 death, and the very idea that some COVID-19 deaths were overlooked in New Brunswick was patently absurd.

Am I suggesting that the unprecedented surge in unknown deaths in Canada is related to the vaccines? Don't be ridiculous. That vaccine deaths are the only category that takes forever to be recognized (if ever), and these unusual spikes in unknown deaths arrived at the same time as the vaccination bandwagon was rocking is purely coincidental. Get your mind out of the gutter.

From Taiwan to Toronto, the vaccine injury puzzle was not readily solved. The insidious trend was for authorities to drag their heels investigating and reporting vaccine injuries (in Canada, was this done so that more people would make the 'right' choice and take more shots?). The case could be made that those obstructing the discovery and disclosure of vaccine injuries were acting within a black or influence op. Please decide for yourself which agencies may have been doing the influencing. It could also be the case that this vaccine injury situation was yet another example of how the WHO's global reach had run amok.

In May 2022, the WHO released a report saying that the world's actual COVID-19 death toll was nearly 15 million compared to the 5.4 million deaths that had been officially reported at the time.[503] While the WHO may have stretched the limits of believability by clumping so many 'excess mortality' deaths under its COVID-19 umbrella, Dr. Samira Asma, from the WHO's data department said, *If we don't count the dead, we will miss the opportunity to be better prepared for the next time.* '[504] These words were oddly reminiscent of that of Freeland and Trudeau when they suggested the pandemic represented an 'opportunity.'

By 'better prepared,' what Asma may have meant was that the WHO was meeting soon to discuss changing *International Health Regulations'* and, expected by 2024, was their new *'International Treaty on Pandemic Prevention, Preparedness, and Response.* '[505] It only made sense when trying to convince members of the need for these new WHO pandemic powers that a higher COVID-19 death count was more persuasive than a lower one. Even with their elaborate models, the WHO conceded *'estimating the true mortality burden of COVID-19 for every country in the world is...difficult'* and *'Attributing deaths, direct or indirect, to COVID-19 is problematic.* '[506] A difficult proposition or not, the WHO set their mind to finding more 'with covid' deaths.

The WHO came up with the idea of comparing 'excess deaths' relative to deaths expected during 'normal times.' The WHO, at the end of their massive model documents, admitted they didn't adjust for heatwaves and global conflicts, which other modellers were doing at the time, and they also failed to comment on the myriad of other questions relating to excess morbidity. For example, did the WHO consider increases above expected rates during 'normal times' in things like suicide and overdose? Did they adjust for government lockdowns and mandates being indirectly responsible for deaths due to delaying or withholding care as some hospitals shuttered operations and nurses and doctors were forced to sit at home rather than work? Finally, did the WHO adjust for the Quebec phenomenon, one of the only Canadian provinces to openly acknowledge COVID-19 deaths could be overstated by 40-50%? No. Of course not. Instead of adjusting for government overreach contributing to excess mortality, or considering the vaccines played a role in at least some deaths, the WHO rationalized, like the 'experts' in Alberta and New Brunswick, that these unknown deaths were COVID-19 deaths. Moreover, the WHO affirmed its COVID-19 death coding mandates were beyond reproach.

"Some deaths that are attributable to COVID-19 have not been certified as such because tests had not been conducted prior to death. Deaths may also have been mistakenly certified as COVID-19, though this is less likely."[507]

And there you have it. It is 'less likely' that deaths with COVID-19 were overstated because the WHO model makers said so. At times during the pandemic, my fondness of models waned to the point where 'models' became a euphemism for 'man-made lies.' If Canada is anything like a microcosm of many other places in the world, it is not possible that COVID-19 deaths were three times larger than the official estimates. There is plenty of evidence that strongly suggests Canadian COVID-19 deaths are overstated.

To be fair, there are some countries like India and China that likely did downplay COVID-19 deaths. In the case of India, during the 2021 upswing in cases, a local doctor noted:

"Many deaths are not getting recorded, and they are increasing every day...they don't want to create panic."[508]

I cannot vouch for India's COVID-19 data; no one can, but what I can say is that India may be on the WHO's hit list because some are not fond of the country questioning its 'universal legitimacy'. When governments were adopting WHO guidelines to capture as many COVID-19 as possible, you could convincingly theorize that higher deaths were necessary to help spread fear, increase demand for vaccines, make longer-term mandates viable, and help vaccine passport initiatives run smoothly. India was one of the few countries not only resisting vaccine passports but also the WHO's COVID-19 death coding decrees:

"According to sources, the [Indian] government has formed a death audit committee in every district to determine the primary cause of deaths. After the first wave in 2020, the State government issued an order directing an audit of all COVID-19 deaths. Only cases where the primary reason of death is determined to be COVID-19 would be classified as "COVID-19 deaths", the order stated. "The committee, consisting of civil hospital doctors and others, does not count any comorbid death as a COVID-19 death. Only those deaths where the cause is viral pneumonia is considered as a COVID death and counted in the official figures."[509]

Only deaths where COVID-19 is *'the primary reason of death'* should be recorded as COVID-19 deaths. Makes sense to me. By contrast, what doesn't make sense is when the updated WHO COVID-19 death estimates *'includes those who died from other illnesses but could not be treated because of Covid.'*[510] Who determines, exactly, who could not be treated because of COVID-19? Canadian hospitals were operating in crisis mode before COVID-19 came along, and now, because the WHO said so, every medical case that involves a lack of treatment is a COVID-19 death? In July 2022, a man at a Fredericton hospital died after waiting hours in the Emergency Room for care.[511] New Brunswick was also dealing with many cities closing Emergency Rooms due to a lack of staff.[512] From June-July 2022, there were also ER or complete hospital closures in PEI,[513] Ontario,[514] Manitoba,[515] Alberta,[516] BC,[517] and Quebec.[518] Were all these closures the fault of COVID-19 too?

Occam's razor says the WHO didn't care for India's renegade ways and the country's challenge to its COVID-19 sermons, and this was the reason why the WHO singled out and heaped scorn in India's direction. China, on the other hand, which marched to its own drummer and has never produced an honest statistic of any sort ever, was given a pass by the WHO. One wonders why.

India's efforts to classify deaths by the cause of death and not whether someone happened to test positive for COVID-19 was slowly catching on in other parts of the world. For example, consider what Canada's largest province, Ontario, started doing in March 2022:

"...the province will start breaking down deaths into three categories: whether COVID-19 contributed to a death, whether COVID-19 caused a death, or if the cause of death is unknown or missing from provincial data. This change will provide a more accurate representation of deaths that are due to COVID-19 rather than all deaths in people with COVID-19."[519]

You could make the case that this is positive news and that more transparency is excellent. You might also ask who is being fired or arrested for reporting nearly 2-years of garbage data. Anyone?

The overriding aim is not to incessantly denigrate the WHO, or a body I have assailed but actually carry a great deal of ambivalence toward. Rather, the goal is, and will always be, to throw light on the fact that when it comes to COVID-19, the word 'science' has been weaponized. In this respect, elements of the WHO, CDC, PHAC, and countless other organizations are weapon manufacturers, and when anyone questions their marching orders, they become the enemy. To illustrate this consider Ontario's chief medical officer of health, Dr. Kieran Moore, who, in July 2022, broke from authoritarian COVID-19 conventions:

"At present, we're doing a risk-based approach....there's always a

risk to, to having any therapeutic versus a benefit. You want to make sure there's a very strong benefit versus a risk. If we're an 18-year-old, healthy individual, the risk of getting hospitalized if we have no underlying medical illness is very, very low. We know there is a very small risk one in 5000 that may get myocarditis, for example, and you'd have to have that discussion on the risk-benefit of a complication from the vaccine versus a benefit of decreased hospitalization. For a young, healthy person. "[520]

What Dr. Moore said is that COVID-19 vaccines and boosters may not universally be the best health decision for all age groups or all health conditions. On this point, he is absolutely 100% right. People should talk with their doctor about the risks/rewards of the vaccines, do some research, and make an informed choice that is best for them. By merely suggesting a 'risk-based approach,' Dr. Moore was questioning the government's blanket mandating orders, and he was attacked on social media for doing so.

We should not have the government taking on the role of our doctor. COVID-19 demonstrated that governments are incapable of treating people as individuals and that their insane quest for the 'greater good' can harm minority groups of people. While I consider Dr. Moore's words spot on, remember that he got swept up in the covid-mania in 2021. Moore separated kids from sports based upon their vaccination status, and he segregated kids from attending school (i.e., unvaccinated kids in Ontario could not go to school for ten days after a COVID-19 infection at the school while vaccinated kids could). Where was Moore's 'risk-based approach' that he extolled in July 2022 and back in 2021? Did his hesitancy to speak honestly about the vaccines in 2021 have anything to do with his historical ties to Pfizer?[521]

This idea that medicine can be prescribed by a government or that a one-size fits all box of new medical laws must be followed by doctors is not going away even if the pandemic ends. Rather, many countries are still lobbying for the adoption of the new pandemic response treaty. Such a treaty could make Dr.

Moore's words punishable by the pandemic police.

"WHO is the organization with universal legitimacy to implement the International Health Regulations."

The idea that the WHO should have more say, and not less, about global health decisions is unbearably grotesque. If Canadians can't trust and have their voices heard by elected leaders like Trudeau, Higgs, or Legault, what input would we have if the WHO was awarded more authority? It is not as simple as saying the WHO is anti-science or evil. It's that their financial backers, which can vary year to year, may not always be aligned with the rights and freedoms of individuals. The second largest backer of the WHO is The Bill & Melinda Gates Foundation.[522] I don't want Bill Gates as my doctor. The 6th largest contributor is GAVI Alliance. I don't want GAVI Alliance to be my doctor. Then there is China, whose real bond with the WHO might never be known and that won't allow any other COVID-19 vaccine into the country in favour of its own concoctions. I don't want China to be my doctor (or to look after my pets)! Finally, big pharma often follows the Wall Street tradition of not admitting or denying guilt when they pay out billions to settle lawsuits. I don't want big pharma to be my doctor, either!

This is one of the most serious issues of the entire pandemic. After all, if omicron had not come along, it is plausible all the vaccine passports would still be in place, kids would still be masked all day long, and vaccination and boosters would be mandatory. This pandemic tested our institutions. It froze or obliterated the rights of Canadians and turned otherwise peaceful people against their neighbours. People need to remember that while Dr. Moore seems to be part of the solution today, he and his ilk were a huge part of the problem yesterday. There are only two people that should ultimately oversee your health decisions - you and your doctor.

To recap, according to our government, more than 10,000 serious vaccine injuries have happened in Canada, and there have only been eight cases where the injured have been compensated. Canada was the last G7 nation to adopt a vaccine injury program, and thus far, it has proven to be a national disgrace. When added to the litany of all the other dirty covid-deeds, it is abundantly clear that the Canadian government is not for transparency, scientific discovery, and doing what is in your best interest.

Chapter 29 - Collusion, Contagion, and The Cardinal Sin

When the pandemic first started, a cogent voice grew out of the chaos to tell us the following:

February 28, 2020: *"If one assumes that the number of asymptomatic or minimally symptomatic cases is several times as high as the number of reported cases, the case fatality rate may be considerably less than 1%. This suggests that the overall clinical consequences of COVID-19 may ultimately be more akin to those of a severe seasonal influenza (which has a case fatality rate of approximately 0.1%)..."*[523]

This prophetic voice of wisdom was telling us that on an all-case mortality rate, COVID-19 could end up being no deadlier than a bad flu season. This voice was none other than Anthony S. Fauci. Eleven days later, getting swept up in the pandemonium seizing the globe, Fauci raised his less than 0.1% COVID-19 fatality rate estimate to more than ten times this level. Welcome to COVID-19.

March 11, 2020 - Fauci said COVID-19 is at least ten times "more lethal" than the seasonal flu[524]

The prognosticators, epidemiologists, experts, modellers, or whatever you want to call them, are the group that helped put the word panic into the pandemic. This cohort jumped to reckless conclusions, rushed to publish, and, in many cases, wanted to parlay their know-how into being famous or rich. In October 2020, three doctors signed the Great Barrington Declaration (GBD),[525] contending that repressive COVID-19 policies and the *'devastating effects'* of the lockdowns needed to be stopped immediately. These doctors never made it onto the MSM once. Conversely, people like Fisman and Furness had never treated a patient, yet they lived in the news and were a primary information source for an adoring public. This quarantining of information and cancelling anyone that disagreed with the allowed COVID-19 talking points was theatre of an evil order, and we may never truly know the full extent of this propaganda system. However, what we should do is acknowledge that it happened and, when possible, hold the perpetrators accountable.

Below is an email from then Director of the NIH, Dr. Francis Collins, sent to Dr. Fauci on October 8, 2020:

"See https://gbdeclaration.org/. This proposal from three fringe epidemiologists who met with the Secretary seems to be getting a lot of attention - and even a co-signature from Nobel prize winner Mike Leavitt at Stanford. There needs to be a quick and devastating published takedown of its premise. I don't see anything like that online yet - is it underway?"[526]

Like a mob boss putting out a hit, Dr. Collins gave the order that the GBD needed to be taken out and that the best way to do this was a *'quick and devastating published takedown.'* Fauci followed orders and went to work plotting against GBD and singling out their sympathizers. Collins, Fauci, and their lower-level tactical warriors are part of the reason why even today, many people have never heard of the GBD.

Those that think this was an isolated hit should think again. The NIH didn't care about understanding COVID-19, natural immunity, or about being transparent - they cared about vaccines! In the first year of the pandemic, only 2% of the NIH's grant budget was allocated toward COVID-19 research, while nearly 50% was funnelled into *'pharmaceutical interventions research.'*[527] Moreover, the NIH had been working on coronavirus vaccines well before there was ever really any demand or need for coronavirus vaccines:

November 11, 2021: *"Moderna's vaccine, which appears to provide the world's best defense against COVID-19, grew out of four years of collaboration with research scientists at the N.I.H.'s Vaccine Research Center."*[528]

Like an anxious ball player after years in the minors, the NIH made the determination early in the pandemic that it was time to start taking swings in the big leagues. Once the decision was made that the vaccines were the chosen path out of the pandemic, contradicting this edict became sacrilegious. Remember, comrades, the lockdowns and closures are for the greater good, and the vaccines are going to be a home run!

Rep. Jim Jordon: *"31,000 people [at the CDC and NIH] spending $58 billion dollars a year. Why hasn't our government done a study on natural immunity?"*
Dr. Martin A. Makary: *"If I can be honest, Representative Jordan, I don't think they want to know the answer. It would undermine the indiscriminate vaccine/ vaccination policy for every single human being, including extremely low-risk people."*[529]

With the mission of injecting as much of the world as possible with mRNA, the CDC was charged with suppressing incompatible data and impugning anyone who dared challenge the narrative. The CDC complied.

July 27, 2022 - *"The Centers for Disease Control and Prevention coordinated with social media companies and Google to censor users who expressed skepticism or criticism of COVID-19 vaccines, according to a trove of internal communications obtained by America First Legal."*[530]

Before I was fully awakened in late 2020, I often wondered why Google search results for vaccine side effects and injuries seemed to be limited to certain shot-friendly sources and why so many COVID-19-related videos seemed to go missing from YouTube suddenly. That it was just some good ol' fashion collusion is weirdly comforting, as part of me at the time thought I might be losing my mind.

Facebook was also holding a pandemic hootenanny, and only the pro-vaccine crowd was invited. If you mentioned on Facebook that there were plenty of peer-reviewed studies that said masks could not limit the spread, you were banned. Utter the word 'vaccine' with a disparaging tone - banned. Facebook's truth police even went so far as to ban peer-reviewed papers, including a November 2021 study entitled '*COVID-19: Researcher blows the whistle on data integrity issues in Pfizer's vaccine trial.*'[531] This study was from the BMJ, which has been around for more than 180 years and is one of the most respected medical journals in the world. The BMJ's editor-in-chief was not impressed:

"We should all be very worried that Facebook, a multibillion-dollar company, is effectively censoring fully fact-checked journalism that is raising legitimate concerns about the conduct of clinical trials. Facebook's actions won't stop The BMJ doing what is right, but the real question is: why is Facebook acting in this way? What is driving its worldview? Is it ideology? Is it commercial interests? Is it incompetence? Users should be worried that, despite presenting itself as a neutral social media platform, Facebook is trying to control how people think..."[532]

Also gung-ho to try and control what people thought was Biden's White House, which provided $1 billion to the U.S. Department of Health & Human Services to purchase narrative affirming advertising on TV, Radio, Print, & Social Media.[533] These ads were specifically '*aimed at convincing every American to get vaccinated*'[534] (after March 15, 2021, the White House also kicked in $40 for every dose that anyone administered[535]). These vaccines were going to be a grand slam!

Not to be outdone, The Bill & Melinda Gates Foundation (Gates) was also throwing obscene amounts of money around right before the COVID-19 vaccines went live. Gates' had always donated to causes to harvest influence and favourable coverage in the media,[536] and there is a trail of at least $319 million that went to media for what some say was '*to promote his global agenda.*'[537] However, when COVID-19 arrived, the money became more focused on anything vaccine or pandemic related. For example, despite not receiving much money from Gates in the past, Tshwane University in China received four grants in 2020 totalling nearly $4 million, all of which were COVID-19 or pandemic related. Then there was CNN, which got $3.6 million in September 2020 despite having never been given a grant before. Since the CNN grant Bill Gates has appeared on network at least 20 times,[538] predictably to mostly friendly questions.

Sifting through the 31,000+ grants that have been doled out by Gates can be both cumbersome and fascinating.[539] Ever wonder why people accuse Gates of wanting to biochip people, block part of the sun out by shooting chemicals in the atmosphere, and spray vaccines on people, like pesticides on crops? It is probably because someone read and then (maybe) exaggerated the meaning behind one of these grants.[22] An example is a 2005 grant to Harvard University for $8.7 million *'to develop needle-free vaccination via nanoparticle aerosols.'* The conspiracy inclined are not likely to conclude nanoparticle aerosols could be an excellent and safe way to distribute vaccines.

Along with giving the WHO at least 39 grants totalling more than $274 million in 2020 and GAVI Alliance $1.8 billion as the vaccines launched, here is just a tiny sampling of what Gates was up to in 2020:

March 2020 - University of Washington Foundation - $100,000 *"to support the modeling of COVID-19"*.

March 2020 - Beth Israel Deaconess Medical Center Inc. - $4.3 million *"to establish animal models for COVID-19 infection, to define the pathogenesis and immunology of infection, and to utilize these models to test vaccines and/or therapeutics."*

April 2020 - Biological E. Limited - $4 million *"to respond to the COVID-19 pandemic by developing a SARS-CoV-2 vaccine."*

May 2020 - SK Bioscience Co., Ltd. - $3.6 million *"to develop a COVID-19 vaccine..."*

---

[22] Bill Gates also owns Cascade Investment, L.L.C., which people constantly scrutinize to flush out speculations about Gates' intentions.

May 2020 - Evidation Health Inc - $242 thousand *"to develop a digital biomarker of COVID-19..."*

May 2020 - Karolinska Institutet - $353 thousand *"to develop a COVID-19 vaccine."*

May 2020 - Stanford University - $243 thousand *"to support animated storytelling for Global COVID-19 prevention."*

June 2020 - InnoCore Pharmaceuticals - $1.5 million *"to develop a long-acting biodegradable drug delivery implant."*

June 2020 - PATH - $615 thousand *"to develop a COVID-19 vaccine candidate that could be produced using the existing influenza virus vaccine manufacturing facilities."*

June 2020 - Columbia University - $5 million *"to aid countries responding to COVID-19 with coordinated data and modeling support."*

July 2020 - Novavax, Inc - $15 million *"to evaluate the safety, immunogenicity, and potential efficacy of a candidate vaccine to prevent COVID-19..."*

August 2020 - Institute for Strategic Dialogue US - $199 thousand *"to research public discourse on vaccines in Germany..."*

August 2020 - ProMed Pharma LLC - $942 thousand *"to develop a long-acting biodegradable drug delivery implant."*

August 2020 - University of Washington Foundation - $75 thousand *"to use models to project where COVID-19 cases are likely to be surging in the next 4-12 weeks..."*

September 2020 - Open Cities Lab - $1.6 million *"to help journalists better cover the COVID-19 pandemic in Africa by building a data hub that will improve their ability to identify stories and use visualizations and interactives in their coverage..."*

October 2020 - Northeastern University - $90 thousand *"to forecast 3-month incidence of COVID-19 for 60-120 countries in order to assist COVID-19 vaccine developers with clinical trial site selection."*

October 2020 - Dalberg Catalyst - $2.8 million *"to support global vaccine delivery efforts..."*

November 2020 - PATH - $2.5 million *"to support clinical development of COVID-19 vaccines by Chinese manufacturers..."*

December 2020 - Wadhwani Institute for Artificial Intelligence Foundation - $224 thousand *"to support the use of big data, predictive data analysis, and artificial intelligence in the response to COVID-19."*

Last, and unfortunately not least, was the indiscriminate censorship from the Amazon.com regime. When former New York Times journalist and bestselling author, Alex Berenson, went to sell a booklet about COVID-19 on Amazon, he was greeted with the following:

"Your book does not comply with our guidelines. As a result, we are not offering your book for sale.
Due to the rapidly changing nature of information around the COVID-19 virus, we are referring customers to official sources for health information about the virus. Please consider removing references to COVID-19 for this book."[540]

The world's largest bookseller banned ideas and thoughts about COVID-19 that didn't conform to the 'official sources' of truth. Yes, this happened. A version of this also happened in Canada in June 2022 when Indigo Books refused to carry[541] Andrew Lawton's bestselling book *'The Freedom Convoy: The Inside Story of Three Weeks that Shook the World.'*[542] Indigo declined to say why the book would not be placed on its shelves. Did it have something to do with the fact that founder and CEO of Indigo Books and Music, Heather Reisman, was Chrystia Freeland's Bilderberg buddy?

It may be difficult for some people to fathom that special interests, or a mélange of money and power, had command over the COVID-19 'science' they were being spoon-fed. Quite frankly, many Canadians ensconced in government' curated anxiety may never believe anything but the official story. But the unfortunate truth is that to keep some special interests satisfied, it was compulsory that the WHO, governments, the media, and people like Fauci and Fisman all played their roles. This sanctimonious society of pandemic warriors worked tirelessly to trash any viewpoints remotely related to the GBD, ban people like Dr. Robert Malone from the internet,[543] vilify protesters, and defame anyone that refused to accept the clinical vaccine trials as their lord and saviour. In the beginning, the case could be made that some greater good pro-vaccination deity was being served. In the end, they were just making it up as they went along.

July 7, 2022 - *"Disregard anything we said about 2 doses, it's now 3 doses or more."*[544]

August 2, 2022 - Court Documents Reveal Canada's Travel Ban Had No Scientific Basis[545]

Even as opposing views were suffocated by the tremendous militarized media machine, there were some anomalous strays not conforming to doctrine. This dissent would quickly be deemed heresy and needed to be expunged, with force if necessary. People in Trudeau's office sent notifications to journalists saying they were being watched,[546] Ontario police showed up on a person's doorstep to warn them about their Facebook posts,[547] and in Australia, they arrested people for Facebook posts.[548] Then there were Asian countries, which early in the pandemic arrested at least 266 people for what AFP said was 'fake [covid] news':

"Authorities say criminalisation is needed to curb the online flood of dangerous fake cures and conspiracy theories that the World Health Organization has called an "infodemic.""[549]

That it was the WHO that had coined the new playful Orwellian word 'infodemic' was, of course, not surprising. Early in the pandemic, 132 member states signed a *'Cross-Regional Statement on "Infodemic" in the Context of COVID-19.'* Some of the interesting notes from the statement were as follows:

"In times of the COVID-19 health crisis, the spread of the "infodemic" can be as dangerous to human health and security as the pandemic itself...we call on everybody to immediately cease spreading misinformation and to observe UN recommendations to tackle this issue." [550]

Was it really 'misinformation' to posit that the lockdowns could be doing more harm than the virus itself? Was it also 'misinformation' to factually state the mRNA vaccines were still in Phase 3 clinical trials (i.e., 'experimental')? One of the commandments from the WHO was thou shall *'observe UN recommendations'* because the 'infodemic' is as dangerous as COVID-19. The grandiose audacity was astonishing.

Tedros never did and likely never will concede that much of what was promoted as vaccine gold in 2021 turned out to be foolishly wrong. This is not what pandemic dictators do. Instead, Tedros was back in 2022 rereading his script, this time with the 'monkeypox' outbreak:

July 27, 2022 - *"The stigma and discrimination can be as dangerous as any virus and can fuel the outbreak. As we have seen with COVID-19, misinformation and disinformation can spread rapidly online. So we call on all social media platforms, tech companies, and news organizations to work with us to prevent and counter harmful information."* [551]

On July 23, 2022, the WHO declared the monkeypox outbreak a *'Public Health Emergency of International Concern.'* [552] This was two months after the province of Quebec had already started its monkeypox vaccination program (no, this is not a joke) [553] and nearly two weeks after Quebec surpassed 3,000 monkeypox vaccinations. [554] No word on if Legault and Trudeau are considering mandates and health taxes to combat the monkeypox.

For those catching the drift, debating ideas and scientific discoveries in open forums was never an option with the COVID-19 pandemic. Crushing those that strayed from the narrative was. With greedy corporate powers coalescing with political might and philanthropy dollars, this was a brand of collated collusion, the likes of which had never been seen before. And if Tedros' repetitious monkeypox sermons were any indication, this trend looks set to continue in earnest. Beware of what words and images you allow into your brain, as they may be designed with devious intent.

As the dust continued to settle, more information, like bodies rising to the surface, continued to be discovered. Former White House Coronavirus Response Coordinator, Dr. Deborah Birx, on May 24, 2022, had a massive announcement:

"I had briefed the White House multiple times on the difference between protection from disease and protection from infection. And I said multiple times this vaccine is only being studied for protection against disease, not infection. We didn't test participants in the trial on a regular basis to see if they were asymptomatically and mildly infected..."[555]

Dr. Birx was the one standing beside Maestro Fauci as President Trump berated reporters like Acosta in 2020. Now she was crapping on the vaccine trials. On July 22, 2022, Birx sharpened her story and said, '*I knew these vaccines were not going to protect against infection, and I think we overplayed the vaccines...* '[556] Wow. Along with these shocking soundbites, Birx contended in an interview with *The Center for Strategic and International Studies* that she had been writing to '*people inside the administration*' and contacting media sources to break her vaccine story since February 2021. Dr. Birx was allegedly being shunned.

"What people came back to me and said was that no one wanted to discourage people against vaccination."[557]

Was Birx another shocking whistleblower like former CBC reporter Marianne Klowak? Was she about to become the highest ranking U.S. policymaker to blow the lid off the COVID-19 policy deceptions and show us yet another layer of information suppression? In a word, no.

First off, what Birx neglected to mention is that on multiple occasions in December 2020, she publicly endorsed the vaccines, and she speculated about herd immunity being reached at 70-80% vaccination rates.[558] The idea that Birx knew the vaccines couldn't limit transmission at the same time she was touting herd immunity doesn't mesh. One of her is lying. There is also the lengthy interview Birx gave ABC on December 16, 2020, where there was not even a hint that she knew the shots did not stop transmission:

"I understand how this vaccine was made. I understand the safety of the vaccine. And critically, I understand the depth of the efficacy of this vaccine. This is one of the most highly effective vaccines we have in our infectious disease arsenal. And so that's why I'm very enthusiastic about the vaccine."[559]

To be clear, in December 2020, 'highly effective' for a vaccine didn't mean against hospitalization and death. It meant against transmission (remember, it would take until September 2021 before the definition of 'vaccine' would be changed). Next, on January 24, 2001, no longer employed by the White House, Birx gave a full-length interview on Face the Nation. She only mentioned vaccines once - *'we had great innovation in vaccines.'*[560] In her 2022 account, Birx says she was urgently trying to blow the lid off the great vaccine scandal since February 2021, which was days after she appeared on Face the Nation, where she could have blown the lid then.

That Dr. Birx finally gathered the temerity to say she knew all along the vaccines wouldn't limit transmission around the same time her 2022 book was launching sounded more like opportunism than whistleblowing. And while fact-stretching in a capitalist society is not exactly death penalty worthy, when Fauci was 'taking care' of things, he emailed Birx informing her of the plot against the GBD.[561] All the juicy stuff in the email was redacted, but I don't think Fauci was asking his good friend Birx to help him bake the GBD doctors a cake. Birx is not to be admired or considered brave for coming forward 16 months after she says she knew the vaccines didn't work. She should be investigated and maybe even charged.

What the Birx story highlights is that the 'vaccines are peachy-keen' narrative, even for people that knew it was fictitious and overplayed, was parroted by all policymakers. If you stepped out of the prescribed path, you got gone; it was that simple. Despite her newfound moral compass Birx was a major cog in the systematic covid-collusion that gripped the globe in 2020-21.

One person that did walk her own path was Dr. Naomi Wolf. Dr. Wolf provoked the ire of the COVID-19 narrative mob in part because she *'bombards her 142k followers with messages about vaccine side effects, the profits of big pharma, and the negative impact of masks on children.'*[562] By asking these types of legitimate questions, Dr. Wolf was de-platformed from social media and ostracized. Wolf insightfully encapsulated the situation:

"The rest of the world, at least on the progressive side in the United States, became increasingly cult-like and insular in its thinking since March of 2020. As the months passed, friends and colleagues of mine who were highly educated and who had been lifelong critical thinkers, journalists, editors, researchers, doctors, philanthropists, teachers, psychologists - all began to repeat only talking points from MSNBC and CNN, and soon overtly refused to look at any sources - even peer-reviewed sources in medical journals - even CDC data - that contradicted those talking points. These people literally said to me, "I don't want to see that; don't show it to me." It became clear soon enough that if they absorbed information contradictory to "the narrative" that was consolidating, they risked losing social status, maybe even jobs; doors would close, opportunities would be lost."[563]

I am not saying I agree with all her opinions, only that as Dr. Wolf was standing up for *'human rights, freedom of speech, critical thinking, real science,'*[564] powerful forces were trying to shove her to the ground. The smear campaign launched against Wolf was extensive and ferocious, and news organizations that once adored her would not speak with her. Fellow feminist Trudeau didn't single Wolf out, even though he did think that she was a racist misogynist with unacceptable views.

Collins, Fauci, Birx, the CDC, NIH, big tech, big pharma, the White House, Gates, and a myriad of others colluded inside the fog of covid-chaos to smother any and all voices of dissent. Their influence and reach were so overwhelming that even those that knew what was really going on were too afraid to disagree. Although not said out loud, it became quickly understood that access to media, grants, and advertising dollars went to those that conformed to the COVID-19 narrative. In this respect, the act of shunning and punishing those that questioned the vaccination plan became as contagious as the virus itself, and the very idea of questioning the immaculate vaccines became a cardinal sin.

Ironically, one of the many 'published takedowns' of the GBD arrived before Collins' email to Fauci, and it focused exclusively on how money was influencing the authors of the GBD. The idea that billionaires were supporting the GBD due to some secret master plan to subvert the awesomeness of the vaccines was, of course, laughable. Equally amusing was that one of the authors of this paper had *'received research funding from Gavi, the Vaccine Alliance (Gavi) and the Bill & Melinda Gates Foundation.'*[565] In light of all the lockdown, mask mandates, and vaccine shots failing to contain COVID-19, this article did not age well.

What did improve with age is the ability of doctors to speak their minds freely about COVID-19. The GBD was originally authored and signed by three doctors, with an additional 43 doctors co-signing the declaration. As of January 18, 2022, more than 17,000 doctors and scientists had signed the 'Rome Declaration'[566] which contended, among other once 'unacceptable views', that the vaccines should not be given to kids and natural immunity needs to be recognized. The Rome Declaration provided some evidence that cracks in the narrative were forming.

As for that once cogent voice of wisdom erupting from the chaos to tell us that COVID-19 would likely be no worse than the flu, he is long gone. Taking his place is a psychopath who complains that the tyrannical policies that were a catastrophic failure for more than two years can only succeed if WHO-mandated thoughts are universally accepted. To be sure, dictator Fauci said in July 2022 that due to *'social media misinformation and disinformation, it's very difficult to get people to adhere to common sense Public Health measures.'*[567] One cannot help but wonder why people still listen to this madman. Perhaps it is because they don't think they have a choice. YouTube continues to echo Faucispeak and bans that which is against whatever remnants of the narrative remain:

"YouTube doesn't allow claims about COVID-19 vaccinations that contradict expert consensus from local health authorities or the World Health Organization."[568]

Money, power, and clandestine influencers continue to rule, at least part of the day.

Chapter 30 - The Top Pandemic Dictator

"If you are making wildly disparaging comments about the vaccine and have no public health expertise, you may be responsible for someone's death. Shut up." ~ Steve Edwards, CEO of CoxHealth Hospital in Springfield[569]

I acknowledge I am probably nearing the point when I should shut up. But what Mr. Edwards was unaware of is that, akin to Xi and Trump, I seldom allow what I think are fallacious statements to go unanswered. Those that lied and said these shots could end COVID-19 were responsible for deliberately harming people - wake up, Steve! Hopefully, my habit of growing distressed with those that aggravate me will evolve, and life will revert to some form of calmness. However, I doubt tranquility and Shangri-La are in my immediate future.

This chapter is a grab-bag that didn't make it into the meat and potatoes of the book. Like exiling cobwebs festering in your mind, it is preferable to unpack a closing inundation of anger, bewilderment, and amusement in this space rather than carry it around moving forward. The applicable psychological term might be emotional offloading. This chapter doesn't flow chronologically, but it is necessary to build momentum toward the declaration of the Top Pandemic Dictator (TPD). In the words of freedom fighter Tyson Billings, who spent 116 days in jail after the Freedom Convoy and pleaded guilty to a single charge of counselling to commit mischief, 'Let's Go!'[570]

The first order of business is David N. Fisman. An inordinate amount of time was dedicated looking at Fisman, a person that I believe is so politically destitute he should not even be considered a mathematic modeller. On January 21, 2021, it was reported that Fisman was *'paid by teacher union for arguing against school reopenings.'*[571] Premier Doug Ford expressed concern that this incident was a conflict of interest given that Fisman was on the Ontario Science Table. This was the same Science Table that went from updating us on vaccine injuries in early 2021 to ignoring or delaying these updates by late 2021 (yep, Fisman was on this board, which explains a lot).

Before his trash study that nearly every Liberal politician cheered in 2022,[572] Fisman was playing politics when he resigned from the Science Board in August 2021 or when he claimed his peers were withholding 'grim' COVID-19 projections.[573] At the time, politicians used Fisman's unsubstantiated theatrics to support their vaccine mandate election wedge. What few realized is that before the pandemic turned overtly political, Fisman co-authored a study in May 2020 suggesting that up to *'63% of the Ontario population could catch COVID-19.'*[574] Fisman 2021-2022, who posited that COVID-19 could be controlled, would have most certainly called Fisman 2020 an idiot. This was all politics, folks.

Despite not being elected to anything, Fisman - who previously *'served on advisory boards related...SARS-CoV-2 vaccines for...Pfizer, AstraZeneca'*[575] - had successfully infiltrated multiple channels of influence and exhibited many crafty characteristics of a dirt bag tyrant.

January 27, 2021 - *"I am grateful for the expertise and advice of @DFisman and for the conversations he has had with me." ~* Chrystia Freeland

After Fisman comes the Cardy parade. I've always doubted the idea that some kismet force is propelling us through our brief existence on this planet. But when Cardy's big mouth landed him in hot water, again, I began to doubt my doubts.

January 21, 2021 - Cardy unleashes Twitter tirade against Fredericton police over planned protest[576]

January 25, 2021 - Cardy's tweets about Fredericton police went too far, council says[577]

January 27, 2022 - Police officer union demands Cardy's removal from cabinet[578]

January 27, 2022 - Higgs says Cardy's police criticism uncalled for[579]

January 30, 2022 - Education minister in N.B. under fire over
Twitter thread on how police handled protest[580]
*"On Friday, January 21st, Minister Cardy attempted to influence,
direct and/or interfere with police operations within the
Fredericton Police Force."*

Cardy came even closer than Marco to being canned, yet he
somehow survived. Cardy also received another helping of karma
in mid-2022 when he, still acting like a petulant child, flipped out
about the airline crisis in Canada.

June 13, 2022 - N.B. education minister sparks conversation after
calling for deregulation of airline industry[581]

July 3, 2022 - N.B. cabinet minister blasts Air Canada for
cancellation, calls airline 'incompetent.'[582]

Cardy was right about Canadian airports being some of the
worst. But what he conveniently neglected to mention was that
COVID-19 restrictions were to blame. That a guy who says the
province owns kids would argue for airport deregulation is oddly
amusing. Although not running a country, Cardy and Fisman were
both, especially in their minds, TPDs.

As for the airport craziness, on June 29, 2022, the headline
read, *'Half of domestic flights to Canada's big airports delayed,
cancelled last week.'*[583] Instead of trying to fix the issues, Omar
did an Omar and brought back mandatory random COVID-19
testing to Canada's largest airports.[584] And yes, Omar's record of
punishing decrees while disregarding the rights of Canadians is a
sordid and remarkable trail of dictatorial carnage. However, he is
not eligible for TPD due to not having any idea what he was doing.

The Canadian airport chaos lent credence to the
conspiracists that believed that the pandemic tribulations were

being intentionally planned. Think about it: COVID-19 was still spreading rapidly throughout Canada, and there was no longer any contact tracing apparatus in place. Other than to keep power or control, what could be the motivation for bringing back a policy of randomly testing people? An IPSOS poll said 70% of Canadians thought 'the situation at Canadian airports is an embarrassment to Canada,'585 Angus Reid polling said only 25% of Canadians were still keen on vaccine passports,586 and no one was ecstatic about the ArriveCan app. Clearly, bringing back testing was not for political advantage.

One explanation for ignoring the science and the political winds was that this was still a dictator doing whatever he damn well pleased. Despite variants of the ArriveCan app having already been dropped by most countries long ago, Marco was ordered by Trudeau to sell the app to Canadians, so he did:

"ArriveCan was originally created for the purposes of COVID-19, but it has technological capacity beyond that to really shrink the amount of time that is required when you're getting screened at the border."[587]

Marco knew the ArriveCan app was slowing airport flow. He also knew how to lie. Fully vaccinated elderly Canadians returning home without the ArriveCan app were being harassed and told they had to quarantine for two weeks or risk being fined or arrested.[588,589] This government tracking app had strangely become a badge of honour that Emperor Trudeau planned to keep wearing forever, even as the National Airlines Council of Canada spoke up:

"The Public Health Agency of Canada's legacy pandemic-era health policies like ArriveCan cause significant delays in Canada's customs halls. ArriveCAN creates a confusing, complex journey for travellers and keeps Canada out of step with other countries."[590]

Should the ArriveCan app stick around, the conspiracy theorists will have another 'I told you so' moment. Canada was also a pilot partner for the WEF's *'Known Traveller Digital Identity'* technologies, which included things like biometrics and artificial intelligence to boost security and speed up International travel.[591] That Toronto Pearson Airport was ranked the world's worse for airport delays and was also dabbling in WEF witchcraft was oddly amusing.[592]

As the ArriveCan battle was heating up, Dorothy Shephard was told to vacate her position as Health Minister by Premier Higgs.[593] The move arrived after a man tragically died in a Fredericton hospital waiting room.[594] Despite her limited scope and the fact that she only caused heartache to those in New Brunswick, Shephard is a finalist for TPD, as is Ottawa's Diane Deans. In June 2022, Deans' pulled her name from Ottawa Mayor contention, partly blaming the effects of the Freedom Convoy. The victimized Deans' explained that she was *'shook'* when people started talking to *'politicians like they're not real people.'*[595] Deans' resume for COVID-19 folly stacks up against anyone. And for the record Ms. Deans, zero sedition and treason charges means that you should apologize for spreading misinformation to Canadians.

Next is Dr. Tam, who was repeatedly wrong about her shifting herd immunity goalposts and was always pushing vaccination. In 2019 Tam allowed her WHO pedigree and opinion of the 'anti-vaxxers' fly when she stated, *'they're a small number, but they're spreading misinformation...And they're communicating their opinions in a very emotional way.'*[596] The emotionally adverse Tam was speaking with Chatelaine Magazine, or one of the hundreds of magazines Trudeau had his claws dug into.[597] Tam didn't make idiotic or harassing statements like Legault or Duclos, but she did, slyly, display dictatorial qualities. One of her unusual encounters was in 2020 when she spoke with Santa Clause:

"I would like to officially declare you an essential worker in Canada and clear you to work on Christmas Eve."[598]

Although fairly light and jokey, the idea that Tam had the authority to declare who was an essential worker and clear people to work was a little on the nose. The next year the playfulness of Tam's Christmas banter turned outright creepy:

"Hey, kids, just popping in with an update to let you know everything is shaping up nicely for Christmas Eve. Santa, Mrs. Claus, and all the eligible elves have had their booster shots. Santa and his elves have the best layers of protection; his mask is well fitted, and the sleigh naturally ventilated. So I am happy to report that Santa has the all-clear to take off. I'm also happy to report that all of the reindeer are healthy and symptom-free, but just to be extra sure, Rudolph has had his COVID-19 test to confirm his red nose is not a COVID-19 concern..."[599]

Deeply entangled with the WHO and with by far the most pandemic experience, Tam may have been the key Canadian figure operating behind the curtain and handing Trudeau the script. She is in the running for the TPD list, even if she may not be able to crack the top 10.

Finally, there is Trudeau. What more can be said except to quickly overview the harm this one man helped inflict on kids. Trudeau had become so resolute about the idea of universal vaccination he started pursuing kids with urgency in 2022. Below is one of his speeches, given on January 6, 2022:

"I want to end today by speaking directly to kids, once again. I know many of you are in virtual school again. Many of you have made more sacrifices over Christmas over the holidays. Not seeing your friends, not seeing your loved ones, having to hunker down, having to help out around the house as your parents are working virtually. This is not easy. I know. Almost half of kids across this country have gotten their vaccine from ages five to 12. We need to get more, so please ask your parents if you can get vaccinated. Getting vaccinated protects yourself, protects your family, protects your grandparents, protects vulnerable people, but it also supports our frontline workers who are working incredibly hard are nurses and doctors and people in hospitals who are dealing with a rise in

cases. We know kids across this country, you've been doing the right things over these past long years. And it sucks, but you've been amazing. And we need to keep doing everything we can to get through this... [starts speaking Francais] I'm counting on all Canadians to continue to do the right thing."

At the height of the 2021 mandate/restriction mania, kids were told they could eat again with their friends if they got vaccinated, kids that were not vaccinated were booted from sports teams, and almost all kids in Canada, for a despicably prolonged period, were forced to wear cloth masks all day long. Trudeau created the conditions that made these harsh and psychologically damaging provincial practices possible. And during the entire time, he was reading a script. The above speech was eerily similar to a speech Trudeau gave to kids in March 2020.[600] A quick comparison is below:

March 2020: *"Thank you [kids] for helping your parents...for sacrificing your usual day."*
January 2022: *"Many of you have made more sacrifices over Christmas..."*

March 2020: Do what I say *"not just for ourselves, but for our grandparents, our nurses, our doctors, and everyone working in hospitals."*
January 2022: Do what I say because it *"protects yourself, protects your family, protects your grandparents, protects...nurses and doctors and people in hospitals."*

March 2020: *"Thank you...for trusting in science."*
January 2022: *"...you've been doing the right things over these past long years."*

The script may have evolved from *'social distance and wash your hands'* to *'take your vaccine,'* but the sentiment was the same: *Do as I say; we are all in this together.* But were we really all in this together? Kids that didn't have the shots were treated like second-class citizens, and it was inferred, repeatedly, by our Prime Minister that they had (or their parents) made the wrong choice. I'll come right out and say it - Trudeau's two speeches given 22 months apart were abhorrent and borderline psychopathic. A lot of kids were never worried about COVID-19, at least not until Trudeau's policies became predicated on doing everything humanly possible to make them worried.

In addition to the disturbing speeches, Trudeau also did infomercials where he spoke directly to kids and answered their questions. During one such Q&A on December 3, 2021, a six-year-old named Elana asked if she would still have to keep wearing a mask if she got vaccinated. A great question! Trudeau responded:

"You are going to have to wear a mask, sometimes, but the masks are going to work much better when more and more people are vaccinated."[601]

The perplexed six-year-old was probably thinking, 'what the heck is this guy smoking?' Lord Fauci had once caused an uproar in the U.S. because he tried to awkwardly justify his flip-flopping on whether citizens should be wearing masks. Trudeau got a pass on this logic-defying statement because barely anyone was watching. Another question from nine-year-old Brittany was equally concise, and Trudeau's response was equally baffling:

Question: *"Is the vaccine safe? Is there any side effects I should know about?"*

Trudeau: *"...Canadians can absolutely trust Health Canada and all the scientists, all the doctors who have looked at these vaccines and concluded, without a doubt, that the best thing to do to keep you safe from COVID 19 and to get through this as a country and a community is to get vaccinated."*

'Without a doubt'? Not only was Trudeau breaking WHO law and spreading disinformation, but he was also lying to a nine-year-old girl. In early December 2021, there were plenty of doubts about vaccine efficacy and heaps of vaccine injuries (both reported and many more not reported). Trudeau's non-answer was that of a sleazy salesman, and when he turned to government doctor Abdu Sharkawy it was more of the same:

"Prime Minister hit it on the head very nicely there. When you worry about side effects, we're talking about things like a sore arm. That will probably go away in a few days, you might have a little bit fatigue, and you might feel just a little bit rundown. But that will fade generally within a few days, and like the Prime Minister says, COVID is much, much worse even though it may be less serious in kids in general, it can be very serious and when it is that, it can really lead to some serious problems. And don't forget you can spread the virus to other people as well. So getting the vaccine is the right thing to do not just for yourself, but for everybody else."

An intelligent nine-year-old being told by a government doctor that *'getting the vaccine is the right thing to do.'* Shameful.

The tragic background worth highlighting is that kids suffered during the pandemic in Canada, and it had nothing to do with the virus. In an excellent article entitled *'Lockdown is the world's biggest psychological experiment - and we will pay the price,* '[602] Germany's Dr. Elke Van Hoof raised some interesting questions about the trauma that may result from locking down some 2.6 billion people. In the case of Canada, and more specifically, children, this trauma manifested immediately.

Early on, we knew that the lockdown and school closures would cause some issues in kids and families, and it would not take long before domestic violence was increasing, and studies started reporting that *'families with children <18 at home have experienced deteriorated mental health.* '[603] These initial data also led to a more rounded confirmation that *'the mental health impacts of the pandemic were greater for school-aged children during the first lockdown, underscoring the importance of in-class learning and extracurricular activities for children.* '[604] Responding to this crisis, pediatricians - at least those not saying kids could die from COVID-19 - started to warn of a host of problems in kids, including 'social malnutrition'. But what should have been a wakeup call for Canada to adopt Sweden's approach (in Sweden, schools were never shut, and there was no learning loss[605]) instead was met with more of the same:

"Yet the warning from pediatricians comes as some of their peers in the medical and scientific community call for even stricter measures to stall the spread of COVID-19."[606]

As Canadian policymakers tried to lockdown COVID-19 again and again and again, kids were suffering, largely in silence, again and again, and again. Finally, by late 2021 with child abuse rising and child suicide attempts way up,[607] the alarm bells were starting to ring louder. Fixated on the sound of a truck horn instead of the cries of children, Ottawa still wanted more lockdowns and more vaccination. Of the G10 nations, Canada was the only country that maintained a *'severe degree of restriction from spring 2020 onward,'[608]* and Canada was second to the U.S. for primary and secondary school closures.

"The impact of school closures and other aspects of the pandemic have really taken a heavy toll on children - and children are in a state of crisis."[609]

In early 2022, as Trudeau was telling kids to ask their parents if they could get vaccinated, more than 500 doctors in Ontario were demanding schools stay open *'regardless of case counts'* to stop the harm being inflicted on kids.[610] The Canadian Pediatric Society argued that *'certain decisions and measures pose a far greater risk to children and youth than the virus itself'* and that *'The deteriorating health and well-being of our children and youth is also a public health emergency.'[611]* Instead of responding to the real crisis impacting kids, Trudeau, on January 20, 2022, said that the vaccination rate was 'too low' amongst children,[612] and on January 27, 2022 - which was 'National Kids & Vaccines Day' in Canada - Trudeau let loose the following:

"To all of the parents out there: If you haven't gotten your kids vaccinated yet, please, get that taken care of as soon as you can.

It's the best thing you can do to keep them, and those around them, safe right now."[613]

Maybe Trudeau wanted to offload some of the extra pediatric COVID-19 doses he put a rush order on earlier in the month,[614] or maybe he was so out of touch with reality that he still assumed compelling more kids to take the shots served some purpose. Whatever the case, the manic rush by Trudeau to push more shots into kids' arms, along with his record of tyrannical COVID-19 declarations, earned him runner-up status for TPD.

You may be thinking, if not Trudeau, who could be the TPD? And the award goes to - drum roll...

* Benjamin Netanyahu *

Like a dark horse coming out of nowhere, the former Israeli Prime Minister wins! In the lengthy line of would-be pandemic dictators, Netanyahu is the person most responsible for sparking the COVID-19 vaccine mania, the mandates, and, more generally, flaunting epidemic-level hubris. The world may have been turning Chinese in 2020, but Netanyahu's Israel was the key trendsetter for most of 2021. In one of his most memorable lines from his WEF speech in January 2021, Netanyahu decreed:

"The reason we did well in Israel is one because we purchased a lot [of vaccines] fast. We didn't quibble about the price. I personally got involved... You know, you'll pay a few more dollars for those now, and tomorrow everybody will be paying ten times that much..."[615]

Netanyahu's cocky words and overt vaccine nationalism were novel in January 2021. It was like the Lukid leader sparked a vaccine frenzy similar to the Dutch tulip mania, all by himself. Following his hyperbolic words, Netanyahu went above and beyond many degrees of bonkers to lock down TPD. First, in one of the biggest coincidences in history, Netanyahu postponed his own corruption trial by simply closing the courts on March 15,

2020, due to the pandemic.[616] The outrage was wild. Netanyahu didn't care. Days later, Netanyahu would order that cell phones immediately be tracked due to rising COVID-19 cases. Anyone that didn't like this infringement on freedom could take up their complaint with the courts, which were closed. During a prime-time news conference, Netanyahu explained why he reluctantly had to take this step:

"Up until today, I avoided using these measures in the civilian population, but there is no choice."[617]

A few days later, Netanyahu held another televised event and demanded that since COVID-19 cases were rising, people must stay at home. President Xi could be heard whispering: 'Who the hell does this guy think he is?'

"Under these orders, you, Israel's citizens, are required to stay at home. It is no longer a request, it is not a recommendation, it is an obligatory directive that will be enforced by enforcement authorities."[618]

Following this announcement, protests with more than ten people were broken up, fines were handed out, and arrests were made. This was now a fight for democracy![619]

Given that he was ousted from office on June 2, 2022, Netanyahu oversaw one of the shortest dictatorships in history. But for his brief rule, he was the most ruthless and trailblazing pandemic dictator there ever was. Below is how the top ten list settled.

Top 10 Pandemic Dictators

1. Former Israeli Prime Minister Benjamin Netanyahu
2. Canadian Prime Minister Justin Trudeau
3. President of the People's Republic of China Xi Jinping
4. New Zealand Prime Minister Jacinda Ardern
5. Quebec Premier François Legault

6. French President Emmanuel Macron
7. WHO Director-general Tedros Adhanom
8. Australia (the majority of almost all leaders at one point in time[23])
9. Chief Medical Advisor to the President of U.S. Anthony S. Fauci
10. Minister of Health of Canada Jean-Yves Duclos

Honourable mention goes to Turkmenistan, the *'first country to make vaccination mandatory for all adults'* in July 2021.[620] At one point, Turkmenistan banned the use of the word 'coronavirus' and threatened to arrest anyone wearing a mask or talking about the pandemic.[621] Only Turkmenistan and North Korea dared defy the WHO in supplying the body with absolutely zero COVID-19 statistics. Turkmenistan would have been the clear number one choice, but with no opposition parties permitted, the already totalitarian state didn't do anything out of the ordinary during the pandemic.

---

[23] As recently as April 2022, more than 2-years after the pandemic started, Queensland Chief Health Officer Dr. John Gerrard stated that *'the anti-vaxx group is taking up a disproportionate amount of oxygen.'*

Chapter 31 - The Covid Con

"Only 3.8 percent of Alberta's COVID-19 deaths have involved no comorbidities. More than 74 percent of all COVID-19 deaths in the province have involved three or more pre-existing conditions."[622]

While in ICU, Travis Campbell posted Facebook videos begging people to get vaccinated, apologizing for not being vaccinated, and telling his family that he was probably going to die.[623] The mainstream U.S. media widely covered this story, even though many news outlets neglected to mention that along with testing positive for COVID-19, Mr. Campbell was battling pneumonia, a partially collapsed lung, he had rheumatoid arthritis,[624] and he was obese.[625] With Campbell battling for his life and wishing he had been vaccinated, CNN did at least two large segments (Aug 5, 2021,[626] and Aug 6, 2021[627]). Unfortunately, there is no record of CNN ever reporting that Campbell lived and was released from hospital.[628] The story of a COVID-19 survivor was not as narrative-friendly as an unvaccinated person dying in ICU wishing they had taken the shots.

Like many, I followed Travis' poignant story and was happy to hear that he was doing much better. But as Mr. Campbell continued to eulogize the vaccines and claimed *'the studies are out'* to justify his pro-vaccination perspective, it seemed like he was going a little too far. Then Mr. Campbell, per Michael Jordan, made it personal:

"I don't know how you can accept losing a family member at your hands because you didn't get vaccinated."[629]

As Campbell built his straw man case against the unvaccinated, he somehow completely ignored the fact that he had multiple comorbidities, was unvaccinated, and still managed to live after catching COVID-19. He also neglected to mention that insofar as crystal ball gazing, someone's body mass index or their comorbidities were statistically more accurate tools to forecast death compared to whether someone was vaccinated. What we had here, and I say this as delicately as possible, was a delusional man, perchance even a con artist, that had bought into the COVID-19 narrative with a myopic gusto usually reserved for diehard Canadian Liberals (pardon the politics).

While some may deem my contrarian take on Mr. Campbell as being insensitive, I would counter that blunt honesty is usually preferable to living in fantasy land. If someone wants to lecture others about not taking a vaccine and talks about this in the context of right and wrong life choices, their choices subsequently become fair game. Below are some of Mr. Campbell's words while he was not dying in hospital. Insensitive or not, at the time, some people asked, 'is this a crisis actor?':

"I messed up big time, you guys - I didn't get the vaccine. It was my fault. I could have done research. I could have gotten the vaccine. I could have gotten my kids vaccinated, but I was negligent...I'm trying to talk to you, so you understand that I don't want to go to your funeral and I don't want you to come to mine. The new delta strain...will get you down so fast, you are not going to get back up... I want people to understand that they do have a choice, but they need to make that choice...It's not worth the gamble."[630]

Travis went missing from social media around the same time the vaccines were proving incapable of limiting the spread of COVID-19. According to one of his first updates in many months, in June 2022, he continues to suffer from long-haul-covid, he has trouble breathing, he is battling covid-delirium/dementia, and social media gives him anxiety (I know the feeling, Travis). Travis was back in July 2022 with the caption in a video saying, *'One-year anniversary of defeating COVID-19!! Yeesss!!!'* Rumour has it Fauci was told this message was too optimistic and to take Travis out.

I wish Mr. Campbell the best, and I hope he chooses to read more studies, live healthily, exercise as much as he can,[631] and lose some weight.[632] I talk about Travis Campbell's ordeal because his case helps illustrate how ridiculous the entire pandemic had become. Before COVID-19, people were not telling everyone their medical history, openly trying to persuade strangers to take medical procedures, or sharing vaccine-vanity pictures and stories on the internet. That these odd behaviours became accepted as ordinary could have a lasting impact on democratic societies. This scares me more than anything else.

If this book has helped highlight any facet of the pandemic, it is that healthy people below the age of 65, in particular kids, usually handle COVID-19 just fine. One study looking at seroprevalence surveys from 14 countries found approximately a 99.9973% survival rate for kids aged 0-19 (*before* omicron).[633] The Canadian government says 90% of all COVID-19 deaths are those with comorbidities,[634] and as of July 29, 2022, a total of 57 kids have died from COVID-19 during the entire pandemic.[635] Using the Canadian government's data, this leads to a mortality rate for otherwise healthy kids of approximately 0.0006%. Many Canadian doctors allege that zero children under the age of 20 in Canada have succumbed to COVID-19 unless they had severe comorbidities before catching the virus. However, this cannot be confirmed or refuted using untransparent Canadian government sources.

There is also the possibility that the 57 COVID-19 deaths in kids in Canada are overstated. As highlighted in 'The Undercurrents,' provinces have sometimes gone beyond reason to capture more COVID-19 deaths, and this circus continues today. The most eye-popping example of this is seen in a direct quote from the Canadian Government's website:

"Starting April 7, 2022, British Columbia reports all deaths within 30 days of a positive COVID-19 test [as a covid death], regardless of the cause of death. As a result, deaths are now over-estimated for BC and should not be directly compared to other jurisdictions or to earlier data from BC." (footnote 2)[636]

If this is not evidence of Canadians being lied to, what is? Along with BC purposely producing counterfeit data, consider Alberta, where on October 6, 2021, a 14-year-old boy named Nathanael Spitzer died from a stage four terminal brain tumour, but the province recorded his cause of death as COVID-19.[637] Nathanael's family fought to overturn the COVID-19 cause of death, calling the province's death determination 'fake news'.[638] Chief Medical officer, Dr. Deena Hinshaw, apologized and eventually concurred that Nathanael passed away from brain cancer, not from COVID-19. This story begs the question: How many other deaths have been wrongly recorded as COVID-19 deaths?

"Hinshaw announced the province will no longer report COVID-19 deaths of children until a review process has been completed to confirm the actual cause of death."[639]

The above news was an admission that deaths in children were being reported as COVID-19 deaths before the 'actual cause of death' was known. Instead of being penalized professionally and banned on social media for spreading *'misinformation and disinformation,'* Hinshaw received a $228,000 cash bonus for her COVID-19 scheming in 2021.[640] This was the biggest provincial civil servant bonus ever reported in Canadian history.

Hopefully, these types of stories and stats provide context to why I was upset with pediatricians hustling vaccines by saying kids could die, with Cardy saying kids were fairing much worse with omicron, or even with Mr. Campbell harping about how great the vaccines were for kids. As a matter of reflex, I am not fond of con artists, and I instinctually try to inform others of the truth if I think they are mistaken. When this civilized path falters frustration and anger typically are the natural progression, but I digress.

The notion that healthy people require endless shots of mRNA has always been an absurd idea to me, and, in my humble opinion, the very contention that kids need these shots is bordering on criminal. Young, healthy lives will not be saved with COVID-

19 vaccines, and they may be harmed. If people believe kids need these shots, it is possible they may have been cajoled by forces more potent than they can ever imagine. It is probable that many of these people have been conned.

"...a con artist is a manipulator who cheats, or tricks, others through persuading them to believe something that is not true." ~ Psychology Today[641]

That con artist(s) are responsible for starting the COVID-19 pandemic by intentionally releasing the virus from a lab is not a theory I aspire to spread. There is no direct evidence of a lab leak, and speculations about China *intentionally* manufacturing COVID-19 to infect the world with communism are simply that. However, I have zero hesitation in contending that everything that has happened since COVID-19 came to be aligns perfectly with the conceptualization of a con.

From the beginning of the pandemic, there have been powerful forces tirelessly scheming to deceive and trick people. It started with the WHO, China, and others spreading well-contrived fear-driven information that exaggerated the severity of COVID-19. This manipulation increased exponentially as the mRNA vaccine revolution was set in motion.

While we're on the subject, the mRNA 'gold rush', as Wired Magazine called it in early 2021,[642] was the centerpiece of one of the biggest manias in history.[24] At the height of the euphoria, biotech mergers and buyouts of anything mRNA-related were running wild, scientists speculated mRNA tech might be capable of producing new flu vaccines within weeks, and new mRNA vaccine offerings were in the works for *'HIV, Nipah, Zika, herpes, dengue, hepatitis and malaria.'*[643] The excitement

---

[24] Sona Nanotech Inc., which focused on rapid COVID-19 tests, is an example of the irrational exuberance infecting anything in the markets related to COVID-19. Sona went from trading at 1 cent/share before COVID-19 to $14.45/share by July 2020. At its peak Sona had a nearly $1 billion market capitalization, and no sales.

surrounding mRNA technology, much like the 1990s internet mania, was largely artificial and driven by those looking to profit. And this path to profitability became immensely easier as governments agreed to help pay for the final development and launch of the COVID-19 vaccines. That governments also enlisted to advertise, mandate the shots, and sign indemnity contracts was the proverbial icing on the big pharma-baked cake.

The reach and depth of the vaccine con rival any before it, including Bernie Madoff's $65 billion Ponzi scheme,[644] which is regarded as the largest in history. In 2021 Pfizer reported nearly $37 billion in COVID-19 vaccine sales, easily making it *'one of the most lucrative products in history.'*[645] In 2022 Pfizer forecasts that it will produce $32 billion in COVID-19 vaccine revenues and an additional $22 billion from its COVID-19 oral antiviral Paxlovid. In addition to Pfizer's remarkable vaccine success, Moderna logged $17.7 billion in vaccine sales in 2021,[646] and China's Sinovac Biotech tagged nearly $20 billion (USD).[647] These three vaccine behemoths had more sales of COVID-19 vaccines in 2021 than most countries have GDP, and none of their vaccines were effective at reducing transmission.

Remember Fauci stumbling and getting irritated in 2021 as he learned that vaccine efficacy was rapidly waning, and he realized his new hocus pocus would be selling the idea of perpetual boosters? A couple of other players also knew, even before Fauci, that the mRNA vaccines were not exactly magical.

February 23, 2021 - Pfizer 10K: *"The companies continue to study BNT162b2, including studies evaluating it in additional populations, booster doses, and emerging variants."*[648]

February 25, 2021 - Moderna: *"mRNA-1283 is intended to be evaluated for use as a booster dose for previously vaccinated or infected individuals..."*[649]

Right off the jump, big pharma informed shareholders that profits don't get to be recurring profits if the vaccines were a one-

and-done affair. That booster shots were being examined as the vaccination campaign began raises the spectre of planned obsolescence. You didn't think these shots were intended to help end COVID-19 and do what vaccines have traditionally always done, did you?

That the shots quickly proved incapable of ending COVID-19 is, in the totality of the pandemic discussion, why it was all a giant con. Israel launched the fastest vaccination campaign in history in January 2021,[25] and by June 2021, the vaccines had already suffered a catastrophic failure. If these vaccines had been in bona fide Phase 3 clinical trials and not embroiled in a shady for-profit scheme, the trials would have been discontinued.

June 25, 2021 - *"About half of adults infected in an outbreak of the Delta variant of COVID-19 in Israel were fully inoculated with the Pfizer Inc. "*[650]

It is not a conspiracy theory to posit the COVID-19 vaccines were an abysmal failure. Per Moderna, the primary objective of the shots was to guard *'against symptomatic COVID-19 disease, '*[651] and only months into the trials this objective was unattainable. But the pandemic-vaccine-confidence trick was so cunningly crafted, and those perpetrating the con so heavily invested, failed vaccine or not the narrative would proceed.

As for those conspiring with big pharma, in 2013 the U.S. Department of Defense gave Moderna $24.6 million to *'research and develop potential mRNA medicines,'* in 2016 Gates gave Moderna up to $100 million to *'advance mRNA-based development projects, '*[652] and in May 2020 the FDA 'fast tracked' the final development of the vaccines. Also in May 2020, the White House announced *'Operation Warp Speed,'* and the NIH was charged with creating an *'independent'* data safety board to monitor the trials. By the time Moderna started Phase 3 trials the company had strategic alliances with, *'BARDA, DARPA, the NIH,*

---

[25] In Israel the first dose of the Pfizer-BioNTech COVID-19 vaccine was administered on December 20, 2020.

CEPI and the Bill & Melinda Gates Foundation.' Then there was Pfizer, which before its Phase 3 enrollment process was even completed had *'entered into agreements with various governments to supply over 300 million doses…with options for over 500 million additional doses.'*[653] Sales before Phase 3 clinical trials even start. What could go wrong.

The sway big pharma had and has over the FDA and policymakers are the stuff of legend, and during covid-19 some claimed this influence spread to blackmailing governments,[654] controlling the media, and rigging the safety data. The endless trail of entanglements tells us the very definition of 'big pharma' went supernova when COVID-19 arrived. What, exactly, 'big pharma' represents today is open to interpretation.

As big pharma and their legion of collaborators strong-armed nations into the cult of vaccination, world leaders activated policies, laws, and mandates that did big pharma's bidding. Like waves washing over the world, this onslaught became a self-fulfilling prophecy and popularized the delusion that universal vaccination was vital. Recall that after a few weeks of lockdowns in Wuhan, China, *'the authorities now leap into action at any sign of new infections, if at times with excessive zeal.'* After a few weeks of the new COVID-19 shots hitting the streets, things would never be the same again. The con had been unsheathed.

In Ontario, in 2021, the payment to a medical provider for a flu vaccine was *'$5.00 for each dose administered.'*[655] By contrast, in June 2021, the payment for a COVID-19 vaccine in Ontario was $13 per shot, an additional $5.60 per shot if a *'sole visit premium'* was applicable, and an additional $6 per patient *'facilitation fee'* was dished out to whoever booked the shot.[656] In July 2021, The Ontario Medical Association also started rewarding *'activities related to COVID-19 vaccination,'* which included a $67.75 fee for 20 minutes worth of COVID-19 vaccine counselling,[657] and ten minutes of phone and video vaccine info netting a physician $23.75. Like a bank teller pushing a credit card at the end of your visit, in BC any doctor or 'specialist' could collect a $17.62

'COVID-19 immunization advice fee' for mentioning the vaccines and \$43.55 if the phone call or discussion lasted 15 minutes. These confusing fees were simpler in Alberta, where administering the COVID-19 vaccine was worth \$25 a shot and an additional \$20 if the appointment took more than ten minutes.[658] Why was injecting mRNA into someone potentially compensated at more than ten times the rate of administering a flu vaccine? One word. Science.

For many medical professionals these fees for *'activities related to COVID-19 vaccination'* had a similar allure to the 'cash' jobs at the Ontario Food Terminal. I was entranced by cash work when I was younger, and I would stay after a shift to hand-bomb trailers any chance I could. Ottawa's Dr. Nili Kaplan-Myrth stayed after her shifts to host frequent 'Jabapalooza' vaccine parties, sometimes injecting even 'ineligible patients' with booster shots.[659] Incidentally, Kaplan-Myrth is an ardent advocate for mandatory child vaccination and she is in the running to be an Ottawa School Board Trustee. This would seem to be a conflict of interest as she zealously promotes and administers as many COVID-19 vaccines as possible, for that little extra 'cash.'[26]

Another conflict of interest was when The University of Toronto announced on July 28, 2022, that students living on campus would be required, by decree, to have two shots plus *'at least one booster dose.'*[660] No science was shared to justify this policy, which is contrary to the province's 'risk-based' approach, and there will be no recognition of natural immunity. UofT is where infectious researcher Tara Moriarty works. You may recall that Moriarty erroneously said she sees COVID-19 deaths all the time in New Brunswick. UofT is also where David Fisman and Colin Furness work, where the WHO started its *'Collaborating Centre for Bioethics,'*[661] and where numerous biotech and big pharma adventures have begun. It is not coincidental that the only major Canadian University that is mandating boosters has a myriad of associations with the COVID-19 narrative. UofT is an excellent

---

[26] Dr. Kaplan-Myrth did not respond to multiple requests for comment about her compensation (if any) for administering reportedly 'thousands' of COVID-19 vaccines.

example of why the system of control, the con, will not end until people rise up and end it.

I finally spoke with my union President Jan Simpson on June 25, 2022. I asked why in the world did we selected Colin Furness to represent us in arbitration. Jan said he was the only expert they could get. I said that no expert would be better than having one who undermines our case. For context, of the many defective statements Furness said at arbitration, he asserted that viral loads in infected vaccinated people were up to 20 times lower than in infected unvaccinated people, and that *'Pfizer vaccination reduces transmission substantially.'*[662] This was our expert witness that was supposed to be arguing against the mandates! Perhaps someone should have told Furness that scores of studies had proven viral loads were the same,[663] Fauci confirmed the amount of virus in breakthrough delta cases *'almost identical,'*[664] and not even Pfizer believed their shots could reduce transmission substantially.

I asked Jan if she got the emails I sent on December 1, 2021 and February 3, 2022, where I politely noted Colin Furness was a radical pro-mandate ideologue and there were other experts who would fight for our cause. Jan informed me there were too many emails from members and that everything was forwarded to the lawyers. That our President somehow knew Colin Furness was the only epidemiologist in Canada available or willing to attend our arbitration hearing was deeply troubling given that only the lawyers knew everything else. Before ending our conversation, Jan pledged to let me know the status of my grievances. More than two months later and I have yet to hear back. What was clear to me as we parted ways was that union leaders and representatives were also conned into believing the vaccine mandates were essential, and many were reluctant to come clean and admit that they were hoodwinked.

Even as part of me empathized with Jan's stressful position, another part of me still wanted her to step down and apologize for allowing lawyers and fanatics to cause undue harm to members.

One of the most upsetting things of the pandemic was when policymakers failed to admit their mistakes and also refused to argue why their actions were justified. If someone is passionate, informed, and eloquent on the subject of mandates, I will listen and try to be objective. Leaders lead, they do not hide like the coward Trudeau.

I spoke with many lawyers in late 2021, and all passed on taking up my case(s). The reason one of the lawyers gave me was simple and, at the time, made me think. The lawyer said the law is like an art form, and right now, no judge in Canada will rule against any vaccine mandates. I am reasonably certain this lawyer was drunk at the time, and for some reason, he cursed like a sailor, but looking back, his candour was stunningly accurate. The con was so pervasive and the vaccination solution so universally imprinted upon the minds of the masses that no judge would stray from the status quo. What was required to look at the mandates in a different light was the destruction of the narrative.

The drunken lawyer led me toward an understanding that while mandates themselves cannot supersede existing federal law, that doesn't necessarily mean that mandates are illegal in the eyes of the court. Vaccine mandates were and are, like art, a matter of interpretation and perception. Perceptions can and do change.

An old business adage is that you have to spend money to make money. Big pharma and global governments spent obscene amounts of money to ensure as many people as possible took the COVID-19 shots, and, in turn, this incentivized one of the largest profit sprees any product has ever recorded. That this pandemic paradigm endures even as the original justification for the shots has collapsed makes it a confidence trick instead of following the science. And that this con is being paired with fraudulent information to further a narrative that takes away personal freedoms, limits mobility rights, and aims to destroy medical privacy, is why the con needs to be obliterated, with prejudice.

I was driving around town listening to Pēteris Vasks'
Distant Light when it occurred to me this book really can't end;
there will always be new information surfacing, circling, and
presenting more context and confirmation that the COVID-19
charade was little more than a covid con. Something that can't end
but must epitomizes the agonizing feelings of people as they
watched the covid con develop, while at the same time knowing it
had to end. Personally, this fight has hardened my militarized
mind, jaded my personality, and run off with a part of my
humanity. The entire time I longed for my childhood naivety. It
was indeed bliss.

Chapter 32 - Follow the Money

"In total, over $18 billion dollars of US public funds have been invested in 6 vaccine candidates." ~ U.S. Taxpayers Heavily Funded the Discovery of COVID-19 Vaccines. March 2022[665]

The original sin of complete pandemic control emerged quickly as fear-frozen citizens recoiled from their instinct to resist government overreach. And once it was established that Chinese-style lockdowns were the chosen path to limit the spread of COVID-19, the concept that the vaccines could bring back freedom was born. Lockdowns were the stick, and vaccination was the carrot. This was a simple and well-executed plan.

After the vaccines were in play, mandates, mask restrictions, and vax-passes became some of the standard tools to try and compel the entire population to take the shots. Had the omicron variant not come along and rapidly spread natural infection, all the restrictions and mandates would likely still be in place today.

As mandate-mania crashed and the pipedream of ending COVID-19 with vaccines imploded, what remained was the previously anointed leaders, still intoxicated by the absolute power they wielded only months earlier. The power of the pandemic dictators was bestowed by special interests, and these interests never said the pandemic was forever.

The questions as despot leaders like Trudeau tried to keep hold of power are how much of the script was preordained, how much occurred spontaneously, and who are the main actors and primary originators of the COVID-19 narrative? These heavy questions, like death itself, are being asked by everyone who was impacted by COVID-19, and the answers differ tremendously.

In my opinion, the COVID-19 narrative was essentially a top-down model with a complex (or even indistinguishable) command structure. To help elaborate on this speculation and highlight the type of hierarchy at play, your basic military 'Strategy-Operations-Tactics' command structure[666] will suffice.

The smallest part of the model was the Strategic level (the top), and the largest part of the model was those carrying out orders at the Tactical level (the bottom). In the middle of these two strata were people like Trudeau at the Operations level. The Strategic level planned, planted, and helped nurture the COVID-19 narrative(s). These would be your WHO, WEF, China (initially), big pharma, parts of government, Gates, Soros, etc. Operations were charged with deciphering and deploying the directives passed down by the Strategists, and those in Tactical were expected to follow orders.

Along with this basic three-level command structure, some players were not readily definable and/or appeared to covertly float between levels as they deemed fit. For example, the NIH's budget is more than six times that of the WHO, and no one from the NIH made it into the top ten pandemic dictators list. Similarly, the CDC and FDA had/have massive resources and tons of influence, but beyond shilling, for big pharma, they do not seem to be key architects of the COVID-19 narrative. Then there was NIAID, which started throwing money at more than 24 different *'projects that contributed to their spike protein discovery'* as early as 2000, and finally discovered a *'complete prefusion spike protein of a human betacoronavirus'* in 2016.[667] Akin to a proud parent, NIAID is as staunchly pro-vaccine narrative as any organization. Also in the mix was the U.S. Department of Defense, which, more than a decade before COVID-19 arrived, had been *'making high-risk investments in RNA vaccine technology through its Defense Advanced Research Projects Agency.'*[668] This list of stakeholders and mRNA influencers could grow further, depending on how much you care to dig.

With the above in mind, the real money and power in today's medically mandated world operate behind the scenes. Remember, the unfortunate reality is that when everyone is scrambling around in the dark, people will follow just about anyone who vows they are the light. A cabal of powerful interests and false-vaccine-prophets amalgamated and told us in 2020 that it was time for mRNA to shine. Almost everyone listened and obeyed.

Once the vaccine plan was in place, those that resisted were professionally sabotaged by the bought and paid-for media and torched by the voodoo-vaccine science. As for the world leaders, which mainly resided in Operations, they followed the chain of command and the narrative presented to them because actions, no matter how preposterous, ruled the day. Netanyahu speaking at the WEF streamlined the narrative, the NIH (and countless others) provided the muscle to enforce it, and Trudeau eventually followed the score already being played by Ardern, Macron, Draghi, Morrison, Biden, Frederiksen, Anastasiades, etc. The plodding but catchy tune was - Vaccines - Mandates - Passports - Symbol crash!

Finally, the Tactical level arrested peaceful protesters, injected vaccines into arms for profit, and refused to do anything for the unvaccinated to avoid professional suicide. These Tactical soldiers were regarded as entry-level agents by the Strategic elite, and they were strung along like disposable assets. Those at the highest levels knew once most of those in Tactical were involved in the narrative deeply enough, they would, like stepping into quicksand, be immersed and opt not to struggle for fear of being drowned.

Then there were people like me and most of you, being sloshed to and fro by all levels of government, companies, doctors, and lower-level drones that were just following orders. Our purpose was to take the shots and embrace tyranny. We existed on the exterior of the hierarchy and - like manually picking products and placing them on a skid - were the lowest of the low. The entire edifice relied upon our compliance and all of us (i.e., taxpayers) paying the bill. Terrified citizens didn't even need to be blackmailed, as they would openly pay anything for the chance to end COVID-19.

Some people believe the COVID-19 Strategy-Operations-Tactics command structure can remain erect and evolve into a climate change force, while others believe despite recent setbacks, another COVID-19 blitzkrieg is still to come. What is accepted is the COVID-19 narrative is no longer invincible and that no amount of censorship can conceal the lies and deception that have already been exposed. Perceptions are changing.

One of the reasons why the narrative is no longer all-powerful is because money - the key incentivizing agent that courses through the entire system - is no longer targeting a universal goal. For a brief moment, corporate, political, and philanthropic interests were perfectly aligned in demanding the COVID-19 vaccines be injected into as many arms as possible, no matter the risks. Such alignments, like multiple planetary conjunctions, are usually exceptionally rare and brief.

Do not let this current weakness in the COVID-19 narrative fool you into thinking the entire house of cards is about to come crumbling down. It isn't. The longer-term focus is on a 2030 vaccine plan promoted by the WHO[669] and the CDC.[670] There is also the WEF's 2030 Vision, which is supposed to welcome the fourth industrial revolution,[671] and the NIH is doing a *Healthy People 2030'* thingamajig.[672] Dig even deeper, and 2030 could be shaping up to be one heck of a year, or maybe this is what they want us to think.

Before 2030 arrives, variants of the COVID-19 model are already being rewritten, and reconstruction could be forthcoming. For example, shortly before Australian Prime Minister Scott Morrison lost the federal election in May 2022, he signed a *'10-year strategic partnership'* with Moderna that made Australia *'a critical regional hub for mRNA technology development and production.'*[673] Weeks after Morrison's deal, our dictator, Justin Trudeau, finalized his deal and announced that *'Moderna will build a state-of-the-art manufacturing facility in Quebec to deliver made-in-Canada vaccines.'*[674] Both the Canadian and Australian facilities are projected to be up and running by 2024. Each is expected to have the capacity to produce 100 million doses of mRNA vaccines per year. These plants are in addition to the memorandum of understanding Moderna signed in March 2022 to invest $500 million in a new African vaccine plant,[675] the *'four new subsidiaries'* in Asia announced in February 2022,[676] ongoing European expansion,[677] and new efforts that *'establish large presence in Brazil and Mexico.'*[678] Far from accepting that the COVID-19 pandemic was a one-time phenomenon, Moderna is boldly plotting to ensure its COVID-19 vaccine success is repeated. On August 3, 2022, Moderna announced that it had '*46 programs in development across 43 development candidates, of which 31 are currently in active clinical trials.'*[679] The critical question, at least for stakeholders, is can Moderna's mRNA shots for HIV, cancer, influenza, zika, and many other ailments be as profitable as its COVID-19 product?

Money Changes Everything ~ Cyndi Lauper

This book was my story - the unexpected path my life took for me to forever embrace an anti-mandate and pro-medical-choice dogma. I had questions that I believe warranted being answered by my leaders, my employer, and my union. I still have many questions today. One of the more daunting questions we should all ask is how did so many people accept being injected with an untested vaccine so quickly. Before COVID-19, *'the process of developing a new drug or biologic'* took up to 12 years and cost more than $800 million (USD).[680] Are we really to believe that because COVID-19 was exceptionally contagious and scared a lot of people, we should permanently lower the vaccine safety bar from 12 years down to less than 12 months? Emperor Trudeau weighed in on this issue when he was doing his lying-to-kids tour in December 2021, or shortly before he caught COVID-19 a couple of times.

"People have also heard that these are new vaccines, and they've been done quicker. It usually takes years and years and years for a vaccine. Well, the reason it was able to be done quicker is because we threw more money and more people to do the work than ever have been done before to get a vaccine because it was so important

to get it right. There wasn't any shortcuts taken. There weren't any steps skipped. The full approval was done. It was just done with a lot more people and a lot more attention on it than ever before. So that's how you can know that the vaccines absolutely are safe."[681]

The insinuation that throwing more money at vaccine development produces safe vaccines faster is, like Trudeau himself, repellent. Clinical vaccine safety trials have always taken many years to be completed, because no amount of money can pressure or haggle the hands of time. Contrast Trudeau's words to those of AstraZeneca from February 20, 2021, and decide for yourself if any shortcuts were taken bringing the COVID-19 vaccines to market:

"COVID-19 Vaccine AstraZeneca confirms 100% protection against severe disease, hospitalization, and death in the primary analysis of Phase III trials."[682]

'Follow the money' is overused for good reason: Money made the COVID-19 pandemic possible.

Epilogue

Shortly after June 14, 2022, the day most but not all of the federal mandates were rescinded in Canada, I got the call to return to work. At the time of this writing, I am contemplating my options and pursuing legal advice. Part of me is looking forward to returning to the routine, making some moolah, and having some laughs. Another part of me knows the company and union left people like myself to fend for themselves, and both could easily do it again. I used to think unions fought for all employees, had core beliefs like 'no rollbacks,' and that members could decide for themselves if they wanted to join clinical vaccine trials. Not anymore.

Although only one prominent union figure in Canada has been charged during the COVID-19 fiasco,[27] it is easy to speculate that unions, or their lawyers, were sponsored in some way by the COVID-19 narrative. The alternative is that almost all Canadian unions were in a trance when they entertained the idea that medical choice, informed consent, and workplace contracts could be suspended without consulting workers. I sincerely believe that the majority of workers were and are against vaccine mandates, even though most are not willing or able to lose their jobs over this issue.

If the pandemic taught us anything, it is that the justification for tearing the very fabric of a democratic society apart can be cloaked in seemingly innocent phrases like 'the rights of others.' Greek President Katerina Sakellaropoulou contended that *'the limits of free choice are determined by the rights of others,'*[683] and moments later, Greece weaponized this philosophy and started taxing unvaccinated citizens over 60 years of age. Is the greater good being served by financially punishing the elderly for not accepting a government order to take a vaccine? If democratic societies allow governments to declare when individual rights can

---

[27] Former UNIFOR National President Jerry Dias was charged with 'breach of Unifor Constitution' on March 23, 2022. Dias allegedly accepted $50,000 from a COVID-19 rapid test supplier.

be suspended due to one person or party's interpretation of 'the rights of others,' societies will one day cease to be democratic.

Germany's Ms. Anderson called Trudeau a dictator to usher this book into existence, and it is fitting her excellent freedom speech helps take us out. Like Florida Governor Ron Desantis bravely standing up to the mandates before most in the U.S. did, Ms. Anderson, from the very beginning, stood for freedom. She gave the following speech at EU Parliament in October 2021:

"Whenever a government claims to have the people's interest at heart, you need to think again. In the entire history of mankind, there has never been a political elite sincerely concerned about the well-being of regular people. What makes any of us think that it is different now? If the Age of Enlightenment has brought forth anything, then certainly this: never take anything any government tells you at face value; always question everything any government does or does not do. Always look for ulterior motives and always ask cui bono - who benefits. Whenever a political elite pushes an agenda this hard and resorts to extortion and manipulation to get their way, you can almost always be sure your benefit is definitely not what they had at heart. As far as I'm concerned, I will not be vaccinated with anything that has not been properly vetted and tested and has shown no sound scientific evidence that the benefits outweigh the disease itself and possible long-term side effects, which to this day, we don't know anything about. I will not be reduced to a guinea pig by getting vaccinated with an experimental drug. And I will most assuredly not get vaccinated because my government tells me to and promises in return, I will be granted freedom. Let's be clear about one thing. No one grants me freedom, for I am a free person. So I dare the European Commission and the German government - throw me in jail. Lock me up and throw away the key for all I care, but you will never be able to coerce me into being vaccinated if I, the free citizens that I am, choose not to be vaccinated."[684]

While all of us may not be as fired up as Ms. Anderson is on the topic of vaccines, there are issues that each of us holds dear.

The beautiful thing about a democracy is that we have opportunities to express ourselves on the issues we are most passionate about, usually without fear of penalty. The rule of law and fundamental freedoms and rights should be ideals that all Canadians are passionate about, and when the government seeks to control or ration these basic principles, all Canadians should be alarmed.

As citizens protested the lockdowns in Shanghai, a drone appeared, and over a loudspeaker, the words rang out loudly: *'Control your soul's desire for freedom.'*[685] When freedom becomes the enemy, tyranny is present. What gave rise to pandemic dictators like Trudeau was a globalist groupthink that craftily surmised the greater good would be served by suppressing the soul's desire for freedom.

The argument could be made that the pandemic dictators are not real dictators in the traditional sense of the word; that once the pandemic is gone, they too will vanish. This quaint rationalization is precisely what the pandemic dictators want us to think. No one can be certain that Canadians will reacquire the freedoms lost since March 2020. Canada was one of the most oppressive places on earth for most of the pandemic, and, despite there no longer being an emergency, Trudeau's gang is *still* dictating pandemic policies today. Until government prohibits COVID-19 vaccine mandates, freedom is in doubt.

Even if you sincerely believed all the emergency pandemic policies in Canada were enacted solely for public health motives, remember that despite the mountains of money and thunderous effort - alongside the deception and lies - the majority of Canadians still caught COVID-19. It is not a conspiracy theory to shout that COVID-19 curtailment efforts failed. It is a fact. Are we going to allow politicians and unelected officials to decree closures, mandates, emergency orders, and masking in schools again, given that such activities did more harm than good?

"Canada had among the most sustained stringent policies regarding restrictions on internal movement, cancellation of public

events, restrictions on public gatherings, workplace closures and international travel controls... "[686]

"The price tag of lockdowns in terms of public health is high: we estimate that, even if somewhat effective in preventing death caused by infection, lockdowns may claim 20 times more life than they save." [687]

It becomes easier, in time, to see your mind's thought process and evaluate things once the intensity of the burdens weighing you down, or the pleasures raising you up, have subsided. At the height of the mandate-mania, when Trudeau's hatred started being delivered with kamikaze-like glee, something triggered inside me, and I became trapped inside a black and white world. As the trend toward some semblance of normalcy shows signs of returning, I have been able to step away from this period of darkness. Like many Canadians, I now appreciate that anger and frustration took me down a bleak path and that my ability to effectively navigate negative information in this new-cruel-world order was impaired. I am still in search of new techniques to process the corruption and lies that are being exposed, and I long for a novel refinement process that doesn't raise my blood pressure. Maybe I should take up dancing.

Inside an article on the CBC, it was innocently said that *'Dancing is allowed once again.'*[688] The wording seemed off and made me think. Dancing isn't something that needs to ever be regulated by an elected government. Dancing is something you feel and do when you feel like doing it. The Freedom Convoy agitated those in Ottawa, in particular Trudeau, because instead of a mob acting destructively to fight tyranny, the mob was dancing. The all-night dance parties in front of Parliament were televised on live streams on the internet, and they were magical. Despite being frustrated, flummoxed, and beaten down for many months, these freedom fighters still knew how to best harness and express their freedom-loving spirit. Lines from the corny Lee Ann Womack song seem oddly applicable:

Don't let some Hell bent heart leave you bitter,

When you come close to sellin' out, reconsider,
Give the heavens above more than just a passing glance,
And when you get the choice to sit it out or dance.

I hope you dance...

Touching words. My take is that our existence, when whittled down to its pandemic core, is all about the choice of whether to comply or not comply. I choose not to comply, and in place of embodying wrath, I hope that I can learn the spirit of the dance. I hope you will as well. The freedom to dance must never be subjugated to the constant review by dictators like Trudeau, Netanyahu, or Xi. Ever.

A running theme has been me contacting people and places and never getting a response. I kept an excel file of every call or email, and it is, upon reflection, scary how persistent I was at knocking my head against the wall. Well, on June 7, 2022, this changed when a Health Canada email popped up. Overjoyed, I hurriedly opened the email, anxious about what insights I might find. Part of me thought that if it took this long to respond, they must have some decent insights into some of my queries. The email said the following, in full:

"Thank you for contacting Health Canada
Your recent enquiry has been redirected to the appropriate area
for a response.
Sincerely,
Health Canada | Santé Canada"

One wonders if it took Health Canada more than six months to forward my questions to the appropriate parties how long it will take for tangible answers to come back. Or maybe this email was just another one of Trudeau's mind games.

Finally, two last second updates:

1) On August 22, 2022, Western University became the second major university in Canada to mandate the booster.[689] This

announcement was made after many students had just paid their tuition. Natural infection will not be recognized. Emails and voicemails for comment were not responded to. Is this the world we want to live in?

2) On September 2, 2022, the headline read: *'NACI now suggests Canadians consider a COVID-19 booster every 90 days.'*[690] I didn't think the Watson and Deans show could be topped. I stand corrected.

Keep the faith, fight the power, and end all mandates! The struggle continues...

Endnotes

[1] https://www.thestar.com/news/gta/2021/08/26/when-it-comes-to-empathy-for-the-unvaccinated-many-of-us-arent-feeling-it.html?utm_source=Twitter&utm_medium=SocialMedia&utm_campaign=GTA&utm_content=empathyunvaccinated

[2] https://www.youtube.com/watch?v=cU8Pj_Q_wVo

[3] https://www.europarl.europa.eu/plenary/en/vod.html?mode=chapter&vodLanguage=EN&playerStartTime=20220323-17:40:32&playerEndTime=20220323-18:35:56#

[4] https://www.bnnbloomberg.ca/musk-tweet-comparing-canada-s-trudeau-to-hitler-was-deleted-1.1725152

[5] https://www.cbc.ca/news/politics/european-members-parliament-attact-trudeau-1.6397579

[6] https://www.ctvnews.ca/mobile/politics/european-mps-blast-pm-trudeau-for-handling-of-freedom-convoy-after-brussels-speech-1.5833652?cache=yes?clipId=373266/7.564849/7.564849/7.564849

[7] https://clinicaltrials.gov/ct2/show/NCT04470427

[8] https://clinicaltrials.gov/ct2/show/NCT04368728

[9] https://www.express.co.uk/news/world/1576921/Justin-Trudeau-protest-video-Number-10-visit-Canada-Covid-mandate-vn

[10] https://www.canada.ca/en/treasury-board-secretariat/news/2021/08/government-of-canada-to-require-vaccination-of-federal-workforce-and-federally-regulated-transportation-sector.html

[11] https://www.youtube.com/watch?v=HSA4nUO1P1g

[12] https://tinyurl.com/3rxfryrr

[13] https://www.pfizerclinicaltrials.com/about/how-clinical-trials-work#trialdesign

[14] https://www.ncbi.nlm.nih.gov/pmc/articles/PMC3148611/

[15] https://www.redvoicemedia.com/2021/10/smoking-gun-videos-emerge-of-fauci-and-hhs-plotting-to-stage-massive-health-scare-using-new-virus/

[16] https://financialpost.com/opinion/terence-corcoran-in-canada-follow-the-money-the-ideas

[17] https://financialpost.com/opinion/peter-foster-justin-trudeau-embraces-the-davos-plutocrats

[18] https://www.weforum.org/agenda/2015/11/maurice-strong-an-appreciation/

[19] https://www.weforum.org/agenda/2020/06/now-is-the-time-for-a-great-reset/

[20] https://www.youtube.com/watch?v=n2fp0Jeyjvw

[21] https://www.who.int/director-general/speeches/detail/address-to-the-sixty-ninth-world-health-assembly

[22] https://twitter.com/ZN2_______/status/1537190925608296448

[23] https://www.who.int/classifications/icd/Guidelines_Cause_of_Death_COVID-19.pdf?ua=1

[24] https://www150.statcan.gc.ca/n1/pub/45-28-0001/2020001/article/00087-eng.htm

[25] https://www.medrxiv.org/content/10.1101/2020.11.11.20229872v2

[26] https://www.weforum.org/agenda/2020/12/italy-death-toll-pandemic-covid-coronavirus-health-population-europe/

[27] https://pubmed.ncbi.nlm.nih.gov/33052299/

[28] https://www.medrxiv.org/content/10.1101/2020.11.28.20240267v1

[29] https://www.thelancet.com/action/showPdf?pii=S0140-6736%2820%2932623-4

[30] https://www.cmaj.ca/content/192/34/E982

[31] https://www.france24.com/en/europe/20201219-italy-imposes-lockdown-over-christmas-and-new-year-to-curb-spread-of-COVID-19

[32] https://science.gc.ca/eic/site/063.nsf/eng/98340.html

[33] https://www.canada.ca/content/dam/phac-aspc/documents/services/diseases-maladies/coronavirus-disease-COVID-19/epidemiological-economic-research-data/update-COVID-19-canada-epidemiology-modelling-20210625-en.pdf

[34] https://www.cidrap.umn.edu/news-perspective/2020/07/commentary-my-views-cloth-face-coverings-public-preventing-COVID-19

[35] https://www.mayoclinic.org/diseases-conditions/coronavirus/in-depth/herd-immunity-and-coronavirus/art-20486808

[36] https://www.nih.gov/news-events/news-releases/nih-moderna-investigational-COVID-19-vaccine-shows-promise-mouse-studies

[37] https://www.pfizer.com/news/press-release/press-release-detail/pfizer-and-biontech-announce-data-preclinical-studies-mrna

[38] https://igorchudov.substack.com/p/covid-vaccine-test-animals-were-killed

[39] https://www.drug-injury.com/drug_injury/2011/07/astrazeneca-resolves-most-seroquel-suits-for-647-million.html

[40] https://www.cnbc.com/2020/08/14/the-us-has-already-invested-billions-on-potential-coronavirus-vaccines-heres-where-the-deals-stand.html

[41] https://globalnews.ca/news/7521148/coronavirus-vaccine-safety-liability-government-anand-pfizer/

[42] https://www.cbc.ca/news/politics/thursday-vaccine-injury-compensation-1.6023899

[43] https://www.cbc.ca/news/politics/astrazeneca-approved-1.5929050

[44] https://covid-vaccine.canada.ca/info/regulatory-decision-summary-detailTwo.html?linkID=RDS00772

[45] https://globalnews.ca/news/7815342/health-canada-astrazeneca-covid-death/

[46] https://www.reuters.com/business/healthcare-pharmaceuticals/canadas-alberta-confirms-first-death-linked-astrazeneca-vaccine-2021-05-05/

[47] https://www.cbc.ca/news/canada/british-columbia/covid-briefing-may6-1.6016511

[48] https://nationalpost.com/news/canada/very-little-excuse-to-continue-to-use-astrazeneca-in-canada-infectious-diseases-specialist

[49] https://ici.radio-canada.ca/rci/en/news/1792478/future-of-astrazeneca-COVID-19-vaccine-in-question-in-canada-over-blood-clots-supply-issues

[50] https://globalnews.ca/video/7884395/new-brunswick-reports-2nd-astrazeneca-related-death

[51] https://toronto.ctvnews.ca/ontario-confirms-first-blood-clot-death-in-man-who-received-astrazeneca-COVID-19-vaccine-1.5442160

[52] https://www.cnbc.com/2021/08/12/blood-clots-linked-to-astrazeneca-shot-have-22percent-mortality-rate-study.html

[53] https://clinicaltrials.gov/ct2/show/NCT04516746

[54] https://www.ctvnews.ca/health/coronavirus/when-it-comes-to-vaccine-interchangeability-naci-recommends-using-the-same-type-1.5439707

[55] Ibid.

[56] https://www.cbc.ca/news/health/canada-mixing-COVID-19-vaccines-astrazeneca-pfizer-moderna-naci-1.6048152

[57] https://www.canada.ca/en/public-health/services/diseases/coronavirus-disease-COVID-19/vaccines/safety-side-effects.html

[58] https://www.yalemedicine.org/news/myocarditis-coronavirus-vaccine

[59] https://www.fda.gov/news-events/press-announcements/coronavirus-COVID-19-update-june-25-2021

[60] https://publications.aap.org/pediatrics/article/148/3/e2021052478/179728/Symptomatic-Acute-Myocarditis-in-7-Adolescents?autologincheck=redirected

[61] https://www.nature.com/articles/d41586-021-02740-y

[62] https://www.cdc.gov/coronavirus/2019-ncov/vaccines/safety/myocarditis.html

[63] https://rwmalonemd.substack.com/p/1-in-2680-young-men-develop-acute

[64] https://vaers.hhs.gov/

[65] https://www.canada.ca/en/public-health/services/immunization/reporting-adverse-events-following-immunization/user-guide-completion-submission-aefi-reports.html

[66] https://www.albertahealthservices.ca/info/page16187.aspx

[67] https://www.historyofvaccines.org/content/articles/vaccine-development-testing-and-regulation

[68] https://www.ifpma.org/wp-content/uploads/2019/07/IFPMA-ComplexJourney-2019_FINAL.pdf

[69] https://www.ajmc.com/view/efficacy-of-COVID-19-vaccines-in-real-world-settings-even-better-than-expected-fauci-says

[70] https://www.youtube.com/watch?v=-skA4GhVX7k

[71] https://www150.statcan.gc.ca/n1/pub/91f0015m/91f0015m2021002-eng.htm

[72] https://www.justice.gov/usao-ma/press-release/file/1066111/download

[73] https://www.propublica.org/article/doctors-prescribe-more-of-a-drug-if-they-receive-money-from-a-pharma-company-tied-to-it

[74] https://www.thelancet.com/journals/lancet/article/PIIS0140-6736(21)02183-8/fulltext

[75] https://tinyurl.com/bdz9esf5

76 https://www.cdc.gov/vaccines/vac-gen/imz-basics.htm

77 https://www.miamiherald.com/news/coronavirus/article254111268.html

78 https://www.usatoday.com/story/news/factcheck/2021/11/30/fact-check-merriam-webster-changed-vaccine-definition-accuracy/6354415001/

79 https://www.youtube.com/watch?v=QAkQlZgnbUQ

80 https://www.youtube.com/watch?v=Xm_gLd7MjP0

81 https://abcnews.go.com/GMA/Wellness/meet-young-people-helping-make-COVID-19-vaccine/story?id=74170658&cid=social_twitter_abcn

82 https://www.yahoo.com/lifestyle/meet-kid-heroes-taking-part-191229141.html

83 https://www.cbc.ca/news/politics/freeland-child-care-liberal-convention-1.5980851

84 https://www.albertahealthservices.ca/assets/info/ppih/if-ppih-COVID-19-sag-post-vaccine-transmission-rapid-review.pdf

85 https://www.cbc.ca/news/politics/trudeau-COVID-19-vaccine-passports-1.5947624

86 https://www.youtube.com/watch?v=qjpFe1fdhxU

87 https://www.hrw.org/news/2021/09/28/chinas-use-force-and-coercion-drive-its-COVID-19-vaccination-rate-not-answer

88 https://www.latimes.com/opinion/story/2021-09-29/forced-vaccinations-china-ethics-covid

89 https://www.weforum.org/events/the-davos-agenda-2021/sessions/special-address-by-g20-head-of-state-government-16baf3cc12

90 https://www.wto.org/english/tratop_e/trips_e/techsymp_290621/bown_pres2.pdf

91 https://www.citizen.org/article/pfizers-power/#_ftn57

92 https://twitter.com/justintrudeau/status/1351737740803584005

93 https://pm.gc.ca/en/news/readouts/2021/02/23/prime-minister-justin-trudeau-speaks-prime-minister-israel-benjamin

94 https://www.ctvnews.ca/politics/questions-raised-as-pm-trudeau-keeps-netanyahu-meeting-quiet-1.3773623?cache=yes%3FclipId%3D89531

95 https://www.cbc.ca/news/canada/cansino-deal-canada-nrc-fifth-estate-1.6208241

96 https://www.rcinet.ca/en/2020/08/26/canadas-COVID-19-vaccine-deal-with-china-is-over/

97 https://financialpost.com/diane-francis/diane-francis-questions-mount-over-trudeaus-vaccine-dealings-with-china

98 https://pm.gc.ca/en/news/news-releases/2020/10/23/prime-minister-announces-funding-advance-development-canadian-covid

99 https://abcnews.go.com/Blotter/solyndra-collapse-waste-half-billion-obama-gop-critics/story?id=14424323

100 https://twitter.com/donmartinctv/status/1349031642569048067

101 https://www.cbc.ca/news/canada/summer-vacation-COVID-19-travel-restrictions-1.6022536

102 https://www.nature.com/articles/s41591-021-01661-7

103 https://www.jpost.com/health-science/israel-has-COVID-19-herd-immunity-why-vaccinate-kids-analysis-670352

104 https://nationalpost.com/opinion/rex-murphy-chrystia-freelands-epiphany-that-COVID-19-is-an-opportunity-is-actually-pretty-dark

105 https://www.canada.ca/en/treasury-board-secretariat/news/2021/08/government-of-canada-to-require-vaccination-of-federal-workforce-and-federally-regulated-transportation-sector.html

106 https://health-infobase.canada.ca/src/data/covidLive/covid19-download.csv

107 https://www.gov.mb.ca/covid19/index.html

108 https://toronto.ctvnews.ca/more-than-1-700-fully-vaccinated-people-got-COVID-19-in-ontario-over-the-past-two-weeks-experts-say-it-s-not-a-concern-1.5643324

109 https://montreal.ctvnews.ca/quebec-reports-478-new-COVID-19-cases-nunavik-in-crisis-1.5642188

110 https://www2.gnb.ca/content/gnb/en/corporate/promo/COVID-19/news/news_release.2021.10.0754.html

111 https://news.gov.bc.ca/releases/2021HLTH0066-002045

112 https://www.alberta.ca/stats/COVID-19-alberta-statistics.htm#vaccine-outcomes

113 https://www.ncbi.nlm.nih.gov/pmc/articles/PMC8481107/

114 https://www.rollcall.com/2021/09/22/breakthrough-COVID-19-cases-expected-to-become-more-common-in-coming-months/?fbclid=IwAR2vIXcMaFID8xD65Wi32CLbw6bcorYi5nOH0YeeyHef6Swfhyn_O6JeAWg

[115] https://www.bnnbloomberg.ca/cdc-scaled-back-hunt-for-breakthrough-cases-just-as-the-delta-variant-grew-1.1635073

[116] https://www.youtube.com/watch?v=DNCw8g6aIQI

[117] https://fortune.com/2021/04/01/its-official-vaccinated-people-dont-transmit-COVID-19/

[118] https://www.cnn.com/2021/07/22/politics/fact-check-biden-cnn-town-hall-july/index.html

[119] https://www.cbc.ca/news/world/israel-covid-delta-variant-booster-1.6159472

[120] https://www.canada.ca/en/public-health/news/2021/07/statement-from-the-chief-public-health-officer-of-canada-on-july-23-2021.html

[121] https://www.fnha.ca/about/news-and-events/news/joint-statement-on-misleading-covid-19-information

[122] https://covid19-sciencetable.ca/sciencebrief/vaccine-induced-immune-thrombotic-thrombocytopenia-vitt-following-adenovirus-vector-COVID-19-vaccination/

[123] https://www.ctvnews.ca/health/coronavirus/canada-launches-its-first-national-vaccine-injury-compensation-program-1.5451579

[124] https://torontosun.com/news/national/burial-costs-covered-for-canadians-killed-by-approved-vaccines

[125] https://torontosun.com/opinion/columnists/gunter-the-cbcs-ad-revenue-problem-continues

[126] https://angusreid.org/unvaccinated-covid-sympathy/

[127] https://www.ctvnews.ca/health/coronavirus/canada-launches-its-first-national-vaccine-injury-compensation-program-1.5451579

[128] https://health-infobase.canada.ca/COVID-19/vaccine-safety/#a3

[129] https://www.reuters.com/business/healthcare-pharmaceuticals/sweden-pauses-use-moderna-covid-vaccine-cites-rare-side-effects-2021-10-06/

[130] https://www.nichd.nih.gov/newsroom/news/083021-COVID-19-vaccination-menstruation

[131] https://www.cbc.ca/news/politics/trudeau-promises-1b-vaccine-passports-1.6155618

[132] https://medicalxpress.com/news/2021-10-iceland-halts-moderna-jabs-heart-inflammation.html

[133] https://www.forbes.com/sites/roberthart/2021/11/10/germany-france-restrict-modernas-covid-vaccine-for-under-30s-over-rare-heart-risk-despite-surging-cases/?sh=c54d92a2a8a6

[134] https://www.cbc.ca/news/canada/calgary/covid-jason-kenney-vaccine-passports-1.6098986

[135] https://www2.gnb.ca/content/gnb/en/news/news_release.2021.07.0557.html

[136] https://www.rebelnews.com/ezra_levant_show_november_15_2021

[137] https://www.cbc.ca/news/canada/new-brunswick/sohrab-lutchmedial-cardiac-surgeon-obituary-1.6242359

[138] https://www.ctvnews.ca/health/coronavirus/canada-s-vaccine-injury-support-program-400-claims-since-launch-fewer-than-five-approved-1.5709786

[139] https://www.tga.gov.au/periodic/COVID-19-vaccine-weekly-safety-report-11-11-2021

[140] https://nationalpost.com/health/pandemic-flu-vaccine-not-to-blame-for-five-year-old-toronto-girls-death-judge-rules-after-rare-trial

[141] https://www.mondaq.com/canada/personal-injury/1142998/vaccine-injury-developments-reaffirm-that-proving-causation-remains-a-high-bar?

[142] https://stevekirsch.substack.com/p/covid-vaccine-victim-meet-dr-avindra

[143] https://www.politico.com/news/2021/07/27/biden-vaccine-mandate-federal-employees-consideration-500951

[144] https://www.nih.gov/news-events/nih-research-matters/most-COVID-19-hospitalizations-due-four-conditions

[145] https://cpj.org/2015/04/10-most-censored-countries/

[146] https://www.facebook.com/watch/?v=210918317765323

[147] https://www.youtube.com/watch?v=g2D-4piLnws

[148] https://www.dailycommercial.com/story/opinion/2022/08/05/choice-edwards-propaganda-and-misinformation/10209282002/

[149] https://www.realclearpolitics.com/video/2021/09/02/canadian_pm_trudeau_blasts_anti-vaxxers_im_focused_on_the_health_and_safety_of_the_responsible_majority.html

[150] https://tnc.news/2022/01/04/clip-resurfaces-of-trudeau-calling-unvaccinated-extremists-misogynists-racists/

[151] https://www.macleans.ca/society/typical-vaccine-hesitant-person-is-a-42-year-old-ontario-woman-who-votes-liberal-abacus-polling/

[152] https://nationalpost.com/news/canada/canadas-public-health-agency-admits-it-tracked-33-million-

mobile-devices-during-lockdown

153 https://www.ncbi.nlm.nih.gov/pmc/articles/PMC8481107/

154 https://pm.gc.ca/en/news/news-releases/2021/10/06/prime-minister-announces-mandatory-vaccination-federal-workforce-and

155 https://papers.ssrn.com/sol3/papers.cfm?abstract_id=3949410

156 https://pubmed.ncbi.nlm.nih.gov/34614326/

157 https://www.nejm.org/doi/full/10.1056/nejmoa2114114

158 https://www.medrxiv.org/content/10.1101/2021.08.24.21262415v1

159 https://www.youtube.com/watch?v=soAGhi9KpcQ

160 https://www.thelancet.com/journals/laninf/article/PIIS1473-3099(21)00648-4/fulltext

161 https://www.ctvnews.ca/health/coronavirus/COVID-19-vaccines-reducing-spread-severity-despite-breakthrough-cases-experts-say-1.5643856

162 https://www.theglobeandmail.com/opinion/refusing-to-get-vaccinated-is-selfish/article4356755/

163 https://www150.statcan.gc.ca/n1/pub/82-003-x/2010004/article/11348-eng.htm

164 https://calgaryherald.com/opinion/columnists/opinion-10-reasons-to-book-a-covid-19-vaccination-appointment-for-your-child

165
https://twitter.com/P_McCulloughMD/status/1533082365001613312?s=20&t=v9nLA_dRIIyDOOSsxzdrKA

166 https://www.thelancet.com/journals/laninf/article/PIIS1473-3099(21)00690-3/fulltext#%20

167 https://www.thelancet.com/journals/lancet/article/PIIS0140-6736(21)00947-8/fulltext

168 https://ijhpr.biomedcentral.com/articles/10.1186/s13584-021-00440-6

169 https://www.npr.org/2021/07/06/1013496220/protection-provided-by-the-pfizer-vaccine-may-might-be-fading-israeli-officials-

170 https://www.gov.il/BlobFolder/reports/vaccine-efficacy-safety-follow-up-committee/he/files_publications_corona_two-dose-vaccination-data.pdf

171 https://www.cnbc.com/2021/07/23/delta-variant-pfizer-covid-vaccine-39percent-effective-in-israel-prevents-severe-illness.html

172 https://www.reuters.com/business/healthcare-pharmaceuticals/delta-variant-behind-more-than-80-us-cases-vaccines-still-highly-effective-fauci-2021-07-20/

173 https://www.cnbc.com/video/2021/07/21/fauci-vaccines-are-safe-and-effective-against-delta-variant.html?&qsearchterm=dr.%20fauci

174 https://www.timesofisrael.com/fauci-israel-way-up-there-in-vaccination-seeing-remarkable-drop-in-cases/

175 https://www.cnbc.com/video/2021/07/13/fauci-covid-booster-relates-to-durability-not-vaccine-effectiveness.html?&qsearchterm=fauci%20booster

176 https://www.pfizer.com/news/press-release/press-release-detail/pfizer-and-biontech-confirm-high-efficacy-and-no-serious

177 https://www.cnbc.com/2021/08/12/covid-booster-shot-fauci-says-it-is-likely-everybody-will-eventually-need-a-third-vaccine.html?&qsearchterm=fauci%20booster

178 https://www.medrxiv.org/content/10.1101/2021.08.24.21262423v1

179 https://www.usatoday.com/story/news/factcheck/2020/04/24/fact-check-medicare-hospitals-paid-more-COVID-19-patients-coronavirus/3000638001/

180 https://www.merck.com/news/merck-statement-on-ivermectin-use-during-the-COVID-19-pandemic/

181 https://www150.statcan.gc.ca/n1/daily-quotidien/210712/dq210712b-eng.htm

182 https://www150.statcan.gc.ca/t1/tbl1/en/tv.action?pid=1310039401

183 https://parachute.ca/en/news-release/twice-as-many-people-in-canada-now-die-from-unintentional-poisoning-than-from-transport-related-injuries/

184 https://www.cupw.ca/en/no-cease-and-desist-union-will-continue-defend-members

185 https://www.cbc.ca/news/politics/ei-vax-status-1.6220287

186 https://www.youtube.com/watch?v=6YaT5LBplzc

187 https://www.youtube.com/watch?v=8CVUfAZ6h-Q

188 Ibid.

189 https://thecountersignal.com/nb-minister-of-education-wants-to-ban-unvaccinated-from-schools-and-hospitals/

190 https://www.cbc.ca/news/canada/new-brunswick/COVID-19-new-brunswick-school-child-care-

new-year-omicron-cardy-1.6286557

[191] https://atlantic.ctvnews.ca/n-b-minister-says-to-ignore-federal-vaccine-panel-accept-first-vaccine-offered-1.5414094

[192] https://atlantic.ctvnews.ca/n-b-minister-says-to-ignore-federal-vaccine-panel-accept-first-vaccine-offered-1.5414094

[193] https://www.discovery.co.za/corporate/health-insights-omicron-outbreak-analysis

[194] https://twitter.com/EricTopol?ref_src=twsrc%5Egoogle%7Ctwcamp%5Eserp%7Ctwgr%5Eauthor

[195] https://www.sciencemediacentre.org/expert-reaction-to-press-release-from-discovery-health-giving-real-world-information-on-their-omicron-outbreak-based-on-211000-COVID-19-positive-test-results-in-south-africa/

[196] https://www.npr.org/2021/05/21/999241558/in-kids-the-risk-of-COVID-19-and-the-flu-are-similar-but-the-risk-perception-isn

[197] https://nationalpost.com/news/canada/heroes-of-the-pandemic-new-brunswick-politician-who-crushed-the-COVID-19-curve-is-a-virus-whisperer

[198] https://nationalpost.com/news/canada/heroes-of-the-pandemic-new-brunswick-politician-who-crushed-the-COVID-19-curve-is-a-virus-whisperer

[199] https://twitter.com/FredFarmMarket/status/1468966915519356933

[200] https://www.bitchute.com/video/3JmdmANxrfnB/

[201] https://www.jccf.ca/wp-content/uploads/2021/12/2021-12-14-Ltr-to-Min-of-Justice-and-Public-Safety-NB-FINAL-amended_Redacted.pdf

[202] https://www.jccf.ca/wp-content/uploads/2021/12/2021-12-15-Ltr-to-Fredricton-Farmers-Market_Redacted1.pdf

[203] https://www.jccf.ca/news-release-nb-government-and-farmers-market-back-down-on-mandating-vaccines-for-grocery-shopping/

[204] https://www2.gnb.ca/content/gnb/en/news/news_release.2009.02.0235.html

[205] https://www.whitehouse.gov/briefing-room/speeches-remarks/2021/12/16/remarks-by-president-biden-after-meeting-with-members-of-the-COVID-19-response-team/

[206] https://www.youtube.com/watch?v=-zg1j7Zquoc

[207] https://globalnews.ca/news/8452591/canada-omicron-travel-rules-changing/

[208] https://montreal.ctvnews.ca/quebec-shuts-down-schools-bars-gyms-theatres-as-COVID-19-cases-soar-1.5714268

[209] https://montreal.ctvnews.ca/laval-restaurant-closes-after-at-least-30-infected-in-outbreak-early-testing-shows-omicron-1.5710629

[210] https://www.theatlantic.com/health/archive/2021/12/omicron-sports-leagues-nfl-nba/621079/

[211] https://www.cnn.com/2021/12/19/politics/elizabeth-warren-covid-positive/index.html

[212] https://www.washingtonpost.com/dc-md-va/2021/12/20/gov-larry-hogan-tests-positive-COVID-19/

[213] https://www.nsnews.com/coronavirus-COVID-19-national-news/minnesota-gov-walz-family-test-positive-for-COVID-19-4887210

[214] https://www.espn.com/nba/story/_/id/32832325/toronto-raptors-president-masai-ujiri-tests-positive-COVID-19-says

[215] https://www.cnbc.com/2021/12/20/i-have-covid-jim-cramer-says-he-says-hes-been-triple-vaccinated-and-has-a-mild-case.html

[216] https://tinyurl.com/2ubephmj

[217] https://www.ahajournals.org/doi/10.1161/circ.144.suppl_1.10712

[218] https://www.ahajournals.org/doi/10.1161/CIR.0000000000001053

[219] https://www.factcheck.org/2021/12/no-credible-evidence-COVID-19-mrna-vaccines-dramatically-increase-heart-attack-risk-contrary-to-flawed-abstract/

[220] https://ottawacitizen.com/news/local-news/the-taboo-subject-of-vaccine-injuries/

[221] https://aaronsiri.substack.com/p/fda-doubles-down-asks-federal-judge?s=r

[222] https://www.fda.gov/news-events/press-announcements/coronavirus-COVID-19-update-fda-announces-advisory-committee-meeting-discuss-second-COVID-19-vaccine

[223] https://www.businessinsider.com/fda-panel-backs-pfizers-COVID-19-shot-for-kids-ages-5-11-2021-10

[224] https://www.fda.gov/news-events/press-announcements/coronavirus-COVID-19-update-july-13-2021

[225] https://www.reuters.com/world/americas/canada-will-boost-supply-COVID-19-tests-life-set-get-better-pm-trudeau-2022-01-05/

[226] https://www.quebec.ca/en/news/actualites/detail/COVID-19-pandemic-additional-measures-will-come-into-force-tomorrow-37242

[227] https://globalnews.ca/news/8485740/canadian-army-quebec-COVID-19-vaccination/

[228] https://toronto.citynews.ca/2022/01/07/quebec-covid-vaccine-passport-liquor-cannabis/

[229] https://www.bbc.com/news/world-us-canada-59960689

[230] https://montrealgazette.com/news/local-news/COVID-19-updates-montreal-quebec-new-cases-vaccine-vaccination-booster-shot-omicron-school-students-open-curfew-legault-anti-vax-tax-january-13

[231] https://montrealgazette.com/news/local-news/weve-had-no-choice-but-to-lock-down-reopen-lock-down-reopen-legault-says

[232] https://nationalpost.com/news/canada/canadas-public-health-agency-admits-it-tracked-33-million-mobile-devices-during-lockdown

[233] https://www.cbc.ca/news/politics/duclos-mandatory-vaccination-policies-on-way-1.6307398

[234] Ibid.

[235] https://www.weforum.org/agenda/2019/01/trial-phase-2018-in-basic-income-in-review/

[236] https://www.cpac.ca/episode?id=8429c6a0-0863-4ba3-8515-898a0f27f982

[237] https://www.cbc.ca/news/canada/new-brunswick/new-brunswick-mandatory-vaccines-COVID-19-higgs-1.6310259

[238] https://www.timeschronicle.ca/b-c-will-not-make-vaccinations-mandatory/

[239] https://www.youtube.com/watch?v=pInQUjufYAo

[240] https://www.cbc.ca/news/canada/new-brunswick/new-brunswick-volunteers-COVID-19-pandemic-urgent-1.6347047

[241] https://www.cp24.com/news/feds-make-last-minute-reversal-on-vaccine-mandate-for-truckers-1.5737465?cache=xsfskdnkckf%3FclipId%3D89563

[242] https://www.canada.ca/en/public-health/news/2022/01/requirements-for-truckers-entering-canada-in-effect-as-of-january-15-2022.html

[243] https://www.france24.com/en/france/20220105-macron-says-he-wants-to-piss-off-france-s-unvaccinated

[244] https://www.cbc.ca/news/canada/edmonton/ahs-rapid-testing-vaccine-mandate-covid-1.6297604?fbclid=IwAR1HLBcraV4S024MtFLroQvmzbbDhki5aLhHIVvEZhAzJi1vOtCKFFmsojw

[245] https://www.theglobeandmail.com/canada/article-quebec-to-allow-some-health-care-staff-infected-with-COVID-19-to-stay/

[246] https://www.theglobeandmail.com/canada/article-quebec-to-allow-some-health-care-staff-infected-with-COVID-19-to-stay/

[247] https://torontosun.com/opinion/columnists/brampton-mayor-speaks-out-on-ontarios-misleading-covid-hospital-data?s=08&fbclid=IwAR3ZUEgJAhtGYX0voyoywVliUJnruC2ES5i4WlEVMgsiwxC6ZKVz39NMpNY

[248] https://www.cp24.com/news/ontario-now-distinguishing-between-people-admitted-to-hospital-with-or-for-COVID-19-1.5736010

[249] https://www.cbc.ca/news/canada/nova-scotia/COVID-19-hospitals-health-care-1.6307913

[250] https://www.ctvnews.ca/health/health-headlines/hospitals-overwhelmed-by-flu-and-norovirus-patients-1.1108376?cache=ilazquiulmx

[251] https://www.ctvnews.ca/health/ontario-ers-overwhelmed-as-flu-hits-harder-than-usual-1.2165912?cache=

[252] https://www.thestar.com/news/canada/2017/04/16/surge-in-patients-forces-ontario-hospitals-to-put-beds-in-unconventional-spaces.html

[253] https://www.cbc.ca/news/canada/windsor/hospital-overcrowding-windsor-crisis-1.4503107

[254] https://www.thestar.com/politics/provincial/2019/11/12/ontario-residents-urged-to-get-flu-shot-as-hospitals-brace-for-the-worst.html

[255] https://www.fraserinstitute.org/studies/comparing-performance-of-universal-health-care-countries-2019?utm_source=Media-Releases&utm_campaign=Comparing-Performance-Universal-Health-Care-2019&utm_medium=Media&utm_content=Learn_More&utm_term=700

[256] https://www.cbc.ca/news/canada/new-brunswick/COVID-19-new-brunswick-forecasting-

omicron-technical-briefing-epidemiologist-1.6310738

[257] https://www.cbc.ca/news/canada/new-brunswick/COVID-19-new-brunswick-update-level-3-restrictions-hospitalizations-1.6312937

[258] https://www.cbc.ca/news/canada/new-brunswick/COVID-19-new-brunswick-cosmetology-association-horizon-cleaning-1.6318757

[259] https://www.cbc.ca/news/canada/new-brunswick/COVID-19-new-brunswick-pfizer-pill-paxlovid-volunteers-1.6319782

[260] https://phmpt.org/pfizers-documents/

[261] https://globalnews.ca/news/8801205/quebec-still-reporting-dozens-covid-deaths-dailydeaths-daily/

[262] https://globalnews.ca/news/8497344/COVID-19-saskatchewan-incidental-hospitalization-reporting/

[263] https://winnipegsun.com/news/news-news/two-thirds-of-COVID-19-hospitalizations-incidental-province-says

[264] https://calgary.ctvnews.ca/incidental-COVID-19-transmissions-to-hospital-patients-creates-strain-for-alberta-health-care-workers-1.5744875

[265] https://www.kamloopsthisweek.com/local-news/omicron-variant-leads-to-many-more-incidental-COVID-19-hospitalizations-5017839

[266] https://globalnews.ca/news/514767/28-per-cent-of-hospital-occupied-by-seniors-waiting-for-nursing-home-bed/

[267] https://www.thestar.com/opinion/contributors/2019/11/03/nobody-wins-when-hospitals-become-long-term-care-homes.html

[268] https://atlantic.ctvnews.ca/lengthy-waits-for-nursing-homes-are-stressing-n-s-hospitals-ndp-says-1.3833568

[269] https://toronto.citynews.ca/2022/01/12/canada-poll-unvaccinated-fines/

[270] https://nationalpost.com/news/canada/more-than-one-in-four-canadians-support-jail-time-for-unvaccinated-poll

[271] https://www.westernstandard.news/news/trucker-freedom-convoy-gofundme-raises-over-1m/article_bd2c0ccf-6117-550f-ac0a-a652ac8b6a43.html

[272] https://www.westernstandard.news/news/trucker-freedom-convoy-gofundme-raises-over-1m/article_bd2c0ccf-6117-550f-ac0a-a652ac8b6a43.html

[273] https://www.independent.co.uk/news/world/americas/canada-truckers-freedom-convoy-gofundme-b2004806.html

[274] https://www.youtube.com/watch?v=vDfMybczw1k

[275] https://www.cbc.ca/news/politics/vaccine-mandate-double-down-convoy-1.6326821

[276] https://www.nytimes.com/live/2021/12/30/world/omicron-covid-vaccine-tests

[277] https://www.bbc.com/news/uk-60047438?fbclid=IwAR0Ryc04mViG7y9wr20Rg7XyKMchQpgA_x94MFPAd2K-3cRsXJbhqEE1kvM

[278] https://ca.movies.yahoo.com/COVID-19-downing-street-seeks-164600303.html

[279] https://www.bbc.com/news/av/business-21186386

[280] https://www.itv.com/news/2020-01-19/davos-what-you-need-to-know-about-the-2020-summit

[281] https://www.bnnbloomberg.ca/boris-johnson-s-new-priorities-see-the-u-k-boycott-davos-1.1363867

[282] https://www.express.co.uk/showbiz/tv-radio/1548650/Dr-Hillary-latest-GMB-doctor-antivax-coronavirus-vaccine-latest-vn

[283] https://www.mirror.co.uk/tv/tv-news/gmbs-dr-hilary-says-mandatory-25997679

[284] https://www.bbc.com/news/uk-politics-59952395

[285] https://www.bbc.com/news/world-africa-60039138

[286] https://www.bnnbloomberg.ca/mrna-boosters-don-t-block-omicron-south-african-study-shows-1.1709778

[287] https://twitter.com/cmaconthehill/status/1486842689790300169

[288] https://www.ctvnews.ca/politics/what-does-the-trucker-convoy-hope-to-accomplish-1.5758489

[289] https://www.ctvnews.ca/politics/what-does-the-trucker-convoy-hope-to-accomplish-1.5758489

[290] https://tinyurl.com/57rmxjpk

[291] https://www.independent.co.uk/news/world/americas/trump-jr-truckers-convoy-canada-b2005071.html

292 https://www.washingtonpost.com/opinions/2022/01/28/canada-must-confront-toxic-protest-freedom-convoy/

293 https://nationalpost.com/news/canada/the-canadian-revolution-how-foreign-anti-mandate-sympathizers-are-framing-the-trucker-convoy

294 https://www.reuters.com/business/healthcare-pharmaceuticals/prior-covid-infection-more-protective-than-vaccination-during-delta-surge-us-2022-01-19/

295 https://www.canada.ca/en/public-health/services/immunization/national-advisory-committee-on-immunization-naci/rapid-response-guidance-COVID-19-vaccination-timing-individuals-previously-infected-sars-cov-2.html

296 https://ottawa.ctvnews.ca/heavy-police-presence-as-truckers-arrive-in-downtown-ottawa-1.5757761

297 https://twitter.com/elonmusk/status/1486772334635536395?lang=en

298 https://ici.radio-canada.ca/rci/en/news/1859099/protest-organizers-dig-in-and-say-only-politicians-can-clear-ottawas-downtown

299 https://ottawa.ctvnews.ca/ottawa-s-downtown-core-closed-to-vehicles-as-freedom-convoy-packs-parliament-hill-1.5758807

300 https://ottawa.ctvnews.ca/all-options-are-on-the-table-to-end-truckers-protest-ottawa-police-chief-1.5760880

301 https://www.youtube.com/watch?v=50kHdAumXvA

302 https://www.youtube.com/watch?v=Kjjihr_GCu8

303 https://www.facebook.com/PremierScottMoe/posts/485013612993714

304 https://globalnews.ca/news/8579350/doug-ford-says-ontario-needs-to-learn-to-live-with-covid/?fbclid=IwAR12g1GSCiOmBJ_K28YXhFrf4sNdffEGDiZ5aFQeXWMaQJw21OaNuYOTzOA

305 https://rumble.com/vtkmpp-cbc-tv-suggests-russian-actors-are-behind-freedom-convoy.html

306 https://www.cbc.ca/player/play/2002191939918

307 https://www.youtube.com/watch?v=jGb6GeiuN0c

308 https://ottawa.ctvnews.ca/mobile/video?clipId=2376532&binId=1.1164511&playlistPageNum=1&fbclid=IwAR23oUloEaflOSuwDTwMypvolgzr7ushUPvN9vau3E-15kYyk58BuOnVmxo

309 https://www.youtube.com/watch?v=ozWQW0BiBsY

310 https://nypost.com/2022/02/09/man-78-arrested-for-honking-horn-in-support-of-freedom-convoy/

311 https://globalnews.ca/news/8610512/givesendgo-fundraiser-trucker-convoy-frozen/

312 https://www.cbc.ca/news/canada/toronto/freedom-convoy-2022-donations-frozen-give-send-go-1.6347345

313 https://www.msn.com/en-ca/news/canada/ottawa-protesters-employ-gas-can-subterfuge-to-frustrate-police/ar-AATCY4x?li=AAggNb9&cvid=f5deea6fdad74ebfa9bb751231f0e304#image=2

314 https://www.youtube.com/watch?v=8j0wZ52jrgY

315 https://twitter.com/pnpcbc/status/1493735565690228738?lang=en

316 https://www.cbc.ca/player/play/2000605763636

317 https://twitter.com/dianedeans/status/1493717827144105987?s=20&t=YypVPQYJzxOAv48-MZyLgw

318 https://www.youtube.com/watch?v=Kbcrboh0Bk4

319 https://www.healthline.com/health/migraines-after-covid-vaccine#prevalence

320 https://www.ottawapolice.ca/Modules/News/index.aspx?newsId=1e4940bf-a4cc-47b8-a22a-a3975191957a&lang=en

321 https://twitter.com/GuerrillaRepor1/status/1477624939113029634

322 https://twitter.com/OttawaPolice/status/1494806133646794752

323 https://www.youtube.com/watch?v=akejAM-jZNg

324 https://twitter.com/OttawaPolice/status/1494806139971813376

325 https://www.cbc.ca/news/canada/convoy-protesters-police-tactical-knowledge-1.6345854

326 https://www.youtube.com/watch?v=SUC4ELQnKEE

327 https://www.france24.com/en/americas/20220202-canada-police-warn-of-guns-at-trucker-protest-against-vaccine-mandate

328 https://www.youtube.com/watch?v=F_zQe4pCk30

329 https://globalnews.ca/video/8707012/trucker-protests-interim-ottawa-police-chief-says-no-charges-laid-in-connection-to-loaded-firearms

[330] https://www.theglobeandmail.com/world/us-politics/article-us-offers-homeland-securitys-help-to-end-ambassador-bridge-blockade/

[331] https://www.youtube.com/watch?v=RIfskg7WNLE

[332] https://www.youtube.com/watch?v=pmQghqnni4k

[333] https://www.youtube.com/watch?v=PXHjnsUlZc4

[334] https://sites.krieger.jhu.edu/iae/files/2022/01/A-Literature-Review-and-Meta-Analysis-of-the-Effects-of-Lockdowns-on-COVID-19-Mortality.pdf

[335] https://www.ncbi.nlm.nih.gov/pmc/articles/PMC8933043/

[336] https://www.sciencedirect.com/science/article/abs/pii/S0749597814000983

[337] https://www.theglobeandmail.com/canada/article-quebec-premier-francois-legault-scraps-plans-to-tax-the-unvaccinated/

[338] https://atlantic.ctvnews.ca/new-order-bans-highway-border-blockades-in-nova-scotia-1.5759013

[339] https://calgaryherald.com/news/local-news/two-more-arrested-as-anti-mandate-protests-continue-in-calgary-public-parks

[340] https://www.youtube.com/watch?v=TLTvejNzaTo

[341] https://ottawacitizen.com/news/national/defence-watch/canadian-special-forces-conducted-flights-over-ottawa-protest-despite-military-directive

[342] https://www.cbc.ca/news/canada/ottawa/tamara-lich-chris-barber-ottawa-trial-freedom-convoy-sept-2023-1.6566730

[343] https://www.cbc.ca/news/politics/government-end-vax-mandates-1.6487585

[344] https://www.cbc.ca/news/politics/singh-trucker-convoy-brother-in-law-1.6328689?__vfz=medium%3Dsharebar

[345] https://twitter.com/thejagmeetsingh/status/1486762512473280516?lang=en

[346] https://twitter.com/thejagmeetsingh/status/1487478167652773888

[347] https://www.npr.org/sections/live-updates-protests-for-racial-justice/2020/06/18/880559245/canadian-politician-kicked-out-of-parliament-for-calling-rival-racist

[348] https://twitter.com/thejagmeetsingh/status/1487867911746248704

[349] https://www.ndp.ca/news/jagmeet-singh-speech-emergencies-act

[350] https://nationalpost.com/news/politics/senate-growing-frustrated-by-pressure-to-rubber-stamp-emergencies-act

[351] https://www.iheartradio.ca/cfax-1070/news/trudeau-set-to-revoke-emergencies-act-sources-1.17225495

[352] https://www.youtube.com/watch?v=DyNeZquKrxI

[353] https://www.ctvnews.ca/health/coronavirus/russia-backs-away-from-unpopular-anti-coronavirus-measures-1.5740247

[354] https://www.youtube.com/watch?v=JrMiSQAGOS4

[355] https://www.politico.eu/article/pope-francis-says-war-in-ukraine-perhaps-provoked-or-unprevented/

[356] https://angusreid.org/omicron-incidence-restrictions/

[357] https://pm.gc.ca/en/news/news-releases/2022/03/22/delivering-canadians-now

[358] https://twitter.com/ctvqp/status/1431997913719312387

[359] https://twitter.com/darryl_barton/status/1547607602279825414?s=20&t=6vsSzGHq_J1SSwI6qGLrew

[360] https://www.cbc.ca/news/canada/toronto/justin-trudeau-s-foolish-china-remarks-spark-anger-1.2421351

[361] https://en.wikipedia.org/wiki/Xi_Jinping#Chinese_Dream

[362] https://www.cnn.com/interactive/2020/04/world/wuhan-coronavirus-cnnphotos/

[363] https://www.wired.com/2003/04/beijing-undergoes-sars-lockdown/

[364] https://www.ncbi.nlm.nih.gov/pmc/articles/PMC3823329/

[365] https://www.nytimes.com/2021/02/05/world/asia/china-covid-economy.html

[366] https://www.nytimes.com/2021/02/05/world/asia/china-covid-economy.html

[367] https://www.cfib-fcei.ca/en/media/news-releases/cfib-statement-100-straight-days-winter-lockdowns

[368] https://info.publicintelligence.net/WHO-ChinaMission-COVID-19.pdf

[369] https://www.reuters.com/article/health-coronavirus-un-idUSL2N2BW09O

[370] https://www.politico.com/news/2020/04/14/trump-world-health-organization-funding-186786

371 https://nypost.com/2020/05/06/finally-the-world-is-catching-on-to-chinas-coronavirus-lies/
372 https://www.youtube.com/watch?v=CkCFDDCkG1k
373 https://www.abc.net.au/news/2021-01-03/heres-what-happened-between-china-and-australia-in-2020/13019242
374 https://link.springer.com/article/10.1007/s12140-021-09382-x?fbclid=IwAR3yxg1_Qf6MyNCODUx3XizRxhEKPzqukku9OuBcOhqFPmaE3guZArZHyPk
375 https://www.cbc.ca/news/politics/china-allegations-mail-1.6318115
376 https://www.chinadaily.com.cn/a/202004/24/WS5ea28240a310a8b2411516bf.html
377 https://unctad.org/system/files/official-document/diaeiainf2021d1_en.pdf
378 https://fortune.com/2021/01/17/china-economy-gdp-2020-growth-q4/
379 https://www.weforum.org/events/the-davos-agenda-2021/sessions/special-address-by-g20-head-of-state-government-67e386f2d5
380 https://www.business-standard.com/article/international/upbeat-about-future-xi-says-time-on-china-s-side-as-turmoil-grips-us-121011200295_1.html
381 https://www.wsj.com/articles/china-creates-its-own-digital-currency-a-first-for-major-economy-11617634118
382 https://www.ft.com/content/7511809e-827e-4526-81ad-ae83f405f623
383 https://supchina.com/2020/07/09/with-11-million-tests-china-contains-COVID-19-where-the-u-s-fails/
384 https://www.globaltimes.cn/page/202103/1217876.shtml
385 https://www.scmp.com/news/china/politics/article/3117314/xi-jinping-says-time-and-momentum-chinas-side-he-sets-out
386 https://zenodo.org/record/5075888#.Yu4xTuzMKSr
387 https://www.science.org/doi/10.1126/science.abp8715#con18
388 https://en.wikipedia.org/wiki/Xi_Jinping#Chinese_Dream
389 https://www.republicworld.com/world-news/rest-of-the-world-news/new-zealand-abandons-zero-covid-strategy-amid-spread-of-delta-variant.html
390 https://rumble.com/vo5th1-covid-tyrant-yes-we-want-a-two-class-system.html
391 https://rumble.com/vqf63m-new-zealand-pm-ardern-theres-not-going-to-be-an-endpoint-to-this-vaccinatio.html
392 https://www.reuters.com/world/asia-pacific/skorea-reports-record-new-daily-covid-cases-deaths-kdca-2022-03-17/
393 https://www.bbc.com/news/world-europe-60681288
394 https://www.cnn.com/2022/05/06/china/china-xi-pbsc-zero-covid-intl-hnk/index.html
395 https://www.ndtv.com/world-news/xi-jinping-warns-for-questioning-chinas-zero-covid-policy-2953549
396 https://globalnews.ca/news/7996100/who-decision-covid-vaccines/
397 https://www.bbc.com/news/59882774
398 https://www.theguardian.com/world/2021/nov/02/china-locks-down-shanghai-disneyland-and-tests-34000-visitors-after-single-covid-case
399 https://en.wikipedia.org/wiki/2022_Shanghai_COVID-19_outbreak#Pet_killing
400 https://www.youtube.com/watch?v=3SRuKZ5P1io
401 https://www.bloomberg.com/news/articles/2020-09-17/behind-china-s-epic-dash-for-ppe-that-left-the-world-short-on-masks#xj4y7vzkg
402 https://www.labpulse.com/index.aspx?sec=ser&sub=def&pag=dis&ItemID=803078
403 https://www.theglobeandmail.com/world/article-china-censors-who-chief-after-he-warns-zero-covid-policy-not/
404 https://www.scmp.com/news/china/politics/article/3177050/stop-shanghais-covid-prevention-excesses-academics-urge-online
405 https://www.ctvnews.ca/health/coronavirus/beijing-imposes-mainland-china-s-first-covid-vaccine-mandate-in-face-of-omicron-subvariant-1.5977730
406 https://tinyurl.com/kppbrbay
407 https://www.bloomberg.com/news/articles/2022-07-19/xi-s-strict-covid-zero-policy-in-china-pushes-wealthy-to-leave-country#xj4y7vzkg
408 https://ca.movies.yahoo.com/movies/china-using-qr-codes-try-062102742.html
409 https://home.treasury.gov/data/treasury-international-capital-tic-system-home-page/tic-forms-instructions/securities-b-portfolio-holdings-of-us-and-foreign-securities

410 https://www.businessinsider.in/stock-market/news/chinas-yuan-is-making-headway-a-global-reserve-currency-with-85-of-central-banks-keen-on-holding-the-asset/articleshow/92652273.cms

411 https://www.foxnews.com/world/canadian-mp-claims-honk-honk-code-heil-hitler

412 https://www.rebelnews.com/cbc_hiring_trauma_therapists_for_journalists

413 https://www.cbc.ca/news/canada/british-columbia/covid-restrictions-update-1.6352614

414 https://www.youtube.com/watch?v=6VnXTLv2YOo

415 https://www.cbc.ca/news/politics/freeland-nationalist-scarf-1.6372995

416 https://nationalpost.com/news/canada/did-chrystia-freeland-pose-with-extremist-symbols-or-is-it-russian-disinformation

417 https://thepostmillennial.com/trudeaus-anniversary-pic-shows-vaccinated-couple-masked-up

418 https://twitter.com/AndrewScheer/status/1009594873501175808

419 https://www.youtube.com/watch?v=mJ7MK8NkErM

420 https://ontarioliberal.ca/ontario-liberals-call-for-mask-extension-and-expansion-to-schools-pharmacies-and-grocery-stores/

421 https://www.ctvnews.ca/health/coronavirus/some-vaccine-waste-expected-but-better-planning-needed-expert-1.5870300

422 https://www.cmaj.ca/content/cmaj/194/16/E573.full.pdf

423 https://twitter.com/jdM273/status/1521195653640110087/photo/1

424 https://www.thestar.com/news/gta/2022/04/25/remaining-unvaccinated-increases-risk-to-the-vaccinated-says-u-of-t-covid-study.html

425 https://viralimmunologist.substack.com/p/fiction-disguised-as-science-to-promote?s=r

426 https://twitter.com/realmonsanto/status/1521818641741795328

427 https://twitter.com/MonaFortier/status/1525244861917630464

428 https://greatgameindia.com/moderna-throw-vaccines-garbage/

429 https://twitter.com/realmonsanto/status/1521103871321546753

430 https://www.cbc.ca/news/health/omicron-immunity-canada-covd19-vaccines-1.6428536

431 https://www.covid19immunitytaskforce.ca/the-omicron-tsunami-analysis-of-data-from-blood-testing-suggests-over-17-million-canadians-were-infected-with-omicron-in-only-5-months/

432 https://health-infobase.canada.ca/COVID-19/

433 https://coronavirus.jhu.edu/data/mortality

434 https://regina.ctvnews.ca/fourth-vaccine-doses-could-be-key-to-ending-pandemic-sask-epidemiologist-1.5897360

435 https://ottawacitizen.com/news/ontario-election/liberals-would-add-COVID-19-shots-to-schools-immunization-lists-del-duca-says

436 https://www.cdc.gov/mmwr/volumes/71/wr/mm7117e3.htm?s_cid=mm7117e3_e&ACSTrackingID%5B%E2%80%A6%5D.%2071%2C%20April%2026%2C%202022&deliveryName=USCDC_921-DM80513

437 https://torontosun.com/entertainment/celebrity/joe-rogan-rips-creepy-dictator-justin-trudeau-over-trucker-protest

438 https://www.youtube.com/watch?v=52jT3RS6e5w

439 https://tinyurl.com/mv97cww9

440 https://apnews.com/article/covid-health-africa-united-nations-7491de8c9634ab2ad88cd92ae1050819

441 https://twitter.com/TheRealKeean/status/1523469203939811328?s=20&t=pEB4sItVzZgMe2Cf5LOJOA

442 https://www.cbsnews.com/news/gun-control-canada-trudeau-national-freeze-handgun-ownership/

443 https://www.axios.com/2022/05/31/canada-illegal-drugs-british-columbia-overdoses

444 https://twitter.com/zchagla/status/1526326098161717249

445 https://vancouversun.com/news/local-news/horgan-health-transfers

446 https://fortune.com/2022/05/10/pfizer-ceo-covid-vaccine-booster-shots/

447 https://tnc.news/2022/05/30/jagmeet-singh-flees-brampton-event-over-questions-from-sikh-protesters/

448 https://www.youtube.com/watch?v=QMzeLIBxUGM&t=7s

449 https://torontosun.com/opinion/columnists/gunter-the-freezing-of-accounts-was-political-vengeance?utm_term=Autofeed&utm_medium=Social&utm_source=Facebook#Echobox=1645913

484
450 https://www.youtube.com/watch?v=VqZ5mf5LMf4
451 https://globalnews.ca/news/8920882/emergencies-act-freeland-freedom-convoy-blockades-ottawa/
452 https://www.ctvnews.ca/politics/liberals-to-release-cabinet-documents-to-emergencies-act-inquiry-1.5965951
453 https://www.canada.ca/en/transport-canada/news/2022/06/government-of-canada-and-airport-and-airline-partners-making-progress-on-reducing-traveller-wait-times-at-canadas-major-airports.html
454 https://twitter.com/LloydLongfield/status/1537570251176558593
455 https://tnc.news/2022/06/10/liberal-mps-say-massive-majority-of-caucus-wants-trudeau-to-end-mandates/
456 https://www.jccf.ca/date-set-for-federal-court-to-hear-challenge-to-travel-ban-in-september/
457 https://www.youtube.com/watch?v=ZhqHsyJbVu0
458 https://ca.sports.yahoo.com/news/jt-realmuto-missing-blue-jays-phillies-series-not-going-let-canada-tell-me-put-my-body-130621008.html
459 https://torontosun.com/news/local-news/warmington-liberal-mp-gets-an-f-for-f-bomb-toward-woman-criticizing-vax-mandates
460 https://torontosun.com/news/local-news/warmington-liberal-mp-gets-an-f-for-f-bomb-toward-woman-criticizing-vax-mandates
461 https://www.youtube.com/watch?v=UUNUIzLCvSU
462 https://twitter.com/ryanwhitney6/status/1533797008200310785
463 https://www.cbc.ca/news/politics/canada-more-sustainable-covid-response-1.6339609
464 https://torontosun.com/opinion/columnists/lilley-trudeau-acts-on-his-own-political-science-to-drop-travel-restrictions
465 https://twitter.com/Tinfoil_Travis/status/1535430832831320064
466 https://www.canada.ca/en/treasury-board-secretariat/news/2022/06/suspension-of-the-vaccine-mandates-for-domestic-travellers-transportation-workers-and-federal-employees.html
467 https://twitter.com/OmarAlghabra/status/1535076474310770688
468 https://www.ft.com/content/27def1b9-b9c8-47a5-8e06-72e432e0838f
469 https://www.npr.org/sections/health-shots/2021/12/15/1064202754/omicron-evades-moderna-vaccine-too-study-suggests-but-boosters-help
470 https://www.cp24.com/news/there-is-a-myth-out-there-that-it-s-mild-head-of-ontario-s-science-table-says-of-omicron-1.5704993
471 https://www1.racgp.org.au/newsgp/clinical/omicron-a-significant-challenge-to-two-dose-vaccin
472 https://www.nytimes.com/2021/12/19/health/omicron-vaccines-efficacy.html
473 https://news.harvard.edu/gazette/story/2022/01/no-omicron-immunity-without-booster-study-finds/
474 https://www.cnbc.com/2022/01/06/moderna-ceo-says-people-may-need-fourth-covid-shot-as-efficacy-of-boosters-likely-to-decline-over-time.html
475 https://www.cnbc.com/2022/01/10/pfizer-ceo-says-two-covid-vaccine-doses-arent-enough-for-omicron.html
476 https://www.cnn.com/2022/01/11/health/us-coronavirus-tuesday/index.html
477 https://globalnews.ca/news/8579350/doug-ford-says-ontario-needs-to-learn-to-live-with-covid/?fbclid=IwAR12g1GSCiOmBJ_K28YXhFrf4sNdffEGDiZ5aFQeXWMaQJw21OaNuYOTzOA
478 https://regina.ctvnews.ca/sask-premier-pledges-to-end-proof-of-vaccination-policies-in-letter-to-truckers-1.5759892
479 https://toronto.ctvnews.ca/we-are-done-with-it-doug-ford-says-ontario-is-moving-on-from-COVID-19-1.5782355
480 https://www.nejm.org/doi/full/10.1056/NEJMoa2119451
481 https://globalnews.ca/news/8920039/canada-covid-rules-remaining-2022/
482 https://saskatoon.ctvnews.ca/sask-trucking-association-wants-vaccine-mandates-lifted-at-land-borders-1.5950920
483 https://www.realclearpolitics.com/video/2021/09/02/canadian_pm_trudeau_blasts_anti-vaxxers_im_focused_on_the_health_and_safety_of_the_responsible_majority.html
484 https://spectator.com.au/2022/07/government-is-not-the-divine-source-of-truth/

[485] https://www.cdc.gov.tw/Uploads/275462dd-bfea-43a3-9b30-6f3829851c21.pdf
[486] https://factcheck.afp.com/http%253A%252F%252Fdoc.afp.com%252F9UM2C6-1
[487] https://www.ntd.com/chinas-zero-post-vaccine-deaths-raises-questions_679660.html
[488] https://www.scmp.com/news/china/politics/article/3152922/mother-detained-china-after-pleas-probe-death-vaccinated
[489] https://www.trishwoodpodcast.com/podcast/episode-116-marianne-klowak
[490] https://nationalpost.com/opinion/tara-henley-why-i-quit-the-cbc
[491] https://www.justice.gc.ca/eng/csj-sjc/rfc-dlc/ccrf-ccdl/check/art2b.html
[492] https://www.cbc.ca/news/canada/british-columbia/bc-man-vaccine-injury-payout-1.6472636
[493] https://www.cbc.ca/news/canada/british-columbia/bc-man-vaccine-injury-payout-1.6472636
[494] https://ottawacitizen.com/news/local-news/ottawa-company-that-built-successful-vaccine-booking-systems-working-with-local-businesses-on-safe-return-to-work
[495] https://www.cbc.ca/news/canada/british-columbia/bc-man-vaccine-injury-payout-1.6472636
[496] https://www.cbc.ca/news/canada/british-columbia/vaccine-injury-support-program-COVID-19-pfizer-vaccine-paralysis-1.6496761
[497] https://health-infobase.canada.ca/COVID-19/vaccine-safety/
[498] https://vaccineinjurysupport.ca/en/program-statistics
[499] https://calgary.ctvnews.ca/deaths-with-unknown-causes-now-alberta-s-top-killer-province-1.5975536
[500] https://calgary.ctvnews.ca/vaccines-not-causing-unexplained-deaths-in-alberta-authorities-say-1.5981134
[501] https://www.cbc.ca/news/canada/new-brunswick/excess-deaths-minister-shephard-1.6484641
[502] https://www.cbc.ca/news/canada/new-brunswick/excess-deaths-minister-shephard-1.6484641
[503] https://www.who.int/news/item/05-05-2022-14.9-million-excess-deaths-were-associated-with-the-COVID-19-pandemic-in-2020-and-2021
[504] https://www.bbc.com/news/health-61327778
[505] https://www.consilium.europa.eu/en/policies/coronavirus/pandemic-treaty/
[506] https://faculty.washington.edu/jonno/COVID-Methods-Paper-Revision.pdf
[507] https://faculty.washington.edu/jonno/COVID-Methods-Paper-Revision.pdf
[508] https://www.nytimes.com/2021/04/24/world/asia/india-coronavirus-deaths.html
[509] https://www.thehindu.com/news/national/other-states/coronavirus-COVID-19-deaths-in-gujarat-far-exceed-government-figures/article34352916.ece
[510] https://www.theguardian.com/world/2022/apr/18/COVID-19-india-accused-of-attempting-to-delay-who-revision-of-death-toll
[511] https://www.ctvnews.ca/health/patient-dies-while-waiting-hours-to-be-seen-in-new-brunswick-emergency-department-1.5987414
[512] https://atlantic.ctvnews.ca/multiple-new-brunswick-emergency-departments-close-as-long-weekend-begins-1.5971330
[513] https://www.cbc.ca/news/canada/prince-edward-island/pei-western-hospital-closed-1.6529382
[514] https://london.ctvnews.ca/clinton-ont-emergency-room-closed-for-entire-canada-day-long-weekend-1.5967020
[515] https://winnipeg.ctvnews.ca/i-m-really-angry-staff-shortages-temporarily-closing-some-rural-manitoba-emergency-rooms-1.5972196
[516] https://www.cbc.ca/news/canada/calgary/emergency-room-doctors-staffing-alberta-1.6414034
[517] https://bc.ctvnews.ca/staffing-shortages-lead-to-temporary-closures-of-4-b-c-interior-emergency-departments-1.5992105
[518] https://montreal.ctvnews.ca/6-quebec-ers-to-be-partially-closed-obstetric-and-neonatal-care-scaled-back-this-summer-1.5958129
[519] https://toronto.ctvnews.ca/ontario-is-changing-how-it-reports-COVID-19-deaths-1.5812306
[520] https://www.theepochtimes.com/young-healthy-adults-dont-necessarily-need-2nd-booster-shot-as-risk-of-hospitalization-is-very-very-low-moore_4596802.html
[521] https://www.youtube.com/watch?v=SuO7BneQjiQ
[522] https://www.who.int/about/funding/contributors
[523] https://www.nejm.org/doi/full/10.1056/nejme2002387
[524] https://www.cnbc.com/2020/03/11/top-federal-health-official-says-coronavirus-outbreak-is-going-to-get-worse-in-the-us.html
[525] https://gbdeclaration.org/

[526] https://www.aier.org/article/fauci-emails-and-some-alleged-science/

[527] https://bmjopen.bmj.com/content/12/5/e059041

[528] https://www.nytimes.com/2021/11/10/us/politics/moderna-vaccine-patent-nih.html

[529] https://rumble.com/v12l9x8-jim-jordan-how-much-money-does-the-cdc-and-nih-spend-each-year.html

[530] https://freebeacon.com/biden-administration/how-the-cdc-coordinated-with-big-tech-to-censor-americans/

[531] https://www.bmj.com/content/375/bmj.n2635?ijkey=5914def355da40d2ad246f6cee76a149482844c5&keytype2=tf_ipsecsha

[532] https://www.bmj.com/content/376/bmj.o95

[533] https://www.youtube.com/watch?v=sifGuMTNzhs

[534] https://www.statnews.com/2021/03/15/white-house-unveil-a-wide-reaching-billion-dollar-campaign-convincing-every-american-to-get-vaccinated/

[535] https://www.cms.gov/newsroom/press-releases/biden-harris-administration-increases-medicare-payment-life-saving-COVID-19-vaccine

[536] https://www.cjr.org/criticism/gates-foundation-journalism-funding.php

[537] https://thegrayzone.com/2021/11/21/bill-gates-million-media-outlets-global-agenda/

[538] https://www.cnn.com/search?size=10&q=bill%20gates&sort=newest

[539] https://www.gatesfoundation.org/-/media/files/bmgf-grants.csv

[540] Berenson, Alex. Pandemia: How Coronavirus Hysteria Took Over Out Government, Rights, and Lives. Washington. Regnery Publishing. Pg 163.

[541] https://nationalpost.com/news/canada/indigo-the-freedom-convoy-the-inside-story-of-three-weeks-that-shook-the-world

[542] https://www.amazon.ca/Freedom-Convoy-Inside-Story-Three/dp/1989555934

[543] https://www.foxnews.com/media/dr-robert-malone-joe-rogan-covid-ingraham-twitter-ban-youtube-censorship

[544] https://twitter.com/BernieSpofforth/status/1544204221360242688?s=20&t=cLyu9DyNQS5OJP-LAp5hHw

[545] https://www.commonsense.news/p/court-documents-reveal-canadas-travel

[546] https://www.youtube.com/watch?v=rt15NjokwxY&list=FLeYYXI7uj2R-4yvi2oJfyxg
https://www.youtube.com/watch?v=rt15NjokwxY&list=FLeYYXI7uj2R-4yvi2oJfyxg
le-visit-to-facebook-users-home

[548] https://www.bbc.com/news/world-australia-54007824

[549] https://news.yahoo.com/asia-cracks-down-virus-fake-news-083226238.html

[550] https://www.who.int/health-topics/infodemic#tab=tab_1

[551] https://www.who.int/publications/m/item/monkeypox--COVID-19---other-global-health-issues-virtual-press-conference-transcript---27-july-2022

[552] https://www.who.int/europe/news/item/23-07-2022-who-director-general-declares-the-ongoing-monkeypox-outbreak-a-public-health-event-of-international-concern

[553] https://www.timescolonist.com/national-news/quebec-to-start-vaccinating-contacts-of-monkeypox-cases-as-25-infections-confirmed-5408399

[554] https://montrealgazette.top1tv.net/news/local-news/monkeypox-cases-climb-to-132-in-quebec-thousands-vaccinated

[555] https://www.csis.org/node/65495

[556] https://www.foxnews.com/media/dr-deborah-birx-knew-covid-vaccines-not-protect-against-infection

[557] https://www.csis.org/node/65495

[558] https://twitter.com/JerseyJoe1234/status/1553042621056040960?s=20&t=srytuEkblMT680DJ7Z1F9A

[559] https://abcnews.go.com/Politics/dr-birx-relationship-trump-respectful-public-clear-private/story?id=74760598

[560] https://www.cbsnews.com/news/transcript-deborah-birx-on-face-the-nation-january-24-2021/

[561] https://www.aier.org/wp-content/uploads/2021/12/FauciBirx.pdf

[562] https://www.businessinsider.com/whos-afraid-of-naomi-wolf-2021-6

[563] https://naomiwolf.substack.com/p/is-it-time-for-intellectuals-to-talk

[564] https://www.youtube.com/watch?v=hamLp6P9ys4

[565] https://blogs.bmj.com/bmj/2021/09/13/COVID-19-and-the-new-merchants-of-doubt/

[566] https://doctorsandscientistsdeclaration.org/

[567] https://twitter.com/RNCResearch/status/1554118665146073088?s=20&t=UJ7UV4hQnlWpmCgUwnHKUA

[568] https://twitter.com/RealAndyLeeShow/status/1554496213650591744?s=20&t=UJ7UV4hQnlWpmCgUwnHKUA

[569] https://apnews.com/article/mo-state-wire-michael-brown-business-coronavirus-pandemic-health-b8a5ba4896ab02f441f24ebb7fed5064

[570] https://ottawa.ctvnews.ca/key-freedom-convoy-figure-pleads-guilty-to-counselling-mischief-released-from-jail-1.5947767

[571] https://torontosun.com/news/provincial/science-table-member-paid-by-teacher-union-for-arguing-against-school-re-openings

[572] https://www.beyondthenarrative.ca/that-fisman-study/

[573] https://www.cbc.ca/news/canada/toronto/david-fisman-resignation-covid-science-table-ontario-1.6149961

[574] https://www.cmaj.ca/content/192/19/E497.short

[575] https://www.cmaj.ca/content/194/16/E573

[576] https://www.cbc.ca/news/canada/new-brunswick/cardy-fredericton-police-tweets-1.6323524?cmp=rss

[577] https://www.cbc.ca/news/canada/new-brunswick/fredericton-council-tweets-social-media-1.6326340

[578] https://tj.news/telegraph-journal/101782092

[579] https://tj.news/telegraph-journal/101781091?ref=tw&tjid=67096&date=1643310765773

[580] https://globalnews.ca/news/8583723/education-minister-in-n-b-under-fire-over-twitter-thread-on-how-police-handled-protest/

[581] https://atlantic.ctvnews.ca/n-b-education-minister-sparks-conversation-after-calling-for-deregulation-of-airline-industry-1.5945201

[582] https://globalnews.ca/news/8963838/nb-dominic-cardy-air-canada-incompetent/

[583] https://globalnews.ca/news/8956152/canada-airport-delays-domestic-flight-delays/

[584] https://toronto.ctvnews.ca/this-is-how-travellers-will-find-out-if-they-ve-been-selected-for-a-mandatory-test-at-toronto-pearson-1.5993288

[585] https://www.ipsos.com/en-ca/news-polls/six-in-ten-canadians-avoiding-airports-until-situation-improves-as-seven-in-ten-call-situation-a-national-embarrassment

[586] https://angusreid.org/covid-canada-seventh-wave-restrictions-masks-vaccine-passports/

[587] https://www.cbc.ca/news/canada/windsor/public-safety-minister-in-windsor-cbsa-cross-border-firearms-1.6503872

[588] https://tinyurl.com/4f3xkre4

[589] https://tinyurl.com/5n6k589b

[590] https://www.thestar.com/business/2022/07/06/ditch-the-arrivecan-app-and-let-the-tourists-flow-in-travel-industry-urges.html

[591] https://ktdi.org/

[592] https://toronto.citynews.ca/2022/07/25/toronto-pearson-ranked-worst-airport-for-delayed-flights/

[593] https://www.cbc.ca/news/canada/new-brunswick/higgs-health-minister-1.6522029

[594] https://www.ctvnews.ca/health/patient-dies-while-waiting-hours-to-be-seen-in-new-brunswick-emergency-department-1.5987414

[595] https://www.cbc.ca/news/canada/ottawa/diane-deans-not-running-mayor-1.6499481

[596] https://www.thecanadianencyclopedia.ca/en/article/theresa-tam

[597] https://www.canadaland.com/media-in-trudeaus-10-million-top-up-fund/

[598] https://thepostmillennial.com/watch-dr-theresa-tam-interviews-santa-claus-grants-him-essential-worker-status

[599] https://ottawa.ctvnews.ca/video?clipId=2349086

[600] https://www.cbc.ca/news/politics/justin-trudeau-tells-kids-to-follow-social-distancing-rules-1.5506113

[601] https://www.youtube.com/watch?v=2VyC7fsfBus&t=3s

602 https://www.weforum.org/agenda/2020/04/this-is-the-psychological-side-of-the-COVID-19-pandemic-that-were-ignoring/

603 https://bmjopen.bmj.com/content/11/1/e042871

604 https://link.springer.com/article/10.1007/s00787-021-01744-3

605 https://www.sciencedirect.com/science/article/pii/S0883035522000891

606 https://www.cbc.ca/news/canada/ottawa/social-malnutrition-phenomenon-kids-youth-isolation-COVID-19-1.6013594

607 https://www.cbc.ca/news/canada/hamilton/pandemic-safety-measures-children-teen-health-impact-1.5953326

608 https://www.cmaj.ca/content/194/25/E870

609 https://globalnews.ca/news/8157443/covid-children-abuse-suicide-canada-report/

610 https://www.narcity.com/toronto/hundreds-of-ontario-doctors-have-signed-an-open-letter-asking-ford-to-keep-schools-open

611 https://cps.ca/uploads/advocacy/Remote_learning_in_New_Brunswick.pdf

612 https://www.dailyheraldtribune.com/news/trudeau-says-vaccination-rate-is-too-low-amongst-children

613 https://twitter.com/justintrudeau/status/1486833073446699009?lang=en

614 https://www.ctvnews.ca/health/coronavirus/140m-rapid-tests-enough-pediatric-COVID-19-doses-for-all-second-shots-coming-this-month-feds-1.5728512

615 https://www.weforum.org/events/the-davos-agenda-2021/sessions/special-address-by-g20-head-of-state-government-16baf3cc12

616 https://www.haaretz.com/israel-news/elections/2020-03-15/ty-article/.premium/netanyahu-trial-postponed-by-two-months/0000017f-e24a-d568-ad7f-f36b862c0000

617 https://www.timesofisrael.com/netanyahu-sparks-privacy-concerns-with-move-to-track-corona-patients-phones/

618 https://www.reuters.com/article/us-health-coronavirus-israel-idUSKBN21622D

619 https://www.weforum.org/events/the-davos-agenda-2021/sessions/special-address-by-g20-head-of-state-government-16baf3cc12

620 https://www.bmj.com/content/374/bmj.n1766

621 https://en.wikipedia.org/wiki/COVID-19_pandemic_in_Turkmenistan#Official_communication

622 https://www.cbc.ca/news/canada/edmonton/covid-comorbidities-alberta-spitzer-1.6212510

623 https://www.facebook.com/tcampbell1087/videos

624 https://www.washingtonpost.com/nation/2021/08/06/virginia-man-hospitalized-putoff-COVID-19-vaccine-pleads-people-getit/

625 https://www.dailymail.co.uk/health/article-9866127/Hospitalized-Virginia-man-pleads-shots-COVID-bout.html

626 https://www.youtube.com/watch?v=FQ3WZKT4U-8

627 https://www.cnn.com/2021/08/06/health/coronavirus-virginia-travis-campbell-vaccine-regret/index.html

628 https://www.cnn.com/search?q=%20travis%20campbell&size=10&sort=newest

629 https://www.youtube.com/watch?v=JKukYO4Ih8M

630 https://www.washingtonpost.com/nation/2021/08/06/virginia-man-hospitalized-putoff-COVID-19-vaccine-pleads-people-getit/

631 https://bjsm.bmj.com/content/bjsports/55/19/1099.full.pdf

632 https://nutrition.bmj.com/content/early/2022/01/18/bmjnph-2021-000375

633 https://www.medrxiv.org/content/10.1101/2021.07.08.21260210v1

634 https://www150.statcan.gc.ca/n1/daily-quotidien/210514/dq210514c-eng.htm

635 https://health-infobase.canada.ca/COVID-19/

636 https://health-infobase.canada.ca/COVID-19/archive/2022-07-01/

637 https://edmonton.ctvnews.ca/hinshaw-apologizes-after-alberta-mistakenly-reports-14-year-old-s-cancer-death-was-caused-by-COVID-19-1.5623489

638 https://thepostmillennial.com/alberta-ndp-push-fake-news

639 https://edmonton.ctvnews.ca/hinshaw-apologizes-after-alberta-mistakenly-reports-14-year-old-s-cancer-death-was-caused-by-COVID-19-1.5623489

640 https://www.cbc.ca/news/canada/edmonton/alberta-government-bonus-pay-hinshaw-COVID-19-1.6541822

641 https://www.psychologytoday.com/ca/blog/crime-she-writes/201909/the-art-the-con-and-why-

people-fall-it

[642] https://www.wired.co.uk/article/mrna-vaccine-revolution-katalin-kariko

[643] https://www.wired.co.uk/article/mrna-vaccine-revolution-katalin-kariko

[644] https://www.cnbc.com/2021/04/14/bernie-madoff-dies-mastermind-of-the-nations-biggest-investment-fraud-was-82.html

[645] https://www.theguardian.com/business/2022/feb/08/pfizer-covid-vaccine-pill-profits-sales

[646] https://www.cnbc.com/2022/02/24/covid-moderna-mrna-q4-2021-earnings.html

[647] https://www.bloomberg.com/press-releases/2022-04-29/sinovac-reports-unaudited-second-half-of-2021-financial-results-and-files-2021-annual-report-on-form-20-f

[648] https://www.sec.gov/Archives/edgar/data/0000078003/000007800321000038/pfe-20201231.htm

[649] https://s29.q4cdn.com/435878511/files/doc_financials/2020/q4/Moderna-4Q-2020-Earnings-PR-(02.25.21).pdf

[650] https://www.wsj.com/articles/vaccinated-people-account-for-half-of-new-COVID-19-delta-cases-in-israeli-outbreak-11624624326

[651] https://investors.modernatx.com/events-and-presentations/events/event-details/2020/RD-Day/default.aspx

[652] https://www.sec.gov/Archives/edgar/data/1682852/000168285220000010/R13.htm

[653] https://investors.pfizer.com/Investors/Financials/SEC-Filings/SEC-Filings-Details/default.aspx?FilingId=14483915

[654] https://www.citizen.org/news/report-how-pfizer-silences-world-governments-in-vaccine-negotiations/

[655] https://health.gov.on.ca/en/pro/programs/publichealth/flu/uiip/reimbursement.aspx

[656] https://www.health.gov.on.ca/en/pro/programs/ohip/bulletins/redux/bul210601.aspx

[657] https://www.afhto.ca/sites/default/files/2021-08/OMA%20COVID-19%20Vaccine%20Billing%20Summary-v6_27-Jul-21.pdf

[658] https://open.alberta.ca/dataset/b7bc019f-ab74-4c8d-b7c9-60147f573854/resource/dbb2491a-3645-44ec-922c-7ad5b5fbc93a/download/health-somb-medical-procedure-list-2021-03.pdf

[659] https://www.cbc.ca/news/canada/ottawa/booster-ottawa-family-doctor-1.6282731

[660] https://www.utoronto.ca/utogether/COVID-19-planning-update

[661] https://www.utoronto.ca/news/tags/world-health-organization

[662] https://www.littler.com/files/canada_post_corporation.pdf

[663] https://www.medrxiv.org/content/10.1101/2021.07.31.21261387v1

[664] https://thehill.com/homenews/sunday-talk-shows/565831-fauci-amount-of-virus-in-breakthrough-delta-cases-almost-identical/

[665] https://www.ncbi.nlm.nih.gov/pmc/articles/PMC8426978/

[666] https://www.alcera.ca/en/articles/SOT-The-Strategy-Operations-Tactics-Framework.php

[667] https://www.ncbi.nlm.nih.gov/pmc/articles/PMC4860016/

[668] https://www.ncbi.nlm.nih.gov/pmc/articles/PMC8426978/

[669] https://www.who.int/publications/m/item/implementing-the-immunization-agenda-2030

[670] https://www.cdc.gov/globalhealth/immunization/framework/index.html

[671] https://initiatives.weforum.org/2030vision-network/home

[672] https://health.gov/healthypeople

[673] https://www.minister.industry.gov.au/ministers/taylor/media-releases/partnership-secures-australian-made-mrna-vaccines

[674] https://pm.gc.ca/en/news/news-releases/2022/04/29/producing-made-canada-vaccines-and-creating-hundreds-good-jobs

[675] https://www.cnbc.com/2022/03/07/moderna-reaches-preliminary-agreement-to-build-covid-vaccine-manufacturing-plant-in-africa.html

[676] https://investors.modernatx.com/news/news-details/2022/Moderna-Announces-Plan-to-Expand-Footprint-in-Asia-with-Four-Additional-Subsidiaries/default.aspx

[677] https://www.pharmtech.com/view/moderna-plans-expansion-in-europe

[678] https://www.bloomberg.com/news/articles/2022-02-22/moderna-inks-latin-america-deal-in-bid-to-expand-vaccine-reach#xj4y7vzkg

[679] https://investors.modernatx.com/news/news-details/2022/Moderna-Reports-Second-Quarter-2022-Financial-Results-and-Provides-Business-Updates/default.aspx

[680] Bernice Z. Schacter, New Medicines. How Drugs Are Created Approved, Marketed, and Sold. Praeger, 2005.

[681] https://www.youtube.com/watch?v=2VyC7fsfBus&t=3s

[682] https://www.astrazeneca.com/media-centre/press-releases/2021/COVID-19-vaccine-astrazeneca-confirms-protection-against-severe-disease-hospitalisation-and-death-in-the-primary-analysis-of-phase-iii-trials.html

[683] https://www.ekathimerini.com/news/1162573/president-weighs-in-on-compulsory-vaccination/

[684] https://twitter.com/pbhushan1/status/1454262872175874055?lang=en

[685] https://tinyurl.com/mryh7x3t

[686] https://www.cmaj.ca/content/194/25/E870

[687] https://www.mdpi.com/1660-4601/19/15/9295/pdf?version=1659419794

[688] https://www.cbc.ca/news/canada/british-columbia/covid-restrictions-update-1.6352614

[689] https://news.westernu.ca/2022/08/western-requires-COVID-19-booster-masking-instructional-spaces-this-fall/

[690] https://torontosun.com/news/national/naci-now-suggests-canadians-consider-a-covid-19-booster-every-90-days

Freedom be thy name. BL, DK, FS, HT, JK, JM, JP, JRS, JT, LB, LP, LW, MC, MH, MJ, MK, ML, MO, MW, RE, RP, RT, SMK, SK, ST, SJ, TC, TL.